Narratives of British Socialism

Also by Stephen Ingle

THE BRITISH PARTY SYSTEM

GEORGE ORWELL: A Political Life

PARLIAMENT AND HEALTH POLICIES (*with Philip Tether*)

SOCIALIST THOUGHT IN IMAGINATIVE LITERATURE

Narratives of British Socialism

Stephen Ingle
Department of Politics
University of Stirling

First published 2002 by
PALGRAVE MACMILLAN
Houndmills, Basingstoke, Hampshire RG21 6XS and
175 Fifth Avenue, New York, N.Y. 10010
Companies and representatives throughout the world

PALGRAVE MACMILLAN is the global academic imprint of the Palgrave
Macmillan division of St. Martin's Press, LLC and of Palgrave Macmillan Ltd.
Macmillan® is a registered trademark in the United States, United Kingdom
and other countries. Palgrave is a registered trademark in the European
Union and other countries.

ISBN 0–333–51083–6

This book is printed on paper suitable for recycling and made from fully
managed and sustained forest sources.

A catalogue record for this book is available from the British Library.

Library of Congress Cataloging-in-Publication Data

Ingle, Stephen.
    Narratives of British socialism / Stephen Ingle.
        p. cm.
    Includes bibliographical references and index.
    ISBN 0–333–51083–6
        1. English literature – 19th century – History and criticism. 2. Socialism
    in literature. 3. English literature – 20th century – History and criticism.
    4. Authors, English – Political and social views. 5. Socialism and literature –
    Great Britain. 6. Socialism – Great Britain. 7. Narration (Rhetoric) I. Title.

PR468.S63 I57 2002
820.9'358–dc21   2002025802

10   9   8   7   6   5   4   3   2   1
11   10 09 08 07 06 05 04 03 02

Printed and bound in Great Britain by
Antony Rowe Ltd, Chippenham and Eastbourne

For my family

Contents

Acknowledgements

I should like first of all to thank the publishers for being so patient with this book. For a variety of reasons it took much longer to complete than had been anticipated. One of the principal reasons was my moving to the University of Stirling and though this proved a disadvantage in respect of completion it has turned out to be a bonus in terms of the exchanges I was able to have with colleagues about various sections of the book. In particular I should like to thank Stanley Kleinberg and Andrea Baumeister for reading and commenting on certain sections. I was also greatly helped in a number of very practical ways by Margaret Dickson and Joyce Burn in the departmental office at Stirling and I should like to take the opportunity to thank them. I would like to thank my good friend John Stewart, whose help with final proof-reading was most welcome. Finally I have to thank my wife Margaret who read and reread various drafts for typographical errors over a long period of time. She showed a patience that never stretched quite as far as enthusiasm. Unfortunately I can blame none of these for any shortcomings that this book might have but I doubt I could have managed the thing without them.

Stirling   STEPHEN INGLE

1
Narrative and Politics

Human speech is like a cracked copper cauldron on which we beat
out tunes for bears to dance to, when what we would really like is to
win the compassion of the stars.

(Gustave Flaubert, *Madame Bovary*, part 2, ch. 12)

Shelley may have been thinking wishfully when he declared poets to be
the unacknowledged legislators of the world, Solzhenitsyn exaggerating
when he identified writers as the official opposition in despotic states,
but both took for granted the importance to politics of narrative in the
form of imaginative literature. Why is it, then, that narrative forms –
novels, drama, poetry, film – play so little part in the formal study of
politics?[1] True, there is a growing body of scholars working in the area
where politics and imaginative literature overlap but few institutions of
higher education include this area within their teaching programme.
Students of literature, on the other hand, usually take into consideration the political context within which writers work and also, when relevant, the ideological disposition of those writers. Students of politics,
however, particularly in the English-speaking countries, have on the
whole felt little impulsion to explore the world of narrative to enrich
their understanding of politics. Yet there are at least two areas where a
prima facie case could be advanced for such an exploration, namely the
manner in which writers might enrich the knowledge and understanding of political issues through their function as mass communicators,
and the light they might shed through their literary analysis upon the
nature of ideologies. To put it simply, imaginative writers should prove
of interest to the student of politics both as political commentators and
as political thinkers. Since this seems to be no more than common

sense, we might briefly consider why imaginative literature has had such a low profile, generally speaking, in the study of politics.

Richard Hoggart made a fundamentally important point when he observed that social scientists are often prone to 'mistake the technical boundaries between academic disciplines for divisions within human experience',[2] and so, for example, students of politics would tend to ignore material in disciplines other than their own. Moreover within the discipline itself there exist well-policed borders, principally between empirically and theoretically based 'territories', which may not easily be crossed and any specialism within the discipline which does not fit readily into one territory or another has the potential to become a no-man's land, often empty, usually hazardous, sometimes littered with corpses. The study of literature can find itself in just such a predicament.

Yet there is more at work than sins of omission. That influential group of scholars associated with the behaviourist movement, which tried to make a science of the study of politics, tended to be highly suspicious of those who, unenthusiastic about the benefits of scientific enquiry (in the narrower, quantitative sense), were willing to mix opinion with 'knowledge', intuition with 'objectivity'. And quite understandably so, as W.H. Auden's characteristic claim suggests: 'In grasping the character of a society, as in judging the character of an individual, no documents, statistics, "objective" measurements can ever compete with the single intuitive glance.'[3] Intuitive glances are anathema to political scientists: they strike at the very heart of their expertise and, as Hoggart unerringly noted, 'like the early natural scientists, they fear a relapse into alchemy'.[4]

There are other constraints. It could hardly be said that literary critics, who themselves expostulate on political themes at a whim, welcome the inexpert into their own area of specialism. F.R. Leavis, for example, whilst ready to acknowledge the importance of imaginative literature for the student of politics, goes on to warn: 'No use of literature is any use unless it is a real use; literature isn't so much material lying there to be turned over from the outside, and drawn on, for reference and exemplification, by the critically inept.'[5] At first sight this might appear to be no more than a robust defence of a disciplinary boundary, but we should not be fooled. To take Leavis seriously is to ignore the ordinary reader (who by definition will be 'critically inept'), or at least to rule out the possibility of one ordinary reader discussing a book with another. There has been much recent debate (to which we shall return) on authors' 'ownership' of their texts but Leavis seems to think texts are owned by the critics. We must defend the rights of the critically inept (including students of politics) to turn literature over from the outside, to draw on it and to use it for reference and exemplification if they choose. Traditionally writers earned their living by writing for the critically inept. Indeed in the field of music Leopold Mozart expressly advised his son early in his career not to forget that he was composing for the 'long ears' of ordinary music lovers as well as for the tastes of the musically sophisticated. No great harm seems to have come from the advice.

Another factor which has tended to limit the attention paid by students of politics (and frequently politicians) to imaginative literature is that writers are part of the intelligentsia – they are intellectuals – and in the English-speaking world the influence of intellectuals upon politics has been insubstantial. Jean-Paul Sartre attempted to explain the differential influence of English and French intellectuals as follows:[6]

> In England, the intellectuals are less integrated than we; they form a slightly cantankerous caste, which does not have much contact with the rest of the population. The reason is, first of all, they have not had our luck; because remote predecessors whom we hardly deserve prepared the Revolution, the class in power, after a century and a half, still does us the honour of fearing us a little (very little); it treats us tactfully. Our *confrères* in London, who do not have these glorious memories, do not frighten anyone; they are considered quite harmless; and then, club life is less suitable for spreading their influence than salon life has been in spreading ours…The English writers… claim as free choice the isolation which has been imposed upon them by the structure of their society.

Sartre has nothing to say about the influence of the official academies of art nor does he expand his comments on the continuing influence of the revolutionary tradition in France. Together these factors have encouraged the formation of on the one hand establishment, but on the other, and more importantly, anti-establishment groups of avant-garde artists and men and women of letters. In Britain it is only comparatively recently that artists in general have become more or less dependent for patronage upon a middle class whose artistic attitudes they generally regard as philistine and whose values they consequently conspire, Jimmy Porter-like, to undermine, thereby gaining a certain solidarity.

For all these reasons, then, students of politics have tended not to concern themselves with imaginative literature and yet all the while in the 'real world' the two are overlapping, indeed nourishing each other, as the writing of Swift, Cobbett, Blake, Coleridge, Shelley, Dickens, Kingsley, Ruskin, Morris, Shaw, Wells, Huxley, Orwell and Golding – to name only some of the more obvious – indicates. These writers are all British (if Shaw and Swift will allow) but many overseas writers have also influenced political thinking in Britain. Indeed these writers are clear testimony to what is in any case a plain common-sense proposition – that 'political passions are often nourished by literature and that literary taste is much affected by politics'.[7]

Maureen Whitebrook, in a concise 'state of the art' essay entitled 'Politics and Literature',[8] sets out the various ways in which students of politics may approach the study of literature. They may study literature as a process, considering the economic forces that shape its production and the cultural forces that shape its style. They may study literature as illustration – of certain political conditions or dilemmas. She cites here Koestler's *Darkness at Noon* on totalitarianism or Melville's *Billy Budd* on law versus liberty. They may study literature as (in Whitebrook's words) moral education – how to lead the good life. They may turn to literature better to understand historical processes or events. Rodney Barker does so when outlining the theory and practice of distributivism through the novels of G.K. Chesterton.[9] Anthony Arblaster does so when he uses Eliot's *Felix Holt* to exemplify the nineteenth-century fear of the mob.[10] Politics students may also study literature as political theory. Whitebrook cites Johnson's *Politics, Innocence and the Limits of Goodness*[11] as an example of the use of plays and novels in this manner. Whitebrook is right to suggest that her categories may well blur into each other in practice but for the purposes of analysis each stands more or less independently as a reason why politics students might benefit from the study of literature. Whitebrook is aware that her 'literature project' is a risky business because 'taking literature into Politics ... disturbs a dependence on reason and rationality'. However it does other things: 'it expands the concept of "reality"; it enlarges the vocabulary of politics ... it provides the occasion for ... the imaginative contemplation of political possibilities'. In short it is a thoroughly worthwhile project.

If we accept that narrative in the form of imaginative literature is indeed a suitable focus of study for students of politics, what might they hope to gain from such study that they might not gain elsewhere? Would Arblaster's explanation of the nineteenth-century bourgeoisie's fear of the mob, for example, have been undermined without George Eliot? Clearly students of politics will gain different things from different writers, but is there anything that literature has to offer qua literature? To tackle this question we need to get a handle on what literature is. Kenneth Quin tackles just this topic in *How Literature Works*.[12] 'We expect expert poets or novelists to be particular about the words they use. The more particular they are ... the better the novel or poem is likely to be. But there is more to it than that. A bad novel is still a novel of sorts ... all such texts have something in common: they work in a particular way ... it is because they work that reading them becomes a literary experience.'[13] He goes on to distinguish between literary texts and others (such as works of history) as follows: they occupy different places in our lives; like cars and trucks, for example, we put them to different uses. Recognising a text as literature means recognising that we are being offered a literary experience, so we read a novel differently to how we would read, say, a do-it-yourself manual or indeed a history. (Dr Johnson was disparagingly clear about the differences between literary and historical works.[14])

Getting the most out of literature is an acquired skill and the more we work at it the more it works on us; as T.S. Eliot remarked, every new novel we read modifies our understanding of all the novels we read previously. The reverse is also true, thanks to the 'law of primacy', which holds that earlier experiences are usually more formative. To understand this relationship is to appreciate that, almost by definition, reading imaginative literature must be a process of interpretation and what the reader takes from a novel will only coincidentally be just what the author intended. The reader cannot help taking a sense of a word that the author would not have had, indeed could not have had; history alters the meaning of words and phrases. And not just history. As Eagleton has argued, the reader has a 'socially structured way of seeing the world'.[15] What Eagleton wishes to underline is that literature is part of the superstructure of social oppression and thus 'literary works are not mysteriously inspired, or explicable simply in terms of their author's psychology. They are forms of perception ... and as such they have a relation to the dominant way of seeing the world which is the "social mentality" or ideology of the age.'[16]

So we, writers and readers alike, are at least in some degree prisoners of our own time, our own history and our own social system. But to accept these limitations is not to agree with Stanley Fish's claim that 'interpreters do not decode poems; they make them'. Some literary theorists in the 1950s held that there were no novels, only novelists, and that all readings were misreadings, though some were more interesting than others. There is surely confusion here: if there is nothing with the imprimatur of an official 'reading' there can be no misreading. If all is open to interpretation and any reader's interpretation is as valid as the author's then, as Hirsch suggests, there is no significant difference between a page of *Paradise Lost* and a Rorschach blot.[17]

Whilst we may be persuaded that there can never be a completely 'right' way of reading a novel, Quin is confident that there can be a wrong way. We are not free agents but 'have to come to terms with the restraints the text itself imposes'.[18] It is clear that writers think and write within a particular conceptual framework (field of significance) that cannot be the same as the reader's, and the reader's perspective and sensibilities will enhance, will give a different dimension to, the author's presence within the text. When we read *Road to Wigan Pier*, for example, we – unlike Orwell – may have *Animal Farm* and *Nineteen Eighty-Four* to inform our perspective and sensibilities. But to claim seriously that one may interpret a work of imaginative literature simply as one chooses is, as Quin suggests, to 'trample on the claim – the claim of literary texts in general – to be taken as a social act'.[19] By this he means an act of communication with an accessible structure which is itself the product of human intelligence. Quin is right to insist that 'in every sentence of a novel or a poem, if we know how to read it, we feel the speaking voice of the writer' (what Steiner called their real presence). A text, then, for Quin, has a will of its own, has what Umberto Eco referred to as an intention.

Can we say anything about the nature of that intention? It is, as we have said, an act of communication, but of what? It does not seem primarily to be concerned with the transmission of information; the text itself need not necessarily serve any immediate purpose of this kind. It provides us with facts that may be of no intrinsic value or indeed it may even provide us with misinformation. No; it is primarily concerned with the sharing of an experience. George Orwell made just this point in his essay 'Why I Write'.[20] He elucidated four major motives, though I want to concentrate here on only one of them: aesthetic enthusiasm, which Orwell defines as the 'desire to share an experience which one feels is valuable and ought not to be missed'. For Orwell these experiences tended to be both aesthetic and political, the two being fused. 'My starting point is always a feeling of partisanship, a sense of injustice.' If he wishes to communicate that feeling successfully he knows that it must be transmitted through a shared aesthetic experience: 'so long as I remain alive and well I shall continue to feel strongly about prose style'. He continues: '*Animal Farm* was the first book in which I tried, with full consciousness of what I was doing, to fuse political purpose and artistic purpose into one whole ... looking back through my works, I see that it is invariably where I lacked a *political* purpose that I wrote lifeless books and was betrayed into purple passages, sentences without meaning, decorative adjectives and humbug generally.' Orwell's aesthetic purpose was to produce what he called 'prose like a windowpane' but this was not principally to expose a body of fact or information but an experience – the experience of injustice.

Orwell was convinced that political and historical motives were crucial in his own writing but was well-aware that other writers might have no immediate or clearly formulated end other than the sharing of an aesthetic experience. He talks about communicating a 'pleasure in the impact of one sound on another, in the firmness of good prose or the rhythm of a good story' or a 'perception of beauty in the external world'. The aesthetic experience is crucial. 'Insight into the human condition in the absence of any special ability to create with words', says Quin, 'is clumsy, if possible at all.'[21]

Imaginative writers, then, are concerned to communicate an experience rather than to transmit a body of information and for this to be successful the experience has to be a shared aesthetic experience. It may be argued that other writers – the best historians, for example – are similarly committed. But their primary task is to present and explain facts, in A.J.P. Taylor's uncomplicated formulation, to answer as accurately as possible the question: 'What happened next?' Historians, however eloquently and empathetically they may write, would simply cease to be read if their account of events proved unreliable or their judgements seriously flawed. But the imaginative writer is concerned with what might be thought of as deeper 'truths'. For example, Orwell wrote two essays about his experiences as an Imperial Policeman in Burma, 'A Hanging' and 'Shooting an Elephant'. His first biographer, Bernard Crick, was unable to prove to his own satisfaction that Orwell the young Imperial Policeman had actually participated in either event which he described.[22] The stories, then, could have been phoney; the author might have made them up. But Orwell had more important fish to fry than historical authenticity in that narrow sense: he wanted to depict the destructive nature of imperialism; this was far more important than historical authenticity. Orwell was concerned, perhaps above everything else, to express what has often been called 'literary truth'.

What sense, if any, can be given to this expression? That a work of fiction might be said to possess or express 'truth' and a non-fictional work to lack or fail to express truth is so universally borne out by experience as to be unarguable. Truth in this context relates to statements concerning human experience. These truths may emanate from any field of experience, psychological, sociological or political, for example. What gives a work literary force is that this experiential truth is expressed in what might be called an aesthetically true manner. Self-evidently literary truth is not the same thing as truth. A literary account may contain many statements – that such-and-such characters exist, for example – that are demonstrably false, and other statements that are true – about, say, a real place or actual event – but which are nevertheless irrelevant to the novel's purpose. Indeed a novel can be considered to have literary truth when no corresponding state of affairs obtains in the real world. So literary truth and truth are not the same. E.M. Forster claimed that it is the *internal consistency* of a work that makes it true. When we enter the world of literature we inhabit 'a universe that only answers to its own laws, supports itself, internally coheres, and has a new standard of truth'. A work of literature, then, is 'true if it hangs together'.[23] Perhaps. But consider for a moment the following. If such a work, though apparently coherent, bore no relation at all to the readers' experience, how could they possibly make a judgement on its internal consistency? What measure or model would they use?

What *can* we say about literary truth? A novel, for example, cannot be said necessarily to convey truth in the sense of presenting verifiable evidence, but it can tell us about human experience in a different way. Indeed it could be said that some general statements about human experience cannot always be stated objectively and the whole point of turning to narrative forms such as imaginative literature is 'to convey *by illustration* a general truth that cannot be stated explicitly'.[24] Or to put it more modestly, cannot be better stated explicitly. This consideration weighs especially in accounts of complex moral dilemmas. Imaginative writers such as Balzac and Stendhal – especially the former – regarded their works as historical. Stendhal subtitled *Le Rouge et le Noir* 'A Chronicle of the Nineteenth Century' and Balzac's *Comédie Humaine* was subtitled 'A Study of Nineteenth Century Manners'. Clearly theirs was not history in the sense of being an investigation of various verifiable events that occurred. Not 'true' in the ordinary sense then. However, they regarded their creative enterprises as offering literary truth that could provide a valuable new dimension to historical or political interpretation. Auerbach's substantial claim is that such work has 'taken over the methods and duties of science'.[25] These novels do add to our knowledge of social conditions and relationships but they cannot surely be said to equate in any meaningful sense to scientific enquiry. Althusser's argument that science gives us knowledge and art gives us experience remains the more generally appropriate conclusion regarding literature even of this overtly historical kind. But experiential truth provides an important dimension to our full understanding of history and politics. Analysing the literature of her own country, the New Zealand political historian Margaret Clark wrote of one novel: 'There you have it. At the heart of this work of the imagination the author places an intensely political question – indeed the central political question of contemporary New Zealand – how shall Maori and Pakeha live together?'[26]

When John Barrell explores the ideas of experience and literary truth, he speaks of 'truth to experience' and implies by this that a fictional experience is only valid (true) if it resembles an actual experience. Walter Benjamin argued that the whole purpose of narrative was to eschew the transmission of information for the sharing of experience.[27] Indeed a literary work succeeds to the extent that it represents experiences which we have had ourselves and helps us better to understand those experiences. In Tolstoy's description of a public execution by guillotine he speaks of understanding what was happening 'not with my mind but my whole being'. It was this *feeling* that he sought to convey. Barrell argues: 'Thus to judge the text's "truth to experience" is, after all, the same thing as to judge its value.' Such claims would make little sense to critics such as Richard Rorty who wish to 'take the halo' off words like truth which, he claims, simply do not exist outside the structure of sentences.[28] By the power of what Nietzsche referred to as its 'mobile army of metaphors', literature, says Rorty, can be as insightful as philosophy.

However, as Michael Fischer points out,[29] since Rorty regards both disciplines as 'imprecise, capricious and methodologically dishevelled', he might be said to leave literature not strengthened by the comparison but only made equally impotent. Rorty's respect for the poetry of Philip Larkin indicates that he fully recognises Larkin's truth to experience, but he applauds the latter's unwillingness, as he sees it, to rise above the contingent. At a man's death, says Larkin, his life appears to have no purpose 'since it applied only to one man and that man dying'. But Rorty is mistaken: is it not precisely because we recognise the universality of Larkin's despair that his poetry does indeed rise above the contingent, speaking the truth of our own experience, and echoing that much earlier poet John Clare who spoke of 'the shipwreck of my life's esteem'?[30]

If it is accepted that there is such a thing as literary truth which rises above the contingent it might nevertheless be argued, harking back to the earlier debate, that what makes a novel 'true' is the reader's reading of it. Reflection indicates that this cannot be wholly the case however. It is perfectly intelligible to say that a certain reader is unable to appreciate the truth of a novel because they are lacking in experience or intelligence or sensitivity. If this suggests that the truth-value of literature is somehow inherent, it does not follow that the literary truth of a work is the monopoly of the writer. It is clear that an author might be unaware of some literary truth that their work conveys to many readers. Indeed if they could these writers might want to challenge the 'truth' that these readers see. Yet it is surely inconceivable that readers in general would form an understanding of a work's 'truth' which was totally contrary to the author's intentions; rather any disagreement would be likely to concern the appropriateness of some literary truth to a broader span of experience than that envisaged by or indeed available to the author.

Consider George Orwell's *Animal Farm*: it was the author's intention to create a parable of the Russian revolution of 1917 and the subsequent establishment of the Stalinist state, but many readers have read the fable much more widely, as making a statement about the nature of revolution itself.[31] Eric Auerbach used the example of Cervantes' *Don Quixote* to make the same point more fully: 'For centuries – and especially since the romanticists – many things have been read into him, which he hardly foreboded, let alone intended. Such transforming and transcendent interpretations are often fertile. A book like *Don Quixote* shows a new face to every age that enjoys him.'[32] A different face, perhaps, but the same personality. On the other hand it behoves the reader to tease out the original intentions and meanings of the author and to try to grasp what the work might have meant to their contemporaries. This will not limit but inform subsequent interpretations.

It is clear from the foregoing that literary truth consists of an attempt to make fictional statements that encapsulate an understanding of some important aspect of human experience. Those who deal in them attempt to portray literary truths as possessing a veracity and significance which the accumulation of factually supportive statements might not. History seeks accuracy and is based upon verifiable evidence. Collingwood noted that what it says is localised in space and time and there is, or should be, only one historical world. Not so imaginative literature. Writers, as Sartre argued, write for all people of all times. They strive after truths of their own but they want, above all, to make them available to us all. Dickens or Kingsley or Gaskell were attempting to convey truths to their audiences about social conditions in England (indeed Gaskell said apropos *Mary Barton*: 'I'm sure I *believe* I wrote the truth') but their themes had far wider significance. Eagleton might remind us that Gaskell's 'truth' was ideological in the Marxist sense, but this is surely not a problem. After all Lukacs argued that it was precisely 'the view of the world, the ideology or Weltanschauung underlying a writer's work, that counts'.[33] It is not as if readers would simply accept Gaskell's 'truth': as we have seen, they would be reinterpreting it in terms of their own (equally ideological) experience.

Imaginative writers – novelists, for example – are not primarily concerned to tell us about character X and character Y and the relationship between X and Y. These writers make a claim *outside* the story of the characters and their relationship; they are to be seen as representing more than their individual selves. This is a distinguishing truth even when novels pretend not to be novels: *Robinson Crusoe* and *Moll Flanders* are overtly autobiographies, *Clarissa* a series of letters, and *Ivanhoe* a history. But these are no less obviously fiction than, say, Dickens's *Martin Chuzzlewit*. Dickens was concerned with the 'reorganisation of reality, that made no pretence at reporting fact; a fiction which was whimsical, comic, discursive, bordered on fantasy – and yet was true to the human condition'.[34] There are no laws to govern the shape and style of novels, as readers of Bulgakov or Joyce would gladly testify. Marxist–Leninist dogs may talk in novels but it *is* important that if they want to be heard, they talk with conviction, and their story should not collapse through internal inconsistencies: it must above all be both intelligible and engaging.

A literary text, says Quin, is the product of a decision: a decision to tell us certain things and not to tell us others.[35] This decision must to some extent be a moral one (he distinguishes between moralists and moralisers: imaginative writers are invariably the former, only rarely the latter) because it reflects a reorganisation of experience so as to make a statement about 'reality'. Unlike philosophers and theologians, for example, imaginative writers do not put their cards on the table; but they have a game plan all the same. Some profess no moral authority, though even to say as much is to adopt a moral position. Mordecai Richler does not beat about the bush: 'every serious writer is primarily a moralist and only incidentally an entertainer'.[36] He may be right, despite the danger of tautology, but it is worth bearing in mind that some writers are more serious than others and the primary expertise of all of them, after all, is with words. Literary critics speak of a work's field of significance, which serves not only to orchestrate the narrative but also to provide its moral and literary perspective. We see an imaginative work as part of moral and literary traditions and knowledge of these tends to shape the way we think about it. Those whose field of significance is fundamentally moral and political are likely to have most impact on us; they 'make us see life with a new clarity … our insight has been sharpened, our understanding of the human condition subjected to a significant renewal'.[37]

This draws our argument back full circle to the student of politics. Having established a case for narrative in the form of imaginative literature as a fruitful field of enquiry for the student of politics, we need to

consider whether we can usefully offer advice as to what kinds of literature might be most fruitful for them to measure against their own experience, a question whose answer has much to do with considerations of
the value or truth of a particular work.

We might intuitively expect that works whose field of significance
was overtly political would be of most interest to the student of politics.
This is not necessarily the case. All writers can be said to be 'committed'
in a specifically political sense, according to Charques.[38] Even those
who 'make a show' of detachment are 'the tacit supporters of the pre-
vailing system'; they are 'the servants of the propertied class'. In a sense
Charques is right: if writers who devote their lives to communicating,
communicate nothing at all about contemporary political events or
relationships then it is fair to conclude that, for whatever reason, they
have come to terms with the existing social/political structure. Rosemary
Woolf, too, shows the extent of writers' commitment in her own field,
unlikely though it might at first seem, of medieval literature – she speaks
of 'art for doctrine's sake'.[39] Yet if all writers are committed, they are
clearly not all equally committed – beyond, that is, the commitment
implied in William Golding's observation that literature actually forces
a form – the writer's – on life which is itself in fact 'a formless business'.[40] If writers introduce specifically political themes into their work
and these themes are important to the work, it makes sense to call them
committed. It makes no sense at all to assume that those who do not do
so are equally committed – that is, to the status quo. What matters, in
short, when distinguishing between the field of significance of writers is
the intensity of commitment. George Gissing's *Demos*, for example, can
be seen as overtly politically committed in a sense that *The Nether World*
is not.

Then should the students of politics concentrate on writers with a
'high commitment score'? Not according to Orwell, who would himself
score as highly on commitment as any recent British writer. Orwell
commented that in the politically charged atmosphere of the 1930s 'a
novelist who simply disregards the major public events of the moment
is generally either a footler or a plain idiot'.[41] Even so, Henry Miller,
whose meeting with Orwell had stimulated this comment, was readily
acknowledged by the latter to be neither. Though he sought the protec-
tion of bourgeois democratic society whilst disclaiming all responsibility for it, says Orwell, Miller was an important writer who, by his
passivity to experience, had been able to get close to portraying the
reality of everyday life. In another essay Orwell similarly took Dickens
to task,[42] criticising the 'utter lack of any constructive suggestion

anywhere in his work' (that is, overt political commitment), and yet here too Orwell was prepared to acknowledge the value of Dickens's political achievements. He concluded the essay by suggesting that Dickens's view on the primacy of reforming human nature might be seen as 'just as "revolutionary"...as the politico-economic criticism which is fashionable at the moment'. Although himself politically committed Orwell accepted the value of writers with different commitments and different levels of commitment, measuring them according to his own standard: that is, their contribution to 'the revolution'. In other words, he thought some of them politically important despite their lack of overt political commitment. An important lesson for the student of politics.

Not merely is overt political commitment no guarantee that the work will be valuable to students of politics, but it may indeed prove positively inimical to their purpose. That is to say, commitment may prove detrimental to the aims of literature and thus open to Julien Benda's charge of treason.[43] Benda argued that modern writers occupy a role in society comparable to that of the medieval clerics or clerks: they are the principal transmitters of values. By accusing the modern clerks of treason Benda was arguing that in so far as they had become the mouthpieces of a particular ideology they were abandoning their independent judgement and thus their integrity. He had in mind the pre-1939 neofascist writers but after the war, in a new edition of his book, the same charge was levelled at the pro-communist writers – including Sartre. More recently others have laid the charge at the door of pro-American liberal writers. What all these writers could be charged with, surely, is the abandonment of what Albert Camus called 'the reserve which befits a good witness', and the subsequent taking on of the mantle of preacher. This must inevitably cause writers, when striving for political consistency, to express thoughts they do not necessarily think. So the clerk may betray his calling by subservience to what Orwell called 'those smelly little orthodoxies', may betray by what he says and what he does not say, by avoiding a political line as well as by taking one. In short, the great treason of the clerk is to be in a false relation to his or her experience and thus inevitably to politics. A false relation to politics implies a false relation to literature.[44] Iris Murdoch observed pithily that bad art is a lie about the world whilst good art is 'in some important sense seen as *ipso facto* true and as an expression of reality'.[45]

If commitment is no sure guide for the students of politics, what is? The answer is in principle straightforward: the long-term impact of the work in question. It is fashionable to argue, as Eagleton does, for example, that '"literature" in the sense of a set of works of assured and unalterable value, distinguished by certain shared inherent properties [a term which might be thought equivalent to long-term impact] does not exist'.[46] Eagleton's argument is that our judgements in these matters are simply our 'socially structured way of perceiving the world' and so *our* Homer is not the Homer of, for example, a fifteenth-century reader (or indeed presumably of Homer himself – or, more probably, themselves) nor *our* Shakespeare that of a Victorian reader (nor, again, of the man himself). Nevertheless the fact that we, like readers in earlier periods, are still reading Homer and Shakespeare implies a clear measure of long-term impact. It would be incredible to believe that Homer or Shakespeare would have been considered great in a variety of times and in countless societies – each one with different socially structured values – for a wide range of substantially different reasons. What endures is specific and identifiable. Many commentators,[47] Eagleton's views notwithstanding, would be willing to accept the notion of 'literature' (a canon of works of long-term impact) and indeed be willing to enumerate the character-istics which, in their view, could be said to constitute such a canon. For practitioners like Vargas Llosa 'literature' *does* exist and he regards arguments to the contrary as 'complete buggles'.[48]

On the other hand it cannot be denied that there are disadvantages to this approach. Any such canon will, almost by definition, tend to exclude certain categories of work: recent works, simply because their pedigree has not been established, and works by socially and politically disadvantaged groups. Some of these works, however, may have such an immediate impact as to force themselves upon our attention even if, for whatever reason, they would fail to achieve long-term impact. The main thrust of my argument, however, is that if we agree that literature will provide the student of politics with an experiential understanding of political issues and dilemmas, then by and large the 'better' the book the richer the understanding. After all, immediate literary impact may be no guide at all to long-term impact. As is well-known, when Flaubert's *Madame Bovary* appeared its success was vastly overshadowed by that of the Feydeau farce *Fanny*, which went into thirteen editions in one year. Long-term impact, however, has overturned the original verdict.[49]

I do not wish to suggest for a moment that all the works we shall be examining here would be generally considered to be great works of literature: some are and some are not. But all have enjoyed a measure of long-term impact and continue to be read many years after they were written. They are worth reading. Second, but only second, each of them has a field of significance that is social/political, and is therefore prima facie of particular interest to the student of politics.

It is hardly necessary to point out that works and writers have been excluded that some readers will feel should have been discussed. Certain issues will no doubt have been treated only briefly or indeed omitted altogether that some readers will feel should have been discussed in depth. The choice of material and themes is essentially subjective and I have pursued writers and themes that seem to me centrally important, that grew out of my own intellectual interests and with which I am most familiar. I would not want to claim anything beyond that.

This book constitutes an attempt to illustrate the contribution which imaginative literature has made to the study of politics. I intend to discuss the political significance of a number of works of literature within a British context and have restricted myself to writers whose names would appear in any review of writing in the period in question: writers who have enjoyed long-term impact, in other words. They are not all British but each was widely read by British socialists. The period in question runs from the 1880s to the 1960s, roughly speaking the period in which socialism emerged as a major political force in Britain, established itself and then began to decline. By concentrating on one society, one period and one ideology we should be able to take stock of narrative's contribution to our understanding of the lifespan of that ideology (and hence by extrapolation its contribution to our understanding of politics). But let me introduce another caveat. Although I shall principally be concerned with people who wrote books of long-term impact, I shall not shrink from making use of other aspects of their works, such as lesser-known books, journalism, essays or letters, wherever I think these will assist our understanding of their literary endeavours.

The body of the work has been organised to deal with the impact of narrative on socialist thought as it developed ontologically in Britain. For many, socialism was primarily a response to poverty. Indeed, before being deported from his homeland, Marx in his final editorial in the *Neue Rheinische Zeitung* had defiantly declared that his last words 'everywhere and always' were to be: 'emancipation of the working class'. Poverty blighted Victorian Britain, and Chapter 2 deals with the picture of poverty painted by socialist writers. Their arguments are both moral and economic and they hoped to arouse the sympathy and compassion of their readers or audiences in order to change the system of capitalism. Others who wrote about these matters drew different conclusions, and their arguments are also considered. Chapter 3 deals with the broad strategic issues concerning the alleviation of poverty: what exactly was to be done with the poor? The very different responses to this question are examined in detail. The next two chapters deal with writers who sought to depict how the injustices of capitalism might be righted. Chapter 4 examines the arguments around the efficacy of revolution, as depicted in narrative literature, as a means of changing society, and Chapter 5 examines accounts of the evolutionary path to social justice. Chapter 6 considers what imaginative writers think a socialist state or society might look like by comparing the ambitions of those we might distinguish as scientific or ethical socialists, and looks at some criticisms of these models. In Chapter 7 we shall be considering the impact of specific historical examples of 'politically important' narratives and will then make some general comments on the nature of that relationship: what can we say about *how* forms of narrative such as imaginative literature might impact upon political thought and indeed political events? We shall end with some observations on the apparent declining political impact of narrative forms. This completes the analysis of literature and the socialist project but it is not the end of the story.

In the Postscript, we shall be taking the story forward. It will have escaped nobody's attention that the works discussed here are predominantly between 50 and 120 years old. We have confined our attention to the trajectory of the ideology of socialism in Britain, and have plotted this trajectory as coming to earth sometime about the 1960s. It might be considered precipitous to date the demise of British socialism as occurring just before the Labour Party was to achieve its second largest parliamentary majority (at that time) but the Labour leadership by the 1960s had recognised that future electoral success would require it to abandon a commitment to the kind of policies that cumulatively might be thought of as 'socialism', either scientific or ethical. To all intents and purposes, Anthony Crosland had written *The Future of Socialism*[50] on the wall, so to speak. No indisputably great literary work with a social/political field of significance has been written in Britain since those days. In many respects the role of the novel and the play in modern Britain as harriers of the social conscience and as visionaries has arguably been usurped by another form of narrative, film. In the Postscript we shall consider cinematic portrayals of the demise of socialism and of the decline of the social forces that had shaped and supported it in modern Britain.

2
'The Terrible Stone Face'

After eighteen months without work, with his family slowly starving, Frank Cavilla cut the throats of his wife and four children with a pocket-knife. Jack London unearthed this gruesome fact when researching for his sociological exploration of the lives of the poor in East London which found expression in *The People of the Abyss*.[1] London was one of a number of writers who might loosely be called social(ist) realists who sought through largely descriptive works showing the evil consequences of capitalism, as they saw them, to gain sympathy for the plight of the poor from a largely middle-class readership and audience. For some these descriptions were a basis for social, political or even ideological analysis, but this was not always so. In any case it is primarily the formal descriptions that we shall be considering in this chapter: we shall be concerned primarily, that is to say, with description rather than prescription.

Poverty as evil

Jack London was employed as a war correspondent and was on his way from the United States to South Africa. He arrived in Britain in the summer of 1902 to discover that the war had ended and that his contract had been cancelled. He threw himself instead into his researches of what he described as a 'huge man-killing machine'. Great towns like London, he said, drew men and women in from the countryside in the search for work. Within two generations their offspring were unfit for strenuous employment. Indeed, as Jack London showed, the Metropolitan Police of some 15,000 officers contained only 3,000 London-born men. In 1902 General Sir Frederick Maurice announced that 60 per cent of volunteers for service in the Boer War had been rejected on medical grounds.

As a direct consequence the government, in that very year, established a committee to consider such matters and, noting among other things that the infant mortality rate was higher in 1900 than it had been in 1859, it concluded that physical deterioration was a price of man's adapting himself, or to be more specific the urban poor adapting itself, to an urban environment.[2] London described in detail his travels to the Poplar workhouse in the company of two tramps, both unemployed artisans, who pick up any piece of food on the way – apple cores, orange peel, greengage stones (for the kernels) – and this in the very heart of the 'greatest, wealthiest and most powerful empire that the world has ever seen'.

London used documentary sources to harrowing effect, for example, a doctor's report to a coroner's inquest on the death of an elderly woman:[3]

> Found deceased lying across the fender on her back ... The body was quite alive with vermin, and all the clothes in the room were absolutely grey with insects. Deceased was very badly nourished ...

And yet London was not primarily a sociologist, he was a novelist and was very clear about his intention, which was to shock his readers. His conclusion was not that of a dispassionate social scientist: 'If it is not good for your mother and my mother so to die, then it is not good for this woman, whosoever's mother she might be, so to die.' London's narrative is remorseless. He provides us, for example, with an official medical description of the physical dissolution and eventual death in considerable pain of normal healthy, well-developed young women who happen to work in white-lead factories. This was a condition explored in an exemplary fashion by Shaw in his play *Mrs Warren's Profession*, in which Mrs Warren, stung by the examples of what happens to her half-sisters who sought respectable employment, decided on a life of prostitution. 'What did they get by their respectability? I'll tell you. One of them worked in a white-lead factory twelve hours a day for nine shillings a week until she died of lead poisoning; she only expected to get her hands a little paralysed.'[4]

Poverty was a theme that Shaw explored at length in his early plays. The earliest, *Widowers' Houses*, first shown in London in 1892, concerns Sartorius, a self-made man of substance, whose headstrong daughter Blanche is engaged to Trench, a well-connected young man of modest means. Sartorius's money comes from the ownership of slum property and, by virtue of his seat on the local council, he is able to ignore most of the municipal sanitary and safety regulations and so maximise his profits. His rents are collected by Lickcheese who, though well-aware of the misery he brings upon the heads of Sartorius's clients, nevertheless feels himself to be in a trap: 'look here, gentlemen: I'm pretty seasoned to the work; but there's money there I couldn't have taken if it hadn't been the thought of my own children depending on me for giving him satisfaction'.[5] Though he truly hates his work, Lickcheese's social circumstances rule out the luxury of any real moral choice: he must do his job. When Trench discovers the provenance of his future father-in-law's wealth he informs his fiancée that they will have to make do with his own far more limited income. But Blanche has no intention of making sacrifices to ease Trench's conscience and simply refuses to marry on this basis. Sartorius points out that far from tyrannising the poor he is in fact providing a service that they are just about able to afford. If the properties were of better quality he would have to charge more and the poor would not be able to afford them. Besides:[6]

> These people do not know how to live in a proper dwelling … You are welcome to replace all the missing banisters, handrails, cistern lids and dusthole stops at your own expense; and you will find them missing again in less than three days: burnt, sir, every stick of them.

But Sartorius's strongest argument is to inform Trench that his own insubstantial income derives from property managed by none other than Sartorius himself. Deflated, indeed humiliated, Trench wonders whether he is 'just as bad' as Sartorius, to which the latter replies: 'If … you mean that you are just as powerless to alter the state of society, then you are unfortunately quite right'. But love conquers all, and in this case Lickcheese makes a suggestion that will secure the financial future and settle the scruples of everybody. Sartorius and Trench will work together to improve conditions in their houses immediately; then they will be in a good position to obtain maximum compensation when the properties are demolished as part of an urban renewal programme planned by the council.

We should be clear that Shaw's intention in writing *Widowers' Houses*, clearly stated in the Preface, was to bring the realities of poverty to the attention of middle-class voters. 'I must warn my readers that my attacks are against themselves, not against my stage figures', since:[7]

> The average Englishman, however honourable and good-natured he may be in his private capacity, is, as a citizen, a wretched creature who … will shut his eyes to the most villainous abuses if the remedy

threatens to add another penny in the pound to the rates and taxes which he has to be half-cheated and half-coerced into paying.

If Shaw really believed his own argument about the incorrigibility of the English middle class he would hardly have bothered to write his play. In fact he believed the opposite, declaring that his true aim in writing *Widowers' Houses* had been to persuade voters to vote for the progressives in the London elections that year.

We have already had cause to refer to *Mrs Warren's Profession* and although it touches on a number of important themes, for example being a play, as Shaw said, about women and for women, one of his principal intentions is much the same as with *Widowers' Houses*: to shock his audience. In fact he hardly got the chance since, apart from a private showing in 1902, the Lord Chamberlain managed to keep the play off the British stage until 1925, some 41 years after it had been written. Nevertheless, as Shaw pointed out in the Preface, though the British public (when they finally got to see the play) would have liked nothing better than to throw the guilt for her profession onto Mrs Warren, the 'whole aim of my play is to throw that guilt on the British public itself'. Shaw's play was roundly criticised as 'wholly evil' because it contained a bold defence of an immoral profession, prostitution.[8] In response he retorted that the play defended Mrs Warren, not her profession. The aphoristic Jeremy Bentham had once claimed that what is politically right cannot be morally wrong, but Shaw's argument is a subtler one: the point of the play is precisely to show us that, given the life choices that society offered her, Mrs Warren's choice of prostitution was a rational, not a moral one. If her decision was as Shaw describes it, 'valid and unanswerable', then plainly society itself was more immoral than the institution of prostitution because it denied her any other rational choice. If he had truly sought to paint prostitution as morally defensible *per se* then Shaw's entire argument would have fallen down. There are, it has to be said, factors which dilute the strength of this argument: unlike the heroine of H.G. Wells's *The Wife of Sir Isaac Harman*,[9] Mrs Warren, having acquired wealth, does not use it to build cheap hostels for young working-class girls and help them secure respectable employment, but instead manages a chain of top-class European brothels. Nevertheless, for Shaw, starvation, disease, dirt and gross overwork are more immoral than prostitution, so for Mrs Warren the choice is between two sorts of immorality. Once again, 'society and not any individual is the villain of the piece'.

The analysis of the nature and effect of poverty is one of the themes of another of Shaw's early plays, *Major Barbara*, first produced in 1905.

A foundling, Andrew Undershaft, who through the operation of some strange trust becomes the manager of a large-scale armaments manufacturing company and a multi-millionaire, dominates the play. His daughter Barbara has become a Major in the Salvation Army, saving souls in London's East End along with her fiancé Cusins, a Professor of Greek. Undershaft has long been separated from his wife and family but the impending marriage of his son brings the family briefly together. As a result of the strained meeting Undershaft agrees to watch Barbara at work at the West Ham shelter, where she is sure she will convert him to her particular brand of muscular Christianity. In return she will visit him at his manufacturing plant, where he is equally convinced that *he* will convert *her* to his well-ordered enterprise which raises its workers above poverty.

Shaw uses Undershaft's visit to paint a vivid picture of poverty by means of introducing us to the lives of some of the poor. Peter Shirley, for instance, is a skilled artisan who cannot find work because he is considered too old – sent to the knackers, he despairs, like an old horse. 'You'd pass still', says Barbara, 'why didn't you dye your hair?' But he has no work, so, secularist though he is, he comes to the Army shelter for food. A fellow worker, whose name – Bronterre O'Brien (the Chartist agitator) Price – indicates the author's approval, tells Shirley that he is only a 'jumped-up, jerked-off...ole working man' who should get off his moral high horse and simply take whatever he can from 'the thievin swine' – that is, the capitalists – who have stolen so much from him. Price's philosophy is to drink whenever he gets the opportunity, to do as little work as possible so as to leave enough to go round for his fellow workers, and finally to do as the capitalist does – 'pinch wot I can lay me ands on'. Shaw will want to build on this working-class pragmatism later but for the moment his aim is to show us broken men and women, people with no hopes for the future, whose lives are dominated by hunger, cold and violence – the violence of the strong against the weak, men against women.

It is to this desperate level that Undershaft descends. He is quickly bearded by Shirley who tells him that it is keeping the Undershafts of the world rich that keeps him and his like poor. Even so, he would not have Undershaft's conscience, not for all his income. And Undershaft pointedly replies: 'I wouldn't have your income, not for all your conscience, Mr Shirley.'[10] Undershaft the gunmaker and his friend Bodger the whisky distiller make substantial donations, both accepted, to the Salvation Army. Barbara, totally disillusioned, leaves the colours, finding herself unable to answer the accusing question of one of the poor: 'Wot prawce selvytion nah?'[11] Her father later expounds his philosophy, that poverty is in fact:[12]

> the worst of crimes. All the other crimes are virtues beside it: all the other dishonours are chivalry itself by comparison. Poverty blights whole cities; spreads horrible pestilence; strikes dead the very soul of all who come within sight, sound or smell of it.

This is Andrew Undershaft's 'Gospel': poverty's daughters, he declares, 'infect our young men with the diseases of the streets, and his sons revenge him by turning the nation's manhood to scrofula, cowardice, cruelty, hypocrisy, political imbecility, all the other fruits of oppression and malnutrition'. It follows that 'our first duty, to which every other consideration ought to be sacrificed, is not to be poor'. We should not be deluded into imagining that Shaw was in any sense standing as a champion of the working class; as we shall see later, his ambition was to abolish the working class as he knew it, largely because, to his way of thinking, it too readily accepted its status.

Shaw wrote as an outsider. He was not from the working-class and indeed was not English, but then most of the novels written about working-class life at this time were written by outsiders, at least in the class sense, such as Arthur Morrison, for example, who wrote the direly pessimistic *A Child of the Jago*.[13] In such books, as Keating reminds us, 'characters and environment are presented so as to contain, implicitly or explicitly, a class judgement'.[14] They were, nevertheless, mostly written by middle-class authors for a middle-class readership. Their objective was spelled out by the young George Gissing: 'to bring home to people the ghastly conditions … of our poor classes, to show the hideous injustice of our whole system of society'.[15]

There was one widely read (autobiographical) novel written about the working class by a working-class author around this time, *The Ragged Trousered Philanthropists*.[16] Robert Tressell, the author, castigated his fellow workers because, like philanthropists, they willingly donated a large proportion of their due earnings to their bosses. They not merely 'quietly submitted like so many cattle' to the existing state of society, but actually defended it and ridiculed its opponents. Tressell himself was a man of whom relatively little is known. Either Irish or more likely Liverpool Irish, Tressell (Noonan to give him his correct name) had emigrated to South Africa where, along with some other Irishmen, he had sided with the Boers in the war against the British. The defeat of the

Boers persuaded Tressell to return to Britain where he lived and worked as a signwriter in Hastings.

Owen, the hero of his novel, is also employed as a signwriter by a firm of painters and decorators, and describes in detail the numerous ruses that the firm employs to maximise its profits. As a consequence the workers can take no pride in their trade. They are alienated from the product of their labour. When they arrive in the morning their thoughts are only of knocking off for breakfast, after breakfast only of dinner, and so on. If their job is not done quickly and cheaply enough the next will go to one of their competitors, such as Pushem and Sloggem, Bluffum and Doemdown, Dodger and Scampit and the like. In such cut-throat competition the firm pays its workers a Ricardian wage, leaving them no prospect of a genuinely rewarding family life. Although Owen may despise their acceptance of this pittance, he shows only too clearly how, at a time of unemployment, the bosses are able to play one man off against another, driving the hourly wage rate down. It is hard to see what individual workers in an industry notoriously hard to unionise could do about it, but Owen is nonplussed by their *acceptance* of the situation as quite normal. 'It can't never be altered ... There's always been rich and poor in the world, and there always will be.'

Tressell's novel gains much of its strength from its obvious integrity and truth to life. As I have said, the work is autobiographical[17] and in the preface Tressell tells us: 'I have invented nothing. There are no scenes or incidents in the story that I have not either witnessed myself or had conclusive evidence of.' Bearing this claim in mind, it is possible that the 'Double Murder and Suicide' headline which Owen reads on a newsagent's placard referred to the very Frank Cavilla whose fate was recorded at the beginning of this chapter. Owen's observation however is incisive: 'the jury had returned the usual verdict, "Temporary Insanity". It never seemed to occur to these people that the truth was that to continue to suffer hopelessly like this was evidence of permanent insanity.'[18] Tressell's eye for detail and his powers of description are formidable and we are left with the certainty that what we read here is true both in the literary and the literal senses and this gives the work great force and poignancy.

The works we have been considering so far have been exclusively pre-1914 and they were unmistakably written to inform middle-class readers and audiences about the conditions in which their fellow citizens had to live. The message was unequivocal: these things should not *be*. Jack London concluded his description of the destitute of East London with the following: 'if this is the best that civilisation can do for the human, then give us howling and naked savagery. Far better to be a people of the wilderness and desert, of the cave and the squatting place, than to be a people of the machine and the Abyss.' Indeed T.H. Huxley, who had once served as a medical officer in the East End, said: 'Were the alternative presented me, I would deliberately prefer the life of the savage to that of those people of Christian London.'[19]

It might seem plausible to suppose that the First World War, which undoubtedly threw the classes together in a common enterprise such as had never happened before, brought an increased understanding of the problems of poverty. For some it did, as Siegfried Sassoon made clear in his *Memoirs of an Infantry Officer*.[20] Sassoon writes that in 1917 he 'was only beginning to learn that life for the majority of the population is an unlovely struggle against unfair odds, culminating in a cheap funeral'. Others learned little or nothing, though Lord Curzon, seeing his troops washing on one occasion, admitted to being amazed at how white were the skins of working-class men. Several postwar writers, however, were as convinced of the necessity of awakening a largely ignorant middle class to the evils of poverty as ever Bernard Shaw had been.

In January 1936 Victor Gollancz commissioned a writer at the beginning of his career, who had already vividly depicted life amongst the poor in Paris and London, to write a book about the conditions of the poor in the north of England. George Orwell's father had served as a civil servant in India and the family had subsequently moved back to live in genteel but straightened circumstances in Suffolk. After a brief period as an Imperial Policeman Orwell had decided to establish himself as a writer and had chosen to live amongst and write about the poor. Hence his commission. With an advance of £500 Orwell set out for foreign parts, taking the train to Coventry and then travelling by foot and bus up to Manchester, staying in cheap hotels and lodging houses. For a southerner with only limited experiences of the North (his sister lived in suburban Leeds), the Black Country and the Potteries in late January must have been a chastening experience. From Manchester Orwell made his way to Wigan where he established himself in lodgings above a tripe shop, locally considered, he proudly tells us, to be a 'right filthy hole'. He spent most of his time in Wigan visiting people's houses, collecting data on living and working conditions from local libraries and so on. In Yorkshire, too, he was to collect statistics, cull newspapers, and above all, meet working and unemployed men. Of all his experiences the most indelible were his trips down mines: for a southern intellectual this was life on another planet. But he stuck to his job. He put together the bones of an account of the lives of the poor, amply supported by narrative *à la* Jack London on the one hand and statistical information on the other. Actually he gleaned something else from his travels, arguably more important, but we shall return to that later.

The fruits of Orwell's labours appeared in *The Road to Wigan Pier*, the first half of which paints a harrowing landscape of destitution and despair. Roused from sleep by the clumping of the mill-girls' clogs on the cobbles outside, Orwell describes the world to which he wakes. He goes on to chronicle the habits of the shop owners, the Brookers, with meticulous (and merciless) accuracy: their meanness of spirit, their self-pity, their squalid life amounting to an 'endless muddle of slovened jobs' and their excruciatingly Pinteresque habit of saying the same thing over and over. Their existence is typified by a set of crumbs whose day-by-day progress down the table is charted by Orwell.

The landscape of industrial Lancashire is no less squalid than the Brookers' house. The lives of the poor are dominated by the inhuman force of industrial detritus; it seems to enter their souls. 'The North', he says, is 'so frightful and so arresting that you are obliged, as it were, to come to terms with it.' Sheffield is unambiguously described as the ugliest town in the world. Although Orwell tells us plainly that the lives of the poor in the North would still be dominated by the prevalent modes of production however pleasant the factories, mills and mines might be, the fact is they are not pleasant: they are oppressively ugly. Orwell's arresting description of a woman unblocking a drainpipe captures in cameo the nature of the lives of so many of those living in industrial squalor:[21]

> I had time to see everything about her – her sacking apron, her clumsy clogs, her arms reddened by the cold ... she had a round pale face, the usual exhausted face of the slum girl who is twenty-five and looks forty, thanks to miscarriages and drudgery: and it wore, for the second in which I saw it, the most desolate, hopeless expression I have seen.

Orwell assures us that this expression shows unmistakably that she *knows* how desperate her situation is. To believe that it is different for 'them'; that brought up in the slums 'they' don't know any better, is to be seduced by a corrupting fallacy. 'She knew well enough what was happening to her – understood as well as I did how dreadful a destiny it was to be kneeling there in the bitter cold, on the slimy stones of a slum backyard, poking a stick up a foul drain-pipe.'

It is Orwell's arresting image of this young woman, ravaged by miscarriages and the burdens of family life, that stays with us, but we cannot ignore the careful collection of data that Orwell uses to build up his picture of working-class housing or of the realities of unemployment. He provides, for example, a statistical analysis of what the poor spend their money on; he uses government statistics to indicate the sheer extent of poverty and malnutrition. He seeks to engage not merely our greater understanding but also our sympathy, pointing out that unemployment means the loss of the ability to feed and clothe one's family, the loss of the sense of contributing, through labour, to the community: the loss of self-esteem.

Orwell was writing to inform middle-class socialists or potential socialists in the south of England, and his technique was to establish his own credentials as 'one of them' and then to take them by the hand, as it were, and show them the world of the poor, a world about as alien to his respectable audience as the underground world of the dreadful Morlocks in H.G. Wells's *The Time Machine* was to the Eloi. His message was just the same as London's: if you and your family could not tolerate such a life, why should anybody have to tolerate it? Orwell's *Wigan Pier* was published by Gollancz's Left Book Club but its influence was felt well beyond that circle.

Just as widely read was Walter Greenwood's novel *Love on the Dole* (1933), a film version of which was banned from public viewing until after the 1939–45 war. Greenwood's story concerns the people of a fictional working-class suburb of Manchester, Hanky Park, and especially the members of the Hardcastle family. Harry, just out of school, and working as a part-time clerk to a local pawnbroker, wanted only to go for an apprenticeship at Marlowe's, a huge engineering works. Engineering, after all, is much manlier than bookkeeping. Eventually he is taken on and joins the harsh world of Marlowe's:[22]

> Such a row. As though a million boys were running stakes along iron railings, simultaneously. Every man stone deaf after a six-month's spell of work there. Phew! But they *were* men.

With both Harry and his older sister in work the Hardcastles lived a reasonably comfortable existence. But Harry grows up, his apprenticeship finishes and he gets his cards – as his parents had predicted – from Marlowe's. They can employ another youngster to do his job more cheaply now that he is qualified. Immediately Harry's relationship with the family is transformed; he is now a liability, not an asset. Worse, his own plans to marry Helen are torpedoed and his easy optimism that he was 'certain to find a berth with persistence' gives way to a 'scaring haunting dread'. His long search ends in complete failure. Unemployment begins to grip him more and more firmly, like a wasting disease, souring his former pleasures, weakening his spirit, transforming his buoyant personality.

> You fell into the habit of slouching, of putting your hands in your pockets and keeping them there; of glancing at people furtively, ashamed of your secret … [but] you knew that your shabbiness betrayed you … breeches backside patched and repatched; patches on knees, on elbows. Jesus! All bloody patches.

Amongst the many unemployed is Larry Meath, a self-educated artisan with strong left-wing views, who is engaged to Sally, Harry's sister. Marriage with no income seemed impossible for them, as it did for Harry and Helen, but for the latter couple there came to be no choice: Helen became pregnant. Harry's father points out that they could not live at home – too many mouths to feed. Larry Meath, meanwhile, a sick man, died after taking part in a demonstration which the police dealt with ruthlessly. Sally, distraught, decided to take her destiny in her own hands. She took up an offer from the local bookmaker, with money and influence, to become his mistress. The family was mortified and her father accused her of whoring, telling her she wasn't fit to be his daughter. She replied that she could feed and clothe herself, could get her brother a job, and that that counted for more than 'being respectable'. Her immoral liaison gave Sally some security and influence, and she was able to get a job for her father, too, which he was not too proud to accept. Yet Greenwood leaves us under no illusion that Sally's decision is not wholly morally reprehensible, and that she also felt this. Even the shiftless Harry felt remorse at having got a job so underhandedly. On his way home from work one evening he saw an old friend:

> He was standing [on the corner of North Street] as motionless as a statue, cap neb pulled over his eyes, gaze fixed on the pavement, hands in pocket, shoulders hunched, the bitter wind blowing his thin trousers tightly against his legs … No influential person to pull strings on his behalf; no wages for him tonight; no planning for the morrow. He was an anonymous unit of an army of three millions for whom there was no tomorrow. Harry faltered, licked his lips then stole away, guiltily, down a back entry, unable to summon the nerve to face his friend.

Even though his own position was secure Harry could not take pleasure from it because he could not claim the customary solidarity with his comrades that had been his of right. Greenwood knows how significant in working-class life this solidarity is, realises too that Harry will feel bitterly the sacrifice that his sister had made. She was no Mrs Warren. Greenwood shows that acting immorally 'works' in the world of Hanky Park and indeed so does criminality. The state is afraid of the potential social disruption that criminals might cause who, having done their time, return to a society that cannot offer a job. So it provides them with job opportunities. The best way to be fed and housed and found employment by the state then is to commit a felony. From a socialist perspective the irony is absolute.

Our writers explore a common theme, the debilitating and demeaning effects of poverty on the human spirit. We do not have to take only their words for it. They built upon a tradition established by earlier writers such as Dickens and Charles Kingsley. There is, moreover, substantial documentary evidence, from various government reports from the 1840s onwards, from Booth's *Life and Labour of the People in London*[23] (researched by, amongst others, Beatrice Webb), the fruits of Rowntree's research in York, *Poverty: A Study of Town Life*,[24] and the later *Minority Report* of the Poor Law Commission in 1908, and in addition a number of government committee reports around the turn of the century, one of which was alluded to earlier. Samuel Hynes, reviewing this evidence, concludes that 'the poor were more wretched and more numerous than at any other time in English history' whereas the rich were richer 'and more conspicuous in the luxuries'.[25] This is an oversimplification because both Booth and Rowntree had a different picture to paint of the better-off working class. Nevertheless it was true of the poor and whilst grounds probably do not exist for any entirely accurate comparisons, most available measures indicated that the position of the working class had deteriorated over the last quarter of the nineteenth century and scarcely improved during the first third of the twentieth.

Poverty as inevitable

The writers we have considered so far leave us in no doubt that the social system that underpins capitalism is immoral and must be changed. Far from being natural, let alone naturally beneficent, the hierarchical structure that characterised capitalism was no more than a device to repress the poor, as the Italian socialist writer Ignazio Silone sought to demonstrate.

His 'peasant's view' shows the 'natural' hierarchy:[26]

> At the head of everything is God, Lord of Heaven
> After him comes Prince Torlonia, Lord of the earth,
> Then come Prince Torlonia's armed guards;
> The come Prince Torlonia's armed guards' dogs
> Then nothing at all. Then nothing at all. Then nothing at all.
> Then come the peasants, and that's all.

Yet others took a different view. 'You are to consider', as Dr Johnson told his travelling companion Boswell, 'that it is our duty to maintain the subordination of civilised society; and where there is gross deviation from rank, it should be punished so as to deter others from the same perversions.'[27] In the following century Thomas Carlye castigated the Chartists for failing to recognise that 'a man has his superiors, a regular hierarchy above him; extending up, degree by degree, to Heaven itself and God the Maker, who made his world not for anarchy but for rule and order'.

George Gissing's fatalism came to mirror Johnson's stance much more closely than Silone's. Gissing as a young man had been a reasonably well-read socialist sympathiser. It is not easy to grasp how and when his attitude changed, though his reading of Herbert Spencer might have had a considerable effect on his thinking. It is certain that he was dismayed by the appearance in a London court of William Morris, whom he greatly respected, on a charge of assaulting a policeman: 'Why cannot he write poetry in the shade?' he queried, 'He will inevitably coarsen himself in the company of ruffians.'[28] What Gissing came to believe, for whatever reason, and to seek to show, is that those who rise above their station are likely to be punished, like Hardy's Jude who mused: 'I may do some good before I am dead – be a sort of success as a frightful example of what not to do … I was, perhaps, after all, a paltry victim to the spirit of mental and social restlessness that makes so many unhappy in these days'.[29] Poor Jude, it will be remembered, had received a letter from the Master of Biblioll college, the only college to bother to reply to his letter seeking to enrol, to the following effect:[30]

> Sir, I have read your letter with interest; and judging from your description of yourself as a working-man, I venture to think that you will have a much better chance of success in life by remaining in your own sphere and sticking to your trade than by adopting any other course. That, therefore, is what I advise you to do.

If only he had taken that advice.

Gissing would certainly have tried to dissuade Jude from seeking a college education; in fact if one central theme emerges from Gissing's work it is that although life tends to be miserable for working people there is little that we can do about it either at an individual or a social level. It is true, as critics have pointed out, that Gissing took no account of 'the rapid development of militant trade unionism and the escalation of industrial conflict',[31] or indeed of other events in working-class history that were going on around him, but given his sense of fatalism it is by no means certain that these factors would have much influenced his judgement about the possibilities for social progress.

Gissing's bleak philosophy infuses all his work even while he clearly sympathises with his working-class characters. 'Who was John Hewett', asks the character of that name in *The Nether World*, 'that he should look for pleasant things in his course through the world? "We are the lower orders: we are the working classes", he said bitterly to his friends, and that seemed the final answer to all his aspirations.' Hewett's son's honeymoon consisted of a one-day visit to the Crystal Palace where he and his new wife watched what Gissing describes as 'the great review of the people' which passed them. Respectable, sober, but so dull:[32]

> See how worn out the girls are becoming, how they gape, what listless eyes they have … Observe the middle-aged women; it would be small surprise that their good looks had vanished, but whence comes it they are animal, repulsive, absolutely vicious in ugliness? Mark the men in their turn: four in every six have visages so deformed by ill health that they excite our disgust.

Unlike her drunken new husband young Mrs Hewett was never able to abandon herself to the 'pleasures' of the day: 'She was thinking all the time that on the morrow it would be necessary to pawn her wedding ring.'[33]

The central character of the story, Sidney Kirkwood, though by no means a revolutionary, cannot accept the injustices of the existing social structure. But with what Gissing describes as the ripening of his intellect he saw 'only more and more reasons to condemn and execrate those social disorders of which his own wretched experience was but an illustration'. Although Gissing's criticisms of the consequences of the social system for the poor are scalding and he portrays their miseries remorselessly, he offers no hope for a juster, fairer order. His characters are all of them doomed. They have only one choice: to accept their lot honourably or dishonourably, as it were. Clara Hewett, self-willed and ruthless, who strikes out from the nether world with hopes to establish a career on the stage, is pulled down at the point of her triumph; acid thrown in her face at the contrivance of a rival destroys her looks and her career and brings her back down to hell. Jane Snowden and Kirkwood himself, who earn our respect for their integrity, are nevertheless shown towards the end of the book to have been thwarted in all their ambitions, crushed intellectually and spiritually.

In his introduction to the Harvester edition of *The Nether World*, John Goode observes that the book was considered by many of Gissing's contemporaries to be a 'valuable document in the cause of reform',[34] and though Gissing himself considered this to be a woeful misreading it is impossible for the reader not to extend sympathy towards many of the characters. They seem to us not so much the victims of personal deficiencies – some 'vicious mole in nature' – as the casualties of a social system created not by God but by a social class anxious to optimise its own benefit. Gissing's intention was to show us what he called 'the destructive futility of philanthropy'. Now, such fatalism might be considered defensible if class divisions were taken to represent stages in evolution, in a Spencerian sense, with the working class as an inferior evolutionary type. This might well have been Gissing's intention, since, as Goode reminds us, Spencer's *The Man versus the State*[35] was published around this time. We know that Gissing had been influenced by Schopenhauer, who had written much earlier on similar themes,[36] and we know he read Spencer.

Demos was regarded by contemporary reviewers as a testament to the Spencerian notion that 'it is by the heart alone that social regeneration is possible'.[37] Here Gissing sets out most fully his beliefs on the limits of social progress. The novel concerns an intelligent, idealist young working-class socialist, Richard Mutimer, whose sudden acquisition of wealth and subsequent adventures form the plot. His capital allows him the opportunity to put into practice his political and social theories. But Mutimer is brought down – crushed – by forces brought into play as a consequence of his own character defects. (This fate is common to Gissing's working-class characters: John Pether, a revolutionary figure in *Workers in the Dawn*, dies the death of an idiot in isolation; John Hewett in *The Nether World*, a much more sympathetic figure, as we have seen, is nevertheless shown to be his own (and his family's) worst enemy, a man whose socialism is accompanied by a streak of cantankerous idleness.) Mutimer puts his newly found wealth into a New Lanark-like community (New Wanley), with a large industrial plant and a new town to house the workforce. Its failure seems to the reader to be inevitable.

What Gissing wants to say is that the working-class is simply not capable, individually or collectively, of self-improvement: to coin a phrase of Wells's,[38] the 'claw of the beast rests upon them'. Gissing's message to the poor is that they should recognise their social and political incapacities and accept with good grace the life to which they have been born. Gissing puts his faith rather in the beneficence and wisdom of the landed aristocracy. The Tory democrat Eldon tells us: 'to the individual poor man or woman I would give my last penny. It is when they rise against me as a class that I become pitiless.' Eldon's class has enjoyed generations of social advantage and as a consequence, as Eldon's mother says, 'our opportunities lead us to see truths to which the eyes of the poor and ignorant are blind'. When New Wanley fails the whole enterprise is simply swallowed up by the English countryside and the natural order is restored.

From what I have said so far it might be concluded that in *Demos* Gissing has presented us with a broad-brush picture of working men who claim to be socialists and who, given the chance to put their ideals into operation, fail, and an equally broad-brush depiction of what might be called traditional Toryism, which, with its sense of *noblesse oblige*, triumphs. In fact the depiction of socialism is, as John Goode points out, 'close to the actuality' rather than broad-brush.[39] The character of Mutimer is modelled, superficially but nevertheless clearly, on the famous radical John Burns. Incidents in the story would have been recognised by contemporary readers; for example, the riot at the end of the book would be understood to represent the Trafalgar Square riot of February 1886 (the year of the book's publication). Indeed the socialism put in place in New Wanley clearly reflects the proposals outlined in the manifesto of the Marxist Social Democratic Federation. So if the socialism depicted for us by Gissing in *Demos* is a straw man, it is nonetheless a painstakingly grafted one.

By way of contrast the Toryism of Eldon is of no political interest at all. At one point Eldon claims disparagingly that when he is conversing with Mutimer he seems to be holding a dialogue with the twentieth-century. If so, it must have been over the dead body of the nineteenth-century, for as far as Gissing is concerned, the bourgeois revolution seems never to have occurred. Where are the Gradgrinds and the Bounderbys? What has happened to the social system that both Marx and Carlyle characterised as being held together by nothing more than the cash nexus? The reader does not have to be a Marxist to appreciate that socialism grew as a response to the bourgeois revolution and makes little sense without it. Disraeli sought to make traditional Toryism appropriate for an industrial age; Eldon (and Gissing) seem unaware of the industrial revolution and its social and political ramifications. Their form of Toryism is crassly anachronistic.

Poverty as inefficiency

One final element in the critique of capitalism and its consequences needs to be considered. It strikes at the heart of capitalism's Panglossian self-justification: that there was no viable alternative. Writers attacking this position urged that capitalism was not merely an immoral economic and social system but an inefficient one. These writers pointed out that there *was* an alternative: socialism. Robert Owen had argued as early as 1827 in his *Cooperative Magazine* that cooperation was economically superior to competition. Indeed, basing their arguments on Marxist and later Jevonian economic theories, leading Fabians actually believed that the inefficiencies of capitalist ownership, production and exchange were so apparent that they, the Fabians, would be able to persuade capitalists of the superiority of socialism.

The principal exponent of this view amongst imaginative writers was H.G. Wells. Wells was one of the greatest writers of his day, described by the *Nouvelle Revue Française* as: 'une lampe qui éclaire la marche du vingtième siècle', though his early career gave no hint of such fame. He had failed to gain a degree at the Royal College of Science and was subsequently prevented from pursuing even the career in second-rate educational establishments to which his failure had condemned him by two haemorrhages of the lung. He was forced to try his hand at writing and within very few years had established an international reputation. In what was intended to be, but never quite became, his early masterpiece, *Tono Bungay*,[40] Wells addressed directly the social and political inefficiencies (inextricably linked) which characterised the capitalist system. *Tono Bungay* is the story of the Ponderevo family and especially of George. George was brought up in a stately mansion where his mother was in service (like Wells's own mother). Bladesover symbolised style and culture but it was based on an hierarchical system that no longer had any rational justification, as young George discovered when he was thrown out after a rough-and-tumble with the son of the owner. Yet Wells shows a sneaking regard for the old aristocratic system and when later the old house is sold to a capitalist, a Jewish entrepreneur, and his family, George reflected that the new owners 'could not have made it, they cannot replace it; they just happen to break out over it saprophytically'. Meanwhile George had been sent to stay with his aunt and uncle who own a chemist's in a small country town (autobiographical again) and when the business failed through no fault of the family's they moved on to London. George followed them and his description of south London as he came in on the train has much in common with Orwell's later description of Sheffield or Wigan, but Wells's focus and his judgement are quite different: 'It is a *foolish* community that can house whole classes, useful and helpful, honest and loyal classes, in such squalidly unsuitable dwellings.'[41]

George's uncle made a great success of London. He invented a cure-all cough mixture, Tono Bungay. This panacea, though entirely bogus, created trade, and therefore work; so Uncle Edward saw himself as a great benefactor. George was not so sanguine: '£150,000 – think of it! – for the goodwill in a string of lies and a trade in bottles of mitigated water. Do you realise the *madness* of a world that sanctions such a thing?'[42] George concluded that capitalism was a spectacle of 'forces running to waste, of people who use and do not replace, the story of a community hectic with wasting, aimless fever of trade and money making and pleasure seeking'. Tono Bungay crashed and so did Uncle Edward. George came out of the crash with some credit and decided to devote his life to science and to progress. He joined the Fabian Society but, like Wells himself, had little confidence in that movement's capacity to shape the future. At the end of the book we find George sailing past the Houses of Parliament in a destroyer which he had designed. He expressed contempt for 'that great pile of Victorian architecture': it represented only a 'feudal scheme overtaken by fatty degeneration and stupendous accidents of hypertrophy' amidst which 'no plan appears, no intention, no comprehensive desire. That is the very key of it all.' Those who know anything of Wells's personal experiences with politics will appreciate how heartfelt was this critique.

It was to be followed up two years later by the partly autobiographical novel, *The New Machiavelli*,[43] which exhibited even more spleen. Remington, the hero, was a young man intent upon achieving political power in order to run the nation's (indeed the Empire's) affairs more efficiently. A leading light on the radical wing of the Liberal Party, he became entirely disenchanted with that party and sought instead to operate through the infant Labour Party. Having become persuaded by the plausibility of socialism he enthusiastically joined the Fabians, where he met the Baileys – a thinly disguised portrayal of the Webbs. At first the Fabians appealed to Remington (as indeed they did to Wells himself) as a small scientifically trained elite enjoying the ear and attention of the powerful. But for Remington and his creator the reality hardly matched the theory. The Baileys did not employ a genuinely scientific approach – they were 'cocksurists in matter of fact; sentimentalists in behaviour' – and the Fabians as a group were nothing more than 'prigs at play'. Remington continued to believe in his own form of socialism but came to have no faith in the Labour movement.

His passion for progress brought Remington at last to the Conservatives, a party torn between a 'rude benevolence of public intervention' and a desire to preserve the existing order. (It not merely stood for the existing order, it *was* the existing order.) When Remington had to explain to his staunchly Liberal wife why he had decided to change party he said that the real enemy of progress was not this or that party, it was general 'muddle-headedness'. This could only be defeated by an aristocracy of understanding and purpose drawn from the ranks of the 'economically powerful and intellectually able', of which he planned to be part. And Remington remained convinced that this aristocracy would be led, no doubt with his guidance, towards a form of socialism.

And what form of socialism? It was for Remington 'the scientific idea, the idea of veracity – of human confidence in humanity – of all that mattered in human life outside the life of individuals.'[44] The basis of Remington's and Wells's socialism was the same as the basis 'upon which all scientific work is carried on ... It is an assertion that things are in their nature orderly, that things may be computed, may be calculated upon and may be foreseen',[45] and its objective was not individual liberty so much as the better ordering of society.

Wells's politics were driven by his scientific knowledge. Mankind was doomed, he argued, as a consequence of pestilence, war, natural disaster or finally the death of the planet, unless he learned how to organise as a species. And capitalism was simply incapable of such organisation. His criticisms of capitalism in *Tono Bungay* and *The New Machiavelli* pale by comparison with *War of the Worlds*[46] in which he depicts the consequences of a Martian invasion. Wells's criticism of how the emergency was handled is withering. Capitalist society's leaders were 'serene in their assurance over their empire over matter' but could it be, he asks, that 'the infusoria under the microscope [feel] the same way?' The comparison is pointed: capitalist man is as incapable of standing in the way of the Martians as would be those infusoria of withstanding the laboratory assistant's thumb. It is not simply national leaders who are criticised but modern man himself. One of the characters, an artilleryman on the run, announced his intention to take to the sewers and to set up alternative societies there. He could not count upon the ordinary citizens to defy the Martians. Ordinary men and women will be well looked after by the

Martians, fed, kept healthy, with all their needs seen to by their masters – who will eventually eat them. The Martians might even keep some humans as pets. Indeed, most men would wonder how on earth they managed before the Martians came. When finally the Martians were defeated it was not by the bravery of the common people, or by the sagacity of their leaders, or by capitalism's advanced technologies, but by viruses – 'the humblest thing that God in his wisdom has put upon this earth'.

For writers like Wells, then, it was capitalism's inefficiencies that earned their scorn more than its alleged immorality, though clearly the two were connected. Wells exposed capitalist society's incapacity to act decisively or to organise itself intelligently in a series of brilliantly original scientific romances of which *War of the Worlds* was only one. *The Time Machine*,[47] *First Men on the Moon*[48] and *Food of the Gods*[49] bristled with images to puncture capitalism's serene assurance 'over [its] empire over matter'. It is clear from Wells's writing that if mankind is to prosper, or even survive, it needs the rigorous discipline of hierarchy and purpose: it needs a highly organised world socialist government administered by a scientifically trained elite. To suggest that such a society could or should be democratic in nature was an absurdity. Wells despised the 'ordinary' in all its manifestations, especially in people, and he rejected it out of hand.

Food of the Gods is a fable that exposes the shortcomings of the world in which Wells lived in the most arresting way. It concerns the discovery of a wonder food, herakleophorbia, which produces in those who eat it not merely greatly increased size but also intelligence. And the inhabitants and institutions of Wells's capitalist world stood shoulder to shoulder against the giants, against change and growth, from the 'invincible inertia of the great mass of the people' to the bankrupt politicians (the 'vote-monsters' for whom the only realities were gatherings, caucuses and votes); to the pedestrian bureaucrats (who could not see beyond the administrative problems presented by the giants); to the aristocracy and the capitalists who could see only threats to their own dominance; finally to the Church whose great truth, *ut in principio, nunc est et semper*, provided a mantra for the whole of capitalist society that represented the absolute antithesis of Wells's faith in progress. Wells was the apostle of change and of growth, and capitalism had ceased to be a vehicle of either. The vehicles of change and of growth in this narrative possess a largeness of spirit in the most obvious way and their task is to bring about change. 'We fight not for ourselves', says one of the leaders of the Children of the Food, 'but for growth, growth that goes on for ever ... that is the law of the spirit.' When asked if the giants' purpose might also be to help the 'little people' he replies with a question of his own: help them fail? No, their responsibility is to the future, to growth. Wells's socialism, then, is about change, and we will have the opportunity to explore the nature of that change later, but for the moment we can be satisfied with calling it world socialism, and capitalist inefficiency stood in its way.

Bernard Shaw, too, was scathingly critical of capitalist inefficiency. It is true that Andrew Undershaft, the armaments manufacturer, is a Shavian hero but it is clear that he is meant to stand for what such men might do if they had vision, not what they were actually doing in Edwardian Britain. If we wish to come to grips with Shaw's views on capitalists as they were, then we should consider the manner in which he portrays the career of his archetypal capitalist, the ruthless Boss Mangan in *Heartbreak House*, or most of the members of the Cabinet in *The Applecart*.[50] Indeed Shaw despaired of long-term progress – which for him as for Wells equated to the establishment of socialism – until an economically equal society made available a much wider pool of naturally gifted leaders.[51]

Conclusions

G.D.H. Cole once described socialism as a 'broad movement on behalf of the underdog'. It was a lot more than that but as far as many socialists are concerned, Marx included, it *was* that. What most of the writers whom we have considered achieved, even Gissing, was to evoke a public awareness of the conditions of the poor and, as a direct corollary, public sympathy. And in the longer run public sympathy will prove a serviceable platform for political action. On completing his investigations in the north of England, Orwell wrote: 'before you can be sure whether you are genuinely in favour of socialism, you have got to decide whether things at the present are tolerable or not tolerable'. The 'you' to whom he refers was the middle-class individual who, by and large, had remained remarkably ignorant of the conditions of the poor. In J.B. Priestley's chilling phrase, 'When it wined and dined, laughed and made love [the middle class] had not yet caught a glimpse of the terrible stone face this world can wear'.[52] As the 1930s wore on, however, they had come to recognise that face and, given the opportunity in 1945, against general expectation, they gave their support to those who at least sought to ensure that the lives of the poor would be transformed and to banish that stone face from the land.

And what had imaginative writers contributed to this development? Bernard Shaw, in his capacity as Fabian pamphleteer, wrote that the collection and publication of authentic and impartial statistical tracts would 'make the public conscious of the evil condition of society'. But Shaw himself wrote plays, and he did so with much the same purpose in mind. Imaginative literature, when it describes the kind of conditions and addresses the kind of issues we have been considering, is close to doing the job that Shaw writes about. But it achieves so much more. No set of figures, no moral statement by even such an eminent figure as Pope Leo XIII, who declared that the obligation upon an employer to pay his workers a reasonable living wage was 'more imperious and ancient than any bargain between man and man', can engage us as completely as Orwell's picture of that young working-class woman unblocking her drain; or Greenwood's depiction of Harry slinking off round a back street rather than face an unemployed friend; or Gissing's juxtaposition of the ease of middle-class life and the desperation of the lives of working-class families (indeed not just the juxtaposition but the dependent relationship between them); or Shaw's analysis of the rationale behind what was later called Rachmanism; or finally Tressell's depiction of the helplessness of the decent working man in the grip of an economic downturn.

Shaw and Wells did not merely criticise capitalism for immorally condemning the majority to a life of overwork and poverty. They criticised it on its own terms, as an efficient modernising economic system. It was nothing of the kind. Shaw's critique represented a ruthless analysis of the character of individual capitalists on stage; Wells condemned contemporary capitalism by a series of brilliant analogies. Together they helped to strip capitalism of its confident self-justification. As a social and economic system, it was, they said, both immoral and inefficient. No treatise in economics and philosophy could match the power or immediacy of Wells's or Shaw's withering attacks on the self-justification of the owning classes – that capitalism, whatever its flaws, was better than any alternative. In brief, capitalist economic efficiency was exposed as just as threadbare as capitalist social morality and imaginative literature stripped away its pretensions as no other form of analysis could.

Characters, situations, relationships fix themselves in our mind in the way that a purely statistical analysis would never do: we are engaged much more fully. And at the end of this debate, as at the beginning, we are *forced* to confront Jack London's question concerning that vermin-infested corpse: if it is wrong for your mother or mine to die like this, how can it be right for anybody's mother to die like this?

3
Power to the People?

There was agreement amongst many of the writers we considered in the last chapter that the alleviation of poverty was both a moral and economic imperative. However, the alleviation of poverty (progress) can be seen to present a paradox. Does 'progress' require a powerful state to act on behalf of working people to improve their living and working conditions? Or does it rather require an enabling state to facilitate, through its own withering away perhaps, the proletariat's attaining its own self-declared interest? To put it more pithily: should the proletariat be given what it 'needs' or get what it 'wants'? Since the writers we considered were for the most part socialists we might have expected some agreement as to how this paradox is to be resolved. In fact this is not so, and the contradictions in their approaches suggest not simply different conceptions of socialism and capitalism but different conceptions of human nature.[1]

It is common to draw a distinction between two schools of socialist thought which might conveniently be called scientific and ethical.[2] Always ambiguous and imprecise, this categorisation represents an attempt to distinguish between two approaches that really are different and whose differences need to be understood. The first is represented preeminently in the United Kingdom by the Fabian Society and more especially by two of its most imaginative and influential polemicists, George Bernard Shaw and H.G. Wells.

Fabians and workers

Bernard Shaw was one of those young intellectuals who had gone to Henry George's celebrated lecture on the nationalisation of land to the Zetetical Society in London in 1883. Having subsequently attended meetings of Hyndman's Democratic Federation to discuss these issues further, he found himself introduced to the work of Karl Marx. This was an event which 'converted him to socialism, turned him into a revolutionary writer, made him a political agitator, changed his outlook, directed his energy, influenced his art, gave him a religion, and, as he claimed, made a man of him'.[3] The year 1883 was an eventful one for Shaw, since he not only found himself a religion and a sense of purpose but, under the influence of the theatre critic William Archer, also discovered his vocation. The failed novelist soon became, in his own modest estimation, Britain's most popular playwright since Shakespeare. Archer and Shaw collaborated on the first act of *Widowers' Houses*; thereafter Shaw was his own man, though the early influence of Henrik Ibsen, always denied by Shaw, is palpable.

The Fabian Society, which grew in 1884 out of the shell of a group known as the Fellowship of the Good Life, was dedicated to 'educate, agitate and organise' so as to bring about, according to Shaw, a 'tremendous smash up of society'.[4] In their origins, if Shaw is to be believed, the Fabians were 'just as insurrectionary as the Federation' (Hyndman's Democratic, later Social Democratic Federation or SDF). But Shaw's own revolutionary credentials were soon put to the test. On Sunday November 7 1887 (one of Britain's 'Bloody Sundays') he found himself next to the radical socialist and feminist Annie Besant at the head of a column of marchers making for an illegal demonstration in Trafalgar Square. The column immediately in front was scattered by the police, and fleeing workers, recognising Shaw, asked him to take a lead. Shaw told them to make their own way into the square and when scuffling broke out around him, he edged away and joined a group of onlookers, earning the historian Cunningham Graham's barb that he had been the first man to run away on Bloody Sunday. Shaw was 31, a good age for a revolutionary leader, but these events had convinced him that such was not his destiny and he was right to be 'acutely aware of my disgraceful exposure as an incompetent windbag'.[5] Any tendency that Shaw or any of his fellow Fabians might have felt to lead a socialist insurrection died on 7 November 1887 and he became a 'non-combatant in an age of combative mass movements'.[6]

In fact an insurrection on behalf of the working-class was never likely to have appealed to Bernard Shaw. It is true that for twelve years Shaw spoke at public meetings on average three times each week, and by common accord he was one of the best public speakers of his day. More often than not his audience was substantially working-class and he often spoke, for example, at the dock gates of Poplar and West Ham.

Yet his hatred of poverty, so clearly expounded in his early works, seemed in many respects to extend to a hatred of the poor themselves. The following extract from one of Shaw's speeches states his position unambiguously:[7]

> As to the working classes I believe neither in their virtues nor their intelligence, on the contrary my objection to the existing order is precisely that it inevitably produces this wretched, idolatrous, sentimental, servile, anti-socialist mass of spoiled humanity which we call the proletariat and which neither understands, believes in us or likes us. I am no friend of the working class. I am its enemy to the extent of ardently desiring its extermination.

The thrust of the arguments of the authors we considered in the last chapter was much as Shaw states it here: capitalism can be judged to have failed palpably in terms of both morality and economics because it has produced the industrial proletariat. This being the case, Shaw goes on, it is disingenuous to construct an ideology, still less a plan of action, that owes its inspiration to the ambitions or self-perceived interests of that disadvantaged class. This is why Shaw regarded Marxism as political romance for it postulated the empowering, not long after the inevitably successful revolution, of the (admittedly now politically conscious) proletariat. We shall have the opportunity in a later chapter to explore in depth what Shaw proposed as an alternative course of action but for the present we should be aware that it was highly elitist in nature and not designed to be democratic in any ordinary sense of that word. 'We must eliminate the Yahoo', he concluded, 'or his vote will wreck the commonwealth.'[8] For Shaw and indeed for most of his fellow Fabians, socialism was not about giving power to the people. Rather socialism was a kind of ideological malt extract to be forced down the throat of an unenthusiastic working-class by a strong-armed, well-meaning Fabian care assistant. This was paternalism writ very large. Shaw claimed that the Fabians had never advanced any pretension to represent the working man,[9] and when challenged on the obvious lack of democracy implied by this claim – or disclaimer – he countered that the only meaningful definition of democracy was a political system that aimed for 'the greatest available welfare for the whole population'.[10] No wonder that Shaw, towards the end of his life, called himself a totalitarian democrat hoping for some benevolent dictatorship that would rule on behalf of, but not be responsible to, the working class.[11] If asked by critics why the people should not make their own laws his reply was rhetorical: why should not the people write their own plays?[12] Shaw, like the trade union leader Hipney in *On the Rocks*, was for 'any Napoleon or Mussolini or Lenin ... that has the stuff in them to take both the people and the spoilers and oppressors by the scruff of their silly necks and just sling them into the way they should go'. Power to the people? Not for Shaw: 'The more power the people are given, the more urgent becomes the need for some rational and well-informed super-power to dominate them and disable their inveterate admiration for international murder and national suicide.'[13]

Shaw's proposal for remedial action on behalf of the working-class by a socialist elite makes some sense. If the intention of that elite were to eliminate economic inequalities then surely Shaw's formulation – abolishing the proletariat – is no more than stating the objective in a forthright, not to say Swiftian, fashion. And the kind of workforce that would take its place is depicted in *Major Barbara* at Andrew Undershaft's munitions factory and the township serving it at Perivale St Andrew. When Barbara and her party visit they are struck by the nursing home, the libraries, the schools, the ballroom and banqueting chamber, the insurance fund, the pension fund, the building society, the 'various applications of co-operation'. Undershaft has abolished the working-class and replaced it with a contented workforce which is motivated[14]

> Not by words and dreams; but by thirty-eight shillings a week, a sound house in a handsome street, and a permanent job. In three weeks [the working man] will have a fancy waistcoat; in three months a tall hat and a chapel sitting; before the end of the year he will shake hands with a duchess at a Primrose League meeting, and join the Conservative Party.

Barbara, still concerned to save souls, realises instinctively that these 'fullfed, quarrelsome, snobbish, uppish creatures, all standing on their little rights and dignities' are in a position to exercise moral choice, unlike the 'weak souls in starved bodies, sobbing with gratitude for a scrap of bread' to whom she proffered religion and soup in the West Ham shelter. Undershaft's workforce is relatively prosperous and, within reasonable parameters, equal in terms of income and social condition. Yet the workers have no say whatever in the running of the company. Shaw's socialism, like Wells's, is truly paternalistic and its objective is to emancipate the proletariat from poverty in the certain belief that this will lead to its self-destruction as a class. So, like Wells, Shaw did not seek to empower the working-class: quite the opposite.

Shaw depicted the working-class as feckless. He believed that they could be 'bought off for thirty shilling a week', like Alfred Doolittle, father of Eliza in *Pygmalion*. Morally offended by Professor Higgins's request to take his daughter away to educate her, Doolittle demands his 'rights' as her father: a payment of £5. Assured by Colonel Pickering that Higgins's designs are entirely honourable, Doolittle replies: 'Corse they are Governor. If I thought they wasn't I'd ask fifty.' For the scientific socialist this is not a class to be entrusted with power. And as for Eliza, until she is transformed by Higgins she is considered by him to be incapable of understanding anything. 'Give her orders', he tells Higgins, 'that's what she wants.' Marx failed to understand, says Shaw, that the worker cannot claim and does not seek equality; he simply wants to be a bourgeois: 'Marx never got hold of him for a moment'.[15] George Orwell makes much the same point when talking about the waiters at Hotel 'X' in Paris: they don't despise the wealthy diner, they simply want to be one some day. As Shaw said:[16]

> In nothing is the middle-class origin of the Socialist movement so apparent as in the persistent delusions of Socialists as to an ideal proletariat, forced by the brutalities of the capitalist into an unwilling acquiescence in war, penal codes and other cruelties of civilisation. They still see the social problem, not sanely and objectively, but imaginatively, as the plot of a melodrama, with its villain and its heroine, its innocent beginning, troubled middle and happy ending. They are still the children and romancers of politics.

This is perhaps why the ineffectual John Tanner in *Man and Superman* was so obviously meant to resemble the revolutionary Marxist and leader of the SDF, H.M. Hyndman. What the poor needed above all was a strong, effective leadership that would abolish poverty, the most important by far of all political tasks, for poverty was the 'worst of all crimes'. The poor, said Shaw, 'poison us morally and physically; they force us to do away with our own liberties and to organise unnatural cruelties for fear they should rise against us and drag us down into their abyss'.[17]

So important was this huge task that only a single-minded leadership could manage it. Shaw's consequent admiration for strong leaders led him to draw conclusions which made the Hyndman he had poked fun at a model of common sense. 'Now in Herr Hitler', Shaw remarked in 1938, 'we have clearly no raving lunatic to deal with. He is a very able ruler and on most subjects a very sane one'.[18] As late as 1940 Shaw declared himself to have been a National Socialist before Hitler was born and he expressed the hope that Britain would soon 'emulate and surpass his achievements'.[19] Indeed, even after the Second World War Shaw declared that Lenin, through operating the New Economic Plan, was a Fabian at heart and Stalin, on adopting 'socialism in one country', had become a Fabian Revisionist.[20] And both, he added, were governing for the good of the workers.

Whilst recognising why Shaw might have admired a leader who had abolished unemployment – indeed in a manner of which Undershaft would have approved – it is nevertheless hard not to sympathise with Oscar Wilde's assessment of his compatriot: 'Mr Bernard Shaw has no enemies but is intensely disliked by all of his friends.'

Bernard Shaw was not the only exemplar of scientific socialism amongst major imaginative writers. His contemporary, H.G. Wells, was at least as influential and just as committed to the notion that the poor needed to be guided. Born the fourth child to parents who kept a small shop in Bromley in 1866, Wells won a scholarship to study at the Normal School (later the Royal College) of Science at South Kensington. One of his teachers was Darwin's friend and supporter T.H. Huxley. After a spell of teaching, ill health obliged Wells to consider alternative forms of earning a living and he took to writing. Within a remarkably short time he had established himself as a rising star. Wells considered himself a socialist and for him socialism was like science. It constituted a denial that future human progress depended upon chance and individual impulse; instead Wellsian socialism held that 'things are in their nature orderly, that things may be computed, calculated upon, and foreseen'.[21] Wells sought a 'comprehensive design' for all man's social activities so that mankind could be transformed from what he called a mob into an army.[22]

Like Shaw, Wells looked to a trained elite to manage society and indeed in 1902 he joined a brains trust set up by Beatrice Webb (later satirised by Wells as The Co-Efficients in *The New Machiavelli*) which included the Webbs, Grey, Leo Amery, Milner, Pember Reeves, Bertrand Russell (briefly) and was chaired by Haldane. His depiction of lesser mortals whom such an elite might manage is projected in the brilliantly imaginative novel *Food of the Gods*, in which, as we have seen, everything that is ordinary is held up for our contempt. Ordinary people are a hindrance to Wells's and his new men's project of progress. It was, in Orwell's arresting phrase, the tale of Giant the Jack Killer.

Whilst the heroes of Wells's early social novels, especially Mr Polly, seem to believe that individual freedom is a good to be pursued impulsively and that 'freedom is fundamentally libidinous',[23] his later heroes, though they may occasionally, like Remington, succumb to the drives of the libido, are altogether more serious-minded. They tend to be fixated, as was Wells himself, by that 'most consistently convincing of nightmares – the extinction of the human race'.[24] If the human race was to be saved, it would not be by ordinary people and democracy. The artilleryman in *War of the Worlds* comments on the necessity of controlling 'this oafish crowd … this gaping, stinking, bombing, shooting, throat slitting, cringing brawl of gawky, undernourished riff-raff'. According to Anthony West,[25] the most chilling picture of the ordinary man and woman is presented in *The Island of Doctor Moreau*. The strange people that Prendick meets are in fact beasts who have been taught to conduct themselves like 'people' after the doctor has realigned muscles and sinews to allow them to walk upright. They have been taught primitive speech and to obey some fundamental laws. But they later revert and kill their human captors. Prendick is lucky to escape with his life but, safely home in England, is unable to persuade himself that the men and women he sees around him 'were not also another, still passably human, beast people, animals wrought into the outward image of human souls'.[26] Who would trust such people?

Wells saw himself as a prophet, as a man who could foresee the future and help to save the world – literally – but who was constrained by his contemporaries' indifference and short-sightedness. We see the fate of the prophet played out in imaginative short stories such as *The Country of the Blind* and *The Wonderful Visit*. In the first Nuñez stumbles upon a valley in which live a race of blind people. At first they refuse to believe that Nuñez has the power of sight but finally acknowledge his gift. They will allow him to stay only if he agrees to have his eyes put out. In the second an angel comes to a Sussex village; it is made clear to him that if he wishes to stay a surgical operation to remove the deformities on his shoulders would be highly advisable.

Bestial, blind or simply hopelessly conformist, ordinary people were not the stuff from which a socialist society could be made. Like his fellow Fabian and imaginative writer Bernard Shaw, Wells looked to an elite of like-minded progressives and was absolutely certain that it was 'no good asking people what they want. That is the error of democracy. You have first to think out what they ought to want if society is to be saved. Then you have to tell them what they want and see that they get it'.[27]

Ethical socialists and workers

How different are the views of the ethical socialists. In contrast to the scientific socialists they are convinced that far from being blind or bestial the proletariat possesses some innate political wisdom which requires not abolition by a socialist elite in the name of efficiency or welfare, but nourishment. According to Dennis and Halsey,[28] the ethical socialist believes in the good sense of ordinary people. Indeed they suggest that 'the respectable working class with its ethical–socialist commitment to "fraternity across the board" has provided the mainstay of the British Labour movement over the years'.[29] Dennis and Halsey show a common thread running through a tradition of English political thought, from St Thomas More to Tawney, which stressed the probity, wisdom and humanity of ordinary people and which looked for a political system that incorporated their values. Most of the writers discussed by Dennis and Halsey were essentially Christian in outlook and the editors were anxious to underline this connection.

Not all ethical socialists, however, were Christian. William Morris, for example, described himself as a 'Marxist *contra mundum*' and deployed Marxist analysis to demonstrate the socialist potential of the ordinary people, though from a somewhat idiosyncratically medieval perspective.[30] For Morris it was the capitalist social order that prohibited people from living the good life and not some abstract concept called human nature. Just because the aim of capitalist production was to increase profit and not to provide for need, there was no necessary limit to the extent of labour and the cheaper labour costs became, the greater was the profit. Such a society, lacking any broader social obligation than to maximise profit, encouraged the growth of a small class of wealthy owners of capital (dead men's labour, Morris termed it) who 'consume a great deal while they produce nothing'.[31] They, like many of the middle class, who produce but typically consume more than they produce, have to be kept at the expense of those who do work. The latter are generally employed, said Morris, in producing 'all those articles of folly and luxury, the demand for which is the outcome of the existence of the rich non-producing classes'.[32] The working-class, then, were forced to produce either luxury goods for the wealthy or shoddy goods for themselves. For Morris, capitalism destroyed people's capacity to derive any satisfaction from work, and since this was their most crucial activity, the lives of all men and women, even the consumers of luxury, remain alienated from their true purpose of self-fulfilment. Under such conditions the essential goodness of mankind had no opportunity to manifest itself. But to imagine that the industrial proletariat of nineteenth-century Britain was 'mankind' and the values of that class the embodiment of 'human nature' was nonsensical; as soon call the smoke of London 'the weather', to coin Shaw's phrase. This is an issue Morris took up in his celebrated utopian novel

News from Nowhere:[33]

> 'Human nature!' cried the old boy, impetuously: 'what human nature? The human nature of paupers, of slaves, of slaveholders, or the human nature of wealthy freemen. Which? Come, tell me that!'

Morris's novel will be considered more fully in a later chapter. His importance here is to stand as an example of an ethical socialist who believed profoundly in the 'probity, wisdom and humanity' of ordinary people but who believed, too, that the capitalist system, by its very nature, stultified those virtues.

Of all the writers discussed by Dennis and Halsey, none set out the beliefs and aspirations of ethical socialism more fully or in sharper focus than did George Orwell. Orwell rooted his socialism precisely in the values and lives of ordinary people – not of ordinary people in some futuristic Morrisonian utopia but of ordinary people struggling to survive in twentieth-century capitalist Britain. Orwell does not discuss but takes for granted the reality of a working-class identity. He assumes the viability of the sociological explanation of identity, which is to say that identity 'sutures' an individual, in Stuart Hall's phrase,[34] into a social group whose status is uncontentious, through the processes of socialisation. That social group thus sustains an identity embodying cultural values which are recognisable and (to an extent) predictable.

Orwell, then, assumes that the working-class had such an identity and could thus be said collectively to express an identifiable set of values that he crucially classifies as residual Christianity. In this he could be said to epitomise the views of most ethical socialists. Now this assumption is clearly challengeable but Orwell does not leave the matter here: he wants at the same time to be both more and less specific. More specific in that he tells us in *The Road to Wigan Pier* that the values that he admires actually are to be found chiefly in the better-off sections of the working-class, roughly speaking those families where the man is in employment. Less specific in that he frequently uses the phrase 'ordinary people' to stand as synonymous with better-off working-class, so that generalisations about the latter can be applied equally well to the former. Roughly speaking, then, Orwell's 'working class' constitutes that equally amorphous group which traditional liberal philosophers were accustomed to refer to as 'the people'. What gives 'the working class' or 'the people' an identity is first that, on the whole, they enjoy a standard of living which allows some genuine moral choices to be made – unlike the lumpenproletariat or the unemployed of Hanky Park, for example – and second (and crucially) that they are comprehensively excluded from the structure of power within the state.

Orwell seemed to assume not merely that we can generalise about identifiable, residually Christian working-class values but that they equated with some form of socialism. In an article on Charlie Chaplin, for example, he wrote that the comedian's success was based upon his ability to symbolise 'the ineradicable belief in decency that exists in the hearts of ordinary people ... Everywhere, under the surface, the common man sticks obstinately to the belief that he derives from the Christian culture.'[35] His essay on the cartoonist Donald McGill[36] explored these ideas in greater depth. McGill depicted a world in which all those with incomes of much above or below £5 per week were figures of fun. Superficially, perhaps, McGill's is a world of obscenity but in fact his cartoons possessed a meaning only within the context of a fairly strict moral code, the backbone of which was an incorrigible belief in the virtue of marriage and family life, a world 'more traditional, more in accord with the Christian past than [that of] the well-to-do women who still try to look young at forty'. All the double entendres of McGill's world actually presuppose a world in which ordinary people want to behave decently and be good, 'but not too good, and not quite all the time'.

Orwell provides a description of working-class family life in *Wigan Pier* in which he seeks to capture these values which he admires. Most important of all is that of equality, which suffuses both social and family life in working-class communities. Northern towns are, he says far more egalitarian than those in the South. You could go for months in the North without hearing a 'posh' accent, whereas 'there can hardly be a town in the South of England where you could throw a brick without hitting the niece of a bishop'. Working-class homes, moreover, exude a 'warm, decent, deeply human atmosphere'. He goes on:[37]

> I have often been struck by the peculiarly easy completeness, the perfect symmetry as it were, of a working class interior at its best. Especially on winter evenings after tea, when the fire glows in the open range and dances mirrored in the steel fender ... it is a good place to be ...

Working-class family life, he believed, was not dominated by social or financial considerations, nor weakened by the social and geographical mobility that so frequently splinters middle-class families. Even more importantly, family values were integrated into the community where the same sense of unity and equality flourished. Orwell believed that this was the good life: this was 'socialism'.

And if this common culture was deeply patriotic, it had no time for extreme nationalism, or indeed for any extremism. Orwell wrote that he found himself unable to listen to proclamations by 'great men', pious moral platitudes from self-righteous left-wing party leaders, papal pronouncements and the like without also 'seeming to hear, in the background, a chorus of raspberries from all the millions of common men'. Theirs is that wisdom that Orwell sought to portray as 'socialism': not an ideology but a commitment to equality and justice. What socialism needed, he believed, was a propagandist who would talk 'less about "class consciousness" and "expropriation of the expropriators", "bourgeois ideology" and "proletarian solidarity"... and more about justice, liberty and the plight of the unemployed'. Like the judge in the film *The Bonfire of the Vanities*, Orwell attaches substantial political meaning to the word 'decency'. The judge berates his courtroom: 'I'll tell you what justice is. Justice is the law. Law is man's feeble attempt to set down the principles of decency. And decency is not a deal, and angle, a contract or a hustle. Decency is... in your bones. Now you go home. Go home and be decent people.' For Orwell decency was in the bones of the powerless.

We accepted for the purposes of argument that at least at the time when Orwell wrote, the working-class was cohesive enough to be assigned an identity. True, it became an imprecise identity as soon as we took account of the way Orwell used it – as a synonym for 'ordinary people'. Orwell wrote of the working-class in *Wigan Pier* and elsewhere as the only true enemy of totalitarianism precisely because of these values. 'All over England, in every industrial town, there are men by scores of thousands whose attitude to life, if only they could express it... would change the whole consciousness of our race.'[38] Orwell was often accused of inconsistency, not to say treachery, as a socialist writer, but in his attachment to working-class values he remained perfectly consistent. He adopted the role of spokesman for working-class values at the beginning of his writing career and never departed from it. If his championing of the working-class in *Wigan Pier* and *Homage to Catalonia* is unambiguous, even in his supposedly anti-socialist works, *Animal Farm* and *Nineteen Eighty-Four*, the values of the working-class survive. *Animal Farm* illustrates the resilience and compassion of ordinary working 'people' (the carthorses) and contrasts this with the ugly face of tyranny under its disconcerting make-up of ideology. In *Nineteen Eighty-Four* Orwell depicts a society without values – a society from which the working-class, pointedly, has been excluded. At the beginning of the novel Winston Smith extols the proles' revolutionary potential, reminding us of Animal Farm's Boxer. Winston says 'they need only to rise up and shake themselves, like a horse shaking off flies. If they chose they could blow the party to pieces.' Although it is true that O'Brien convinces him during the interrogation that the proles would never revolt, not in a thousand years, not in a million, so long as he is capable of thought Winston remains convinced that their values will at least survive. The proles' instinctive loyalty was not to any ideology or creed or party but to each other; there was a moral force and hence a potential political value in their code of decency: if there *was* any hope, it lay with the proles.

Orwell's association of working-class values with socialism was far from universally accepted by other socialists. Indeed Orwell and his ideas were deeply distrusted by many on the left. On closer inspection this is hardly surprising. After all Orwell constructed a form of socialism which expressly excluded most of them. Consider *Wigan Pier*: following his analysis of the lives of the poor in Yorkshire and Lancashire Orwell sets out, in the second half, to savage the kind of people who had financed his journey north, the Left Book Club. He castigates ordinary middle-class socialists with his descriptions of 'fruit juice drinkers, sandal-wearers, sex-maniacs, "Nature Cure" quacks, pacifists and feminists, vegetarians, birth-control fanatics and Labour back-stairs crawlers' and disparages them as 'flocking towards the smell of progress like bluebottles to a dead cat'. Orwell makes it absolutely plain that for socialism to succeed it must dissociate itself from 'progress' and it must send every 'vegetarian, teetotaller and creeping Jesus home to Welwyn Garden City'.

Before he completed *Wigan Pier* the Civil War had broken out in Spain, a war described by Louis McNeice as the 'touchstone of the Left's ambition', and Orwell, though married for only six months, felt compelled to join the 2,000 or so British volunteers who went to fight the fascists. He brought two abiding memories back from Spain. One fitted exactly his own version of socialism and he became intoxicated by the atmosphere of Barcelona under what he believed, perhaps erroneously, to be workers' control. 'I have seen wonderful things', he wrote to Cyril Connolly, 'and at last really believe in socialism, which I never did before',[39] but the other was of the 'treachery' of the communists and the slavish support given them by British left-wing intellectuals and the eventual and probably inevitable failure of the Spanish revolution. In rejecting revolution as the way to achieve socialism (and we shall be considering this aspect of Orwell's thought in greater detail later), just as he had rejected middle-class moderation, Orwell was once again cutting himself off from a mainstream of socialist thinking and antagonising its adherents.

His Spanish experiences, however, did more than expose the futility of revolution; they awakened him to the role of intellectuals, particularly of ideologists, in achieving, or, as he preferred to believe, preventing the achievement of, socialism. In his Eton days Orwell was said to have promoted himself as the 'new Bernard Shaw'. He had read all the works of both Shaw and Wells; they were his early heroes. But intellectual socialists such as the Fabians were, as we have established, anything but democratic. Indeed, as we have seen, they made no claim to be democratic in any sense that Orwell would have recognised: they were unashamed elitists. Ideology, socialism as much as any other, was nothing more than a guise for these intellectuals offering a spurious justification for their natural 'totalitarian' instincts. In this savage attack on (mainly British) socialist intellectuals, especially in *Wigan Pier*,[40] Orwell cut himself off from the Fabian tradition of state socialism, thereby turning his back on yet another mainstream of socialist thought.

Orwell not merely rejected these possibilities for socialism but actually pilloried them in his writing. No wonder then that when he rooted his own version of socialism in the values and lives of ordinary people, Orwell made many enemies. 'He was a sick counter-revolutionary fink', says the radical student in Saul Bellow's *Mr Sammler's Planet*, 'it was good he died when he did.'[41] For Orwell, though, 'working-class' socialism is knowable – it is non-ideological, non-utopian, non-progressive and non-(probably anti-)intellectual. It cannot be systematised into an ideology or even a programme for action because it represents less a set of philosophical premises, let alone precise policy goals, and more a frame of mind. This frame of mind is not shared by starry-eyed middle-class progressives, revolutionary socialists or intellectuals and ideologues. The latter may well construct poverty programmes, for example, but for them poverty was something to be abolished from above, if necessary by force, thus finding their natural shape in a totalitarian rule intensely destructive of the values Orwell cherished.

If this belief in the values of ordinary people could be said to constitute Orwellism, does it constitute a coherent form of socialism? A crucial consideration must surely be the almost total absence in his work of any analysis of how the values of working people could operate *in politics*. After all, in his day the Labour Party was to some substantial degree a working-class party – indeed he said as much[42] – and the trade union movement, to a very large degree, was a working-class movement. If Orwell believed that true socialism, as a set of values that could be put into operation, resided in the values of the working-class, his case would have been immensely strengthened had he analysed these organisations and showed how working-class values permeated them and made them significantly different structures of power. He did no such thing, and we might feel justified in concluding that it was because he thought they were not different. Even Machiavelli championed private virtue and his compatriot Umberto Eco unerringly put his finger on the problematic relationship between private and public virtue: 'How are we to remain close to the experience of the simple, their operative virtue, the capacity of working towards transformation and betterment of their world?' asks William of Baskerville and suggests it can only be achieved through the actions of 'the community of the learned'.[43] This was not a problem that Orwell pursued, though it is crucial to his politics. The reason for this failure might be that Orwell as an ethical socialist was much more concerned with ethics than with socialism. His basic interest was not in political institutions and outcomes so much as in human conduct, and his abiding concern, it can be argued, was a moral one: the effect on Western man of the perceived decline of Christian moral values.

Perhaps the most powerful metaphor in all of Orwell's work, which occurs not once but twice,[44] concerns a wasp eating jam from Orwell's breakfast plate. The fastidious breakfaster cuts the wasp in two with his table knife but the wasp, unaware of this unkindest cut, continues to eat, the jam trickling out of its oesophagus. Only when it tried to fly away did the wasp grasp the nature of its dreadful fate. 'It is the same with modern man', wrote Orwell, 'the thing that has been cut away is his soul.' In forsaking his belief in the afterlife, modern man had lost his soul. Now, a believer can accommodate himself to the fact that man who is born of woman has but a short time to live and his life is full of misery; after all, it is the next life that counts. But, says Orwell, 'to admit that life is full of misery when you believe that the grave really finishes you' – well, that's quite another matter.[45] Indeed, Dostoevsky's Ivan affirms 'there is no virtue if there is no immortality'. How to encourage men to act morally when there remained no fear of everlasting retribution for wrongdoing: this was Orwell's most abiding concern.

Orwell regarded as supremely ironic the notion that modern man had liberated himself from superstition. The reality was, he wrote, that in refuting the myths of religion, man had wittingly sawn away the branch on which he was seated. 'But unfortunately there had been a little mistake. The thing at the bottom was not a bed of roses but a cesspool full of barbed wire.'[46] So much for liberation! What was to be done? As Orwell saw it the problem was to 'restore the religious attitude while accepting death as final', and working-class socialism as he defined it was to be the solution to that problem. Dostoevsky's Alyosha, we may recall, said something similar: that socialism really entailed building a modern Tower of Babel without God.[47]

Was Orwell right to identify the working-class as the repository of ethical socialism or, in his own terms, Christian 'decency'? Whatever he may have written, working-class life, especially in the north of Britain, was manifestly unequal in terms of gender. Orwell has little to say about this beyond referring to the fact that unemployed men generally did nothing to help with household chores, not wishing to be thought 'Sally Annes'. But this was the tip of the iceberg: there was simply no aspect of working-class life in which men and women were equal. Moreover Orwell was either strangely blind to, or chose to ignore, the manifest tyranny of father–son relationships. D.H. Lawrence, himself the son of a miner, knew differently. Finally Orwell said nothing about the violence which had always been part and parcel of working-class life:[48] had he forgotten Dickens's *Barnaby Rudge* with its description of the Gordon Riots? Had he read no account of the mayhem at soccer games between major rivals? Did he really not know of the bitterness and violence which tore working-class communities apart, such as the London dock strike of 1911?

Even if we were to grant, however, that on balance Orwell's assumptions about working-class virtues in the 1930s were justified, we still need to consider the following possibility: however successfully working-class values might operate, in reality they represent the defence mechanism of a community under pressure. In Aldous Huxley's novel *Point Counter Point*,[49] Illidge, a working-class communist, observed that when you live on less than £4 per week you've 'dammed well got to behave like a Christian'. Without financial resources, the support of one's neighbours is necessary to deal with life's problems. The working-class of the 1990s, however, is generally more affluent than that of the 1930s: the accretion of greater wealth has had its effect, as has the post-1945 welfare state, with its health, housing, education, income support and unemployment policies. Cumulatively better welfare provision has tended to erode working-class communities in a comprehensive manner. The almost tribal social framework into which the great majority of working-class children were born until the 1960s exists now in only a relatively small number of well-defined inner-city areas whose identity would often be defined by ethnicity as much as class. Although the developments referred to all took their effect after Orwell's death, he did not address the possibility that the values he admired were largely a response to poverty and so be unlikely to survive the advent of the welfare state. Orwell was always clear about his opposition to 'progress' because of its impact on working-class life and values, but he did not oppose welfare.

Finally, did not Orwell really know all this? Did he really, as some have suggested, have some hopelessly romantic notion of what working-class or 'ordinary' life was like? Whilst we cannot rule this possibility out, it does seem unlikely that a writer and journalist who was credited with the 'best nose of his generation' should have laboured for so long under such a very obvious misapprehension. There is an alternative explanation. Might it not be the case that the working-class, the 'ordinary people', were in fact Orwell's most enduring literary creation? Consider, in mitigation, Orwell's reaction to the dialogue on abortion between the gangster Pinkie and his even more limited (Orwell's phrase) girl-friend in Greene's *Brighton Rock*.[50] Both agree that abortion is immoral. It is simply incredible, thundered Orwell (who would certainly have agreed with them), that 'the most brutish, stupid person can, merely by having been brought up a Catholic', be capable of distinguishing between the moral categories of good and evil. Yet in *Wigan Pier* Orwell insists that a *working-class* Catholic, though he may not be able to open his mouth without uttering a heresy, has 'the heart of the matter in him'. Could Orwell really have believed that though Catholics (who at least would have had the Catechism knocked into their heads as children) could not distinguish right from wrong by virtue of their religious background, working-class people, by virtue merely of having been born in Sheffield or Wigan, would apparently have insights into moral complexities that have concerned philosophers through the ages? Could there be a better example of doublethink?

Orwell must have known perfectly well what the limits of the 'decency' of ordinary people were but he had his own reasons for purveying this particular myth. He built a decency myth to put at the centre of his 'socialism'. He built it from the values that he believed to exist in communities of ordinary people but like all artists he was selective in what he included and excluded from his picture. He sought to smuggle the Christian values by which he set such store into modern political discourse in an acceptable modern guise. And he felt that he had compelling reasons to do so: after all, as Raymond Plant argues, 'we have no clear idea how conceptions of the good can be rationally grounded ... nor how the normative aspects of any account of human nature could be supported rationally'.[51] Orwell tried to ground a conception of the good in a series of metaphors drawn from the lives of ordinary people, and if he failed overall, his efforts were not without some success.

Orwell believed that those in power, including elitist socialists, invariably abused it. He wanted socialists above all to learn that lesson and to this end he created his decency myth, locked into the identity of the working-class. It is of considerable interest but of less political importance that that identity and those values were partly Orwell's creation.

He created them to assist in building a 'decent' society, or in 'grounding the good', in Plant's phrase. But finally he was a moralist, and if he was a socialist in any meaningful sense, then certainly more of an 'ethical' than a scientific one. Richard Rees, a good friend, perceptively compared Orwell to the French writer and moralist Simone Weil; both understood the balance of society at any time and were prepared to add their weight to the lighter scale. His position was like that of justice; he was a 'fugitive from the victor's camp'. More positively Orwell's task was to confront scientific socialists with an image or icon of the values that he believed their policies would sacrifice. That image or icon depicted a working-class which, he claimed, lived out these values. Like all myths, though it contained substantial contradictions and confusions it might also have been based upon a fundamental truth. And like all myth-makers George Orwell kept quiet about the contradictions, even at the expense of being classed confused or romantic, because he passionately believed that if there was any hope for a decent society based upon Christian (or what today we would call Judaeo-Christian values) values, it lay with *his* proles. That was why, for Orwell, power should be given to the people.

Workers and socialism

So far we have dealt with Orwellism as perhaps the most fully articulated version of ethical socialism. We have concentrated on the journalistic descriptions of working-class life in the north of England, the glimpses of Barcelona in the early days of the Civil War and the depictions of the working-class in Orwell's later novels. However it is in the novel *Coming Up for Air*[52] that Orwell gives the fullest picture of the lives of ordinary people. If we wish to examine the identity of Orwell's 'ordinary people' and assess the extent to which their values might offer the basis for a new style of politics, we could do no better than consider this work.

True, Orwell is not writing about the industrial proletariat here, but as we have seen, on many occasions he quite specifically links the better-off working-class with 'ordinary people'. As Bernard Crick commented on the cover of the most recent edition, the novel's excellence resides partly in 'the argument that hope lies with the common people'. It is clear that the book wants us to compare the arid, alienated life of a typical suburban bourgeois of modern capitalism to the rich, fulfilling lives of ordinary people living in an earlier small-town community, and to draw our own conclusions.

George Bowling, the novel's central character, is a lost soul. He is transfixed by the fear of approaching war and its consequences, but equally transfixed by the aridity of his life under capitalism. In terms of the alienation of the central character the novel resembles *Nineteen Eighty-Four*. Bowling, shaving with his bluntish razor, looks out onto his garden, the ten yards by five of grass, with a privet hedge around it and a bare patch, worn by his children, in the middle. He reflects that the same back garden, same privets, same grass, is to be found behind every house in Ellesmere Road.[53]

> Do you know the road I live in? Even if you don't you know fifty others like it... Long, long rows of little semi-detached houses... the stucco front, the creosoted gate, the privet hedge, the green front door... [and] in every one of those little stucco boxes there's some poor bastard who's never been free except when he's fast asleep.

Chief amongst George Bowling's dissatisfactions is his wife Hilda. This state of affairs, however, is not unique to Bowling. We are led to believe that under modern capitalism this is standard. In response to his own question: why did he marry her? he replies: for no good reason. 'But why did you marry yours? These things happen to us.' Middle-class women, he goes on, don't look for excitement or novelty, or even joy in life. They want only the security of middle age. Sometimes, he tells us, he lies on his bed wondering about women: 'why they're like that, how they get like that, whether they're doing it on purpose'.[54] But in reality Bowling's (and everyone's) marital discontents are merely emblematic of his hatred of the whole lifestyle which he thinks is imposed upon people by the capitalist system. He fantasises about erecting a huge statue to the building society that made Ellesmere Road and his lifestyle inevitable: in one hand it would hold an enormous key – to the workhouse – and in the other a 'whole cornucopia out of which would be pouring radios, life-insurance policies, false teeth, aspirins, French letters and concrete garden rollers'.[55]

Bowling detests his lifestyle and the world that frames it. He hates capitalism's thrusting modernity, its slickness, its enamel and its chromium-platedness, and above all its streamlinedness. The capitalist world is symbolised for Bowling by the hamburger he eats in a milk bar. 'I'd bitten into the modern world and discovered what it was really made of... rotten fish in a rubber skin. Bombs of filth bursting inside your mouth.'[56] It is in this state of mind that Bowling, through a chance word connection, becomes suddenly mentally transported back to his childhood home in Lower Binfield. It is life in pre-1914 Lower Binfield that provides Bowling with the context from which he criticises modern capitalism.

Lower Binfield lay in a valley near the Thames, a small market town dominated by Binfield House, 'The Hall', home of the local aristocratic family. In strictly economic terms Lower Binfield was part of a rapidly developing capitalist system and yet to all intents and purposes it represented the opposite – continuity. Its social structure and behaviour had changed little in hundreds of years. He evokes the sounds, sights, tastes and above all smells of a country childhood with loving skill. What he seeks to do above all, however, is to recreate in pictures the sense of family life in a community, just as he had in the North. Life was not easy but it was, says Bowling, 'good'. Central to the good life was Bowling's mother. 'When you saw her cooking you knew that she was in a world where she belonged, among things she really understood.'[57] His father, a seed merchant, meanwhile, busied himself with 'men's work' though both parents were able to find time on Sunday afternoons to read the papers. His mother especially liked an old-fashioned women's magazine, no doubt squeezed out of production now, says Bowling, by something more 'streamlined'.

Lower Binfield was not a society of equals but, in the author's words, of 'big social distinctions' (and even bigger gender distinctions to which the author does not draw attention) and yet it represents for Orwell a real community. To be a boy was to be bound up 'with breaking rules and killing things...the hot sweaty feeling of one's clothes...the sour stink of the rubbish dump...the stamping on young birds, the feel of the fish straining on the line – it was all part of it. Thank God I am a man, because no woman ever has that feeling.'[58] Certainly not in Lower Binfield anyway. But better than anything, even the blowing up of toads with bicycle pumps, was the fishing. Fishing, says Bowling, is the archetypal activity of that civilisation. Even the names of the coarse fish had a poetic ring; they were made up by men who had never heard of machine guns. 'If you gave me the choice of having any woman you care to name', Bowling concludes, 'but I mean *any* woman, or catching a ten pound carp, the carp would win every time.'

Why was life better in Lower Binfield, for it certainly was not softer? Precisely because of the sense of community and continuity. 'For ever and ever decent God-fearing women would cook Yorkshire pudding and apple dumplings on enormous coal ranges, wear woollen underwear and sleep on feathers.'[59] You could accept death when you knew that the things that you cared about would continue after our death.

Your sense of good and evil would remain good and evil. You did not feel that the moral ground was shifting beneath your feet. Compare this certainty to Bruno's despair in Houllebecq's *Atomised* who, looking at his infant son, muses:[60]

> By the time he grows up, the rules I live by will be meaningless – the world will be completely different. If a man accepts the fact that everything must change, then his life is reduced to nothing more than the sum of his own experiences – past and future generations mean nothing to him... For a man to bring a child into the world now is meaningless.

Eventually George Bowling decides that he must pay a secret visit to Lower Binfield simply to refresh his spirits but when his car finally turns from the familiar, he discovers Lower Binfield to be unrecognisable. 'Oh yes', he tells us, '*you* knew what was coming. But *I* didn't.' The small market town had been engulfed by new buildings and was dominated by two new factories. He had to ask the way but his respondent was no help: she answered in a Lancashire accent you could 'cut with a spade'. Bowling felt that a 'kind of enemy invasion had happened behind my back'.[61] Everything had changed, including his father's former shop, now a teashop. Only the church was the same: same pews, same smells, even the same vicar. Worse followed as Bowling explored the area, going, for example, to his favourite river where he fished in solitude as a boy. What he finds now is caravans, teashops, ice-cream stalls – a riverside Margate. And men fishing every five yards of the river, having to compete with canoes, rowing boats and motor launches all making a fearful noise. It was the working-class at play and Bowling's judgement was crisp and certain: 'crowds of bloody aliens'. All in all, his Lower Binfield had degenerated, swollen 'into a kind of Dagenham'.[62]

Bowling had come looking for something that did not exist in capitalism's 'streamlined milk-bars with the radio playing', only to find that it no longer existed in Lower Binfield either. One last, desperate effort to rescue the past remained to him. He must visit the secret pool behind The Hall, where the largest carp were to be found; surely its remoteness and seclusion would have saved it. Its fate, in fact, is even worse: it had been drained and used as a refuse tip. The Hall, moreover, had been sold and had become Binfield House: as Bowling unceremoniously calls it, a 'loony bin'. No, the good life was over and the bad times were coming. And the 'streamlined' men were coming too. George Bowling motors back to Ellesmere Road thoroughly deflated and defeated.

Parenthetically Lower Binfield represented just the kind of society so roundly detested by Alfred Polly. There are many points of comparison between the two novels: it can hardly be coincidental that Orwell reverses the thrust of Wells's story, with the hero running *to* the solid, small-town, lower-middle-class kingdom *from* which Polly had fled. Moreover Bowling sought to escape from the very kind of modernity that Orwell associated with Wells. It is true that Orwell juxtaposed Lower Binfield's timelessness and security against Bowling's fears of the uncertainties of war and the horrors of fascism, true that images of warplanes are everywhere. Fundamentally, however, the comparison is with modern capitalism; Bowling's great rage is against modernity. If only he could persuade one of the bombers to release its friendly bombs (actually made in Lower Binfield's factories) to fall on West Bletchley. He is encaged by his marriage, his family, his house and his job – just like everybody else. Above all, he has lost contact with the purely sensory pleasures of the country, with what Orwell elsewhere refers to as 'the surface of the earth'[63] and Whitman called 'the primal sanities'. And the word which Bowling used to conjure up the intensity of his dislike of modernity is: *streamlined*. Bowling is a precursor of Winston Smith, though he looks more like Parsons. He cannot love the big brother of modern capitalism, which circumscribes his life at every level.

Orwell's dismissive picture of modern capitalism represents something akin to an updating of William Morris's pictures of a community threatened by an earlier stage of capitalism or 'commercialism'. Morris depicted a society incarcerated within subsistence housing and vile working conditions, with people's lives dominated by overwork. Orwell's modern victims have, by and large, escaped from dire poverty only to become reincarcerated in Ellesmere Road and its bland, streamlined, meaningless existence.

Coming Up for Air provides Orwell's only detailed picture of the community life of ordinary people he claimed to admire. Unlike the snapshots of Wigan and Sheffield with their 'symmetrical' working-class lives and their air of equality, the reality of Lower Binfield is quite other. It is based on social inequality. Since time immemorial it has been dominated by The Hall, symbolically overlooking all. Orwell says little about it or its owners, itself an interesting omission. When the aristocratic dominance it represents is finally gone it is replaced by a lunatic asylum. The dominant social value of the community is self-help, but neighbours and family will help each other only up to a point. Above all, it is a man's world and the woman's task is to serve the family. This family represents as formal and rigid a hierarchy as any of Shaw's or Wells's.

What is more, the world of Lower Binfield is exclusive. When Bowling rejects the riverside scene he witnesses on his return as just another Margate, when he refers dismissively to the Lancastrian invasion and when he speaks of working people enjoying themselves noisily as a crowd of aliens, we feel the true weight of this prejudice. Like many traditional communities Lower Binfield was enclosed, bound together by its dislike of outsiders. If we were to look for a literary/political parallel to Bowling's depiction of his birthplace after its development the obvious one is New Wanley in *Demos*.[64] Gissing paints a grim picture not only of the blight of Victorian 'modernity' but also of the political application of working-class values in political action.

All in all the picture of Lower Binfield suggests that Orwell's ordinary people do not possess an identity of common values that will withstand modernity, still less fascism or totalitarianism. The old world of toleration and common decency, the world of Chaplin and McGill (if indeed it had ever really existed), could not offer a model of ethical socialism in practice because it had died.

Conclusions

Back finally to the contradiction with which we began. Given the imperative of creating a more equal society, we analysed the form of that equality: whether a politically informed and trained elite should seek to create a society of economic and social (but not political) equality by abolishing poverty, or whether the aim should be to build a society in which ordinary people could control their own lives. Should experts acting on their behalf transform the people, or should a society be developed based upon the egalitarian values of ordinary people? We pursued these two approaches – those of the scientific and ethical socialists – as advanced by some of the most celebrated British political writers of the late nineteenth and twentieth centuries, all avowed socialists. We examined the inconsistencies in their thinking and discovered that their own imaginative writing fully exposed their contradictions.

Shaw's emancipated worker – a man like Henry Straker in *Man and Superman*[65] – would never accept for long a position in a society in which he enjoyed no political power. Straker dismissed Octavius's claim to believe in the dignity of labour with a wave: 'that's because you never done any'. Straker himself was the product of a polytechnic and when Tanner accuses him of despising Oxford his reply was disarmingly patronising: if you want to learn to be a gentleman Oxford is fine, but if you want to learn to do something useful you had better go to a polytechnic.

Even in matters of more general education he is Tanner's superior. When the latter reminds him of Voltaire's line that whatever was too silly to be said could be sung, Straker admonishes 'it wasn't Voltaire. It was Beaumarchais.' Does Shaw want us to believe that Straker recognises Tanner as his natural and therefore political superior? If he does, his creative powers have defeated his objective. Straker may recognise the social necessity of his domestic servitude but he would be hardly likely to submit to the claim to run the state of a man like Tanner who so palpably mismanages his own life. Straker stands as a witness to the implausibility of Shaw's vision of Perivale St Andrew, of a working-class, that is to say, emancipated from economic subjugation but politically in thrall to a class or group of allegedly superior wisdom. Yet Shaw and his Fabian colleagues must be taken seriously: after all it was they who established the London School of Economics and Political Science (LSE) precisely to produce a scientifically trained elite which, like some modern class of Platonic guardians, would rule in the interests of all, and several of these guardians went on to attain positions of influence within the Labour Party, not the least being Clement Attlee. And yet Shaw's plays are full of leaders to whom no thinking person would dream of entrusting leadership. On the other hand, Shavians might argue that the People's Republic of China, with its massive programmes of modernisation through private ownership and entrepreneurial vigour, constitutes nothing other than a stupendous Perivale St Andrew, its people increasingly better off economically and yet not, with some notable exceptions, concerned with political power.[66] Whether such a state of affairs is sustainable is debatable but it is arguably an example of Shavianism at work.

Orwell too seems effectively to scupper his own even more ambitious project. In creating a myth of working-class decency, a system of values which he equates with socialism, his depiction of the lives of ordinary families in *Coming Up for Air* exposes ordinary people as no more virtuous than the rest of us. But there is an even more fundamental objection to Orwell's model of ethical socialism. Unlike Shaw's and Wells's attempts to abolish poverty (and the poor) or Morris's aspiration to transform society – in each case so that their vision of socialism might flourish – Orwell's socialism becomes not the agent of change but its victim, for its strength is a response to economic and social adversity. Orwell was a forceful opponent of progress, which he dismissively described as making the world safe for little fat men. He knew instinctively that progress, however defined, would signal the end of the class structure that produced a cohesive working-class whose members were equal in one thing above all others: their poverty.

Basic inconsistencies in these narratives might at first be thought to limit their strength. We can be forgiven for concluding that neither the scientific socialists like Shaw or Webb nor the ethical socialists like Orwell successfully answered the question that is the consequence of capitalism's immorality and inefficiency: what to do with or for 'the poor'? But this problem is truly complex and will not permit easy answers. In these narratives the authors evoke images that enlighten and remain with us: Undershaft's visit to the West Ham shelter, Wells's angel contemplating the surgical removal of its wings, Orwell's young mother unblocking the drainpipe. It would be difficult to find a more compelling example with which to conclude than Orwell's depiction of modern man bereft of his traditional moral certainties as resembling that severed wasp on the breakfast plate, still unconcernedly gorging itself on jam. Though they may not resolve our fundamental dilemmas for us, then, imaginative writers provide us with the most penetrating of insights.

4
Narrative and the Sword

When considering what was to be done with or for the poor, imaginative writers did not exclude the possibility of the poor doing something, urgently and vigorously, for themselves, with or without the help of a sympathetic elite. They examined the legitimacy of and the prospects for proletarian revolution, depicted the events of such revolutions and considered their consequences. Indeed there was hardly a socialist who did not believe in the likelihood of revolution of some kind, though they were divided, as in most things, on the legitimacy of *violent* revolution. (I shall use the word revolution to stand for violent revolution in what follows.)

The socialist and revolution

If revolutions represent an instinctive collective response to inhuman treatment – rather like the unplanned uprising of the animals in Orwell's *Animal Farm* – then consideration of their legitimacy seems otiose. Almost invariably, however, justification for such events will have been discussed in principle beforehand, as indeed was the revolution on Animal Farm, and there were many advocates of the legitimacy and efficacy of revolution amongst socialist thinkers. One of the early champions of revolutionary legitimacy in the modern world, Babeuf, argued that throughout history classes and social groups had guaranteed their preeminence by controlling the agencies of state coercion. No such group would yield peacefully to a rival class or group and so would need to be overthrown violently by a superior force. There was no alternative. This argument, as one writer correctly concluded, was 'always an apology for violence from within the precepts of rationalism and never a vindication of it'.[1] That is to say, revolution is to be regarded as an unfortunate but unavoidable necessity. Others, of whom Georges Sorel[2] can be taken as an early modern example, argued that it was only in revolutionary struggle that a group could fully realise its own consciousness. Violence was seen as a creative force and only through decisive action could the people discover their virtue (as well, others would later add, as their consciousness).

Marx himself argued that only the traumatic experience of revolutionary violence would rid the proletariat of the illusion that its interests and those of the bourgeoisie might be reconciled. As Harding suggests, Marx believed that 'the violence of the revolution clarifies the issues, obliges millions to declare their positions, it enormously accelerates the growth of consciousness'.[3] These arguments were picked up later by neo-Marxist writers such as Frantz Fanon,[4] reacting to the collapse of capitalism's so-called final stage, imperialism. Fanon sought to persuade colonial subjects that it was legitimate to want to 'rise up and cut off the heads of the slave-masters, that it is a way to achieve their manhood, and that they must oppose the oppressors in order to experience themselves as men'.[5]

The appeal of this message to men of violence is plain enough but it can also be persuasive to many ethical socialists. The revolution admits of no prevarication: it demands that one take sides – with the exploited. 'I have no particular love for the "idealised" worker as he appears in the bourgeois Communist's mind', said Orwell, 'but when I see an actual flesh-and-blood worker in conflict with his natural enemy, the policeman, I do not have to ask myself which side I am on.'[6] This uncomplicated, not to say simplistic declaration bears further investigation. It can be assumed that Orwell does not wish to imply that in any particular incident the workers are necessarily right and the police necessarily wrong. If anything, he is hinting at the opposite: sometimes it will be impossible to establish rights and wrongs in a particular dispute and sometimes indeed the workers might be in the wrong, but a violent confrontation admits of no calculation; only action (or inaction) is possible. Orwell's philosophical position is that historically the powerful are in the wrong and the powerless in the right. Instinctively, then, he will side with the workers – the people – because in the larger picture they are 'right'. Orwell is legitimising the impulse to violence just as much as Sorel or Fanon. Their justification rested in the historical expectation that revolution will unlock the virtue and the true consciousness of the exploited, and lead to a genuine transfer of power. Orwell had no such expectation but considered himself morally committed to the workers in a struggle that, for much of his life, he regarded as inevitable.

To the scientific socialists the prospect of proletarian revolution could be compelling too. The world being, in Swift's words, a den of dangerous animals, they took it for granted that revolutions would be dominated by political elites. (After the Paris communards surrendered in 1871 French troops were said to have shot prisoners with wristwatches or intelligent faces, for they, the intellectuals, would have been the leaders.) In the modern world that elite would be scientific socialists. On the other hand, precisely because the impulse to revolution is non-rational by nature, revolutions will be difficult to manage. For Marxists and some other scientific socialists, who would see revolutions as part of an inevitable, scientific process, this would not be problematical; others might have no such confidence.

The issue of legitimacy, however, is not the only issue concerning revolution. Another is likelihood of success. Those who argue in support of revolutions tend to make the quite unwarranted assumption that they will be victorious: Marxists, after all, believed that success was historically inevitable. Not only does history suggest that the odds are in reality against victory, but even victory itself does not always imply achieving what was intended: revolutionaries might win, but what will they win? 'A mob of desperate sufferers', said Shaw, 'abandoned to the leadership of exasperated sentimentalists and fanatic theorists [not an essential precondition of revolution, it has to be said] may, at a vast cost of bloodshed and misery, succeed in removing no single evil except perhaps the existence of the human race.'[7] Orwell was no more encouraging. He wrote: 'Throughout history one revolution after another – although producing a temporary relief, such as a sick man gets by turning over in bed – has simply led to a change of masters.'[8]

If we are to consider the narrative treatment of issues of the legitimacy and likely success of revolutions, we will see straight away that they rest on the probability of their being able to secure desired political ends. And we know broadly what these ends are: what we might call in shorthand social justice. Revolutionaries will seek to justify their actions, then, in terms of ends (social justice) justifying means (revolutionary violence). The debate over revolutionary legitimacy then becomes subsumed within a prior debate, that over means and ends. In seeking to consider narrative representations of revolution, especially as they bear on its legitimacy and likely success, we need to begin by considering how imaginative writers have responded to this prior debate over means and ends.

Means and ends

Rubashov, the revolutionary, in Arthur Koestler's *Darkness at Noon*, endorses Machiavelli's recommendation to the 'good man' that to become an effective ruler (or in this case revolutionary) he must learn how *not* to be good. This advice was still the subject of debate nearly half a millennium after Machiavelli wrote.[9] Indeed it became famously central to the debate on America's conduct of the Vietnam War, the so-called 'dirty hands' debate.[10] This phrase had been given prominence earlier by Sartre's play *Les Mains Sales*.[11] Sartre's contention (or at any rate his character Hoederer's) represents the first key principle to be considered in the debate over ends and means: *that politics is a distinctive, autonomous activity* in regard to which the concepts of traditional morality are simply inappropriate. Walzer[12] and others see three possible justifications for such a position: the politician acts on our behalf, speaks in our name, 'lies and intrigues for us'; the politician rules over us, directs our affairs in a comprehensive fashion; finally, the politician threatens or uses violence both for us and perhaps against us – he may kill in our name. No one succeeds in politics without getting their hands dirty and even traditional Christian morality made allowances for this.[13] These characteristics set politics apart from other human activities, and Sartre's play seems to corroborate this principle.

Machiavelli constrains his prince's potentially bloody proclivities by insisting that, when selecting ends and means to achieve them, he must act for the good of the state and not for his own good. But since the criteria by which the state's good is to be assessed are chiefly decided by the prince, the force of such a constraint is limited. It is unlikely that Orwell's Big Brother, for example, would have wrestled for long with the apparent dichotomy between ends and means. Smart argues that democratic political leaders will be subject to more realistic checks when choosing means and ends,[14] though no popular check prevented the democratically elected President Truman from using the atomic bomb to bring the war against Japan to an end. Few political leaders, democratic or authoritarian, would feel the need to take a Kantian position and seek moral rather than consequential justification for their actions.[15] After all, theirs is the autonomous world of politics where these rules do not apply.

But are these features really unique to politics, making it an autonomous activity? Berki argued that any man could face similar problems.[16] The position of princes and politicians or revolutionaries, though undeniably quantitatively different to that of the ordinary citizen, is not in fact qualitatively different. But there are many actors between the levels of the individual and the prince. Would not the bosses of multinational companies or indeed the leaders of any large organisation wish to claim much the same autonomy, indeed would not any person who was required to take important decisions affecting the livelihood of others – any actor in the public realm?

This brings us to an associated principle: *that we can distinguish between the public and the private realm*. In *Homage to Catalonia*, Orwell recounts his unwillingness, when in the trenches, to shoot a fascist because he had his trousers down.[17] 'Our conflict', as Nagel explains, 'is with the soldier not with his existence as a human being.'[18] The incident reflects the individual's (Orwell's) *private* judgement in deciding what steps are proper to achieve desired ends. But what of the British soldier who was later to discover that the wounded enemy he refrained from shooting at Cambrai in 1918 had been Adolf Hitler?[19] Bearing in mind its stupendous public consequences, was Private Tandy's decision a *private* matter? Prominent feminists argue that family life is dominated by structures of power, which are essentially public rather than private and involve crucial decisions being taken by some on behalf of others.[20] If even family life can plausibly be considered to be in the public realm, then the private realm can only certainly exist within the skull. In short there is no 'distinct and clear dividing line' (Hampshire's phrase) between the public and private realm.

In respect of the general and associated features that together delineate politics as an autonomous public realm in which normally good men are *ipso facto* free – indeed required – to act immorally, we can conclude that these features are not self-evident. That such-and-such an act is undertaken in the realm of politics ought not to make it any more immune from moral scrutiny than any other act.

The second basic principle in the debate about ends and means is, to all intents and purposes, the consequentialist argument of the utilitarians: *ends are more important than means*.[21] Public policies are judged not by the intrinsic qualities of the means adopted for their implementation but by their consequences, or ends. It may be necessary to abjure scruples that, in private life, would prevent one from force, or deceit, or of generally using people as means to an end. Machiavelli argued that it was not merely irresponsible but morally wrong for political leaders to be deflected from actions that would eventually conduce to the good of the state by the prompting of their private consciences.[22] In politics (and so in revolutions), he said, 'when the act accuses, the result excuses'.[23]

Robert Penn Warren endorses exactly this position in his novel *All the King's Men*:[24]

> The theory of historical costs, you might put it. All change costs something. You have to write off the costs against the gain ... The theory of the moral neutrality of history. Process as process is neither

morally good nor morally bad. We may judge the results but not the process. The morally bad agent may perform the deed that is good. The morally good agent may perform the deed that is bad. *Maybe a man has to sell his soul to get the power to do good ...*

Plausible though these arguments appear they ignore as many questions as they seem to answer. They assume that some objective measure (utility-sum) can be made of the effectiveness of consequences or ends which does not include a moral judgement. But an end has to be desired and the desirability of an end is unlikely *not* to include a moral judgement. More fundamentally they also assume that we will agree on what actually constitutes a consequence or end. But this is by no means the case. In Aldous Huxley's *Grey Eminence*,[25] for example, Father Louis persuades his Catholic French political masters to support the Protestant Swedish cause, thereby prolonging the barbaric Thirty Years War. Shall we say that the consequence or end of this policy was simply an increase in barbarity? Or was it the eclipse of the Habsburgs as the dominant Catholic power in Europe (the intended consequence)? Or was it instead the consequential terminal decline of Austrian hegemony in Germany? Or perhaps the equally consequential rise of Prussia (and subsequent military defeat of France)? Or was it the consequential rise of German militarism and two world wars? Or even Hitler's death camps? To define an objective as a consequence or end is to state a preference, no more. This has profound but usually overlooked consequences for those who argue that politics is 'the perfection of consequentialist ethics'.[26]

In brief, neither political theory nor imaginative literature gives us the key to unlock the complexities of the debate over ends and means that might then allow us access to a judgement of the legitimacy or likely success of revolutions. But they indicate the complexity of the issues facing revolutionaries. We can now turn to accounts of revolutions and their consequences.

Koestler on revolution

Imaginative writers have constructed narratives upon the themes set out above, none with greater insight than Arthur Koestler. In many respects he was a representative figure of that generation beguiled by the promise of the Russian revolution and later disillusioned by the reality of Soviet show trials, labour camps and the Nazi Soviet Pact. His disenchantment was to inspire three novels, *The Gladiators*,[27] *Darkness at Noon*[28] and *Arrival and Departure*.[29]

The Gladiators is a story of revolution. It concerns a (loosely historical) revolt led by Roman gladiators under the leadership of Spartacus, Crixus the Celt and Zozimos the Essene. At the early stage of revolt, though nominally the leader, Spartacus has no idea of how his men should arrange their affairs effectively; his chief ambition is to avoid the Roman legions for as long as possible. Slowly and despite himself Spartacus begins to contemplate establishing some new social life based on equality and justice. Yet he is unable to prevent his armies from putting two towns to the sword, and so his hopes of some new kind of society seem to have come to a premature end. However he later rationalises these events, seeing them only as 'little truths'. 'And those who recognise only the little truths are very foolish.'[30]

Increasingly Spartacus comes under the influence of Fulvius, a Machiavellian lawyer, who seeks to make him into an effective leader. He explains the operation of the 'law of detours' which states that it will become necessary on occasions for people on a journey to take a direction different to that intended in order to overcome unforeseen obstacles. Then the role of the leader is to proclaim such clarity of vision that even when detours are necessary the majority will follow. 'He who guides the blind ... must harden himself against their sufferings, be deaf to their cries. For he must defend their interests against their own want of reason ... he will have to make detours whose point is lost on others; for he alone can see while they are blind.'[31] Ends will justify means; only the far-sighted can make judgements about means.

Almost willy-nilly, Spartacus and the slaves establish their community, the Sun State, after concluding a treaty of non-aggression with the nearby city of Thurium. Eventually, however, Thurium feels strong enough to revoke the treaty, perceiving the Sun State to be no longer a threat. Strictly against orders, Crixus and his Celts decide to attack Thurium but are bought off by the city dignitaries and persuaded instead to attack another city nearby: Metapontum is put to the sword. Spartacus, following Fulvius' advice, orders the crucifixion of twenty-four of the Celtic leaders. Yet his resolution is mixed with compassion and he has the Celts cut down, though too late to prevent their death.

The slaves hold a mass meeting at which the Essene calls for Spartacus' death. A well-meaning tyrant, he declares, is worse than a man-eating beast. Fulvius, meanwhile, has placed assassins strategically near each Celtic leader: at a word from Spartacus they will cut the throats of his opponents. To Fulvius' dismay Spartacus gives no signal. Instead he addresses the crowd but fails to galvanise them into action. The Sun State has disintegrated and defeat is now inevitable. The slave army is routed and Spartacus himself captured. Recognising his generosity and nobility of spirit the Roman generals offer to spare Spartacus and provide him with an escape route. He cannot accept; he must hand on 'the cup' untarnished to 'the Next One who will come'.[32] Spartacus and his defeated army were crucified, their crosses stretching the length of the Appian Way from Capua to Rome.

Spartacus seems aware, at the end, of his symbolic responsibilities as a leader, yet he had earlier refused the responsibility of stabilising that leadership through bloodshed. Rather than accept what Fulvius recommended, the prospect of a stable but slave-based society whose skies would always be pierced by the crosses of criminals and opponents, Spartacus simply refused to act. Was failure inevitable or did Spartacus choose the wrong means? Koestler himself, in a postscript, does not press the inevitability of failure. What Spartacus lacked, he argues, was a 'programme, a credo' – the equivalent to the Sermon on the Mount.[33] This was what Zozimos had sought: it would have provided a common value system in the name of which sacrifices could be called for and, if necessary, punishment exacted. Spartacus reflects that all revolutions must be abortive until 'knowledge was no longer foisted upon it from the outside but was borne in laboured torment out of its own body, thus gaining from within power over the happening'.[34] Revolution, if it is to succeed, requires a revolutionary consciousness as a prerequisite, not as a consequence.

Darkness at Noon, an account of the consequences of revolution (the post-revolution) is the best-known of Koestler's work; indeed the French edition, which appeared in 1946, was credited with losing for the powerful French Communist Party the general election of that year.[35] Rubashov is a leading revolutionary figure who, like most of the 'old guard', has been arrested for anti-state activities. His task for the Party had been to investigate and destroy those who were not following the current party line. Richard, for example, a young idealist in the German Communist Party, could not come to terms with the lack of support his party had received from Moscow in its hour of need. Richard witnessed the destruction of his own party cell and saw his own young, pregnant wife being taken off by the Nazis. The Party, he claims, made a mistake. Rubashov counters:[36]

> The Party, comrade, is ... the embodiment of the revolutionary idea in history. History knows no scruples and no hesitation. Inert and unerring, she flows towards her goal. At every bend in her course she leaves the mud which she carries and the corpses of the drowned.

> History knows her way. She makes no mistakes. He who has not absolute faith in History does not belong in the Party's ranks.

Following the visit of Comrade Rubashov, Richard was mysteriously betrayed to the Nazis.

Next Rubashov has to deal with Loewy, a proletarian party worker in Belgium. Loewy has to be eliminated because of his opposition to the party line on continuing to ship oil to 'a southern European dictatorship' (Italy) which had invaded a North African state (Abyssinia), despite an international oil embargo. Since the Party had called for an international boycott on trade with that country it would clearly have become embarrassing if local communist dockworkers refused to load Soviet tankers. Rubashov explained that Russia's own industrial development had a higher priority than supporting the embargo, and that capital gained from the deal was essential. The dockers were unconvinced and remained committed to the embargo. Rubashov, however, engineered the expulsion of the leaders from the Party and the denouncement of Loewy as an agent provocateur. The dockers undertook the loading and three days later Loewy hanged himself.

Rubashov, in brief, was a man who would pursue any means to achieve the Party's ends. There was no moral dimension to the decisions he took. The Party was the source of moral certitude: it was the Party that made him infallible.

Rubashov's interrogator is an old comrade, Ivanov, whose task is to persuade Rubashov to accept the charges of treason against him so that the Party can stage a show trial *pour encourager les autres*. Rubashov, we learn, connived at the liquidation of a number of old revolutionary comrades, and did nothing to help his own mistress Arlova when she too was seized by the Party. Ivanov reminds him that whatever he did, he did for the good of the Party and the Party has become convinced that Rubashov himself has become a threat. He should continue to act as he always had – to serve the Party's interest.

Back in his cell, Rubashov begins to ruminate on Ivanov's arguments. In his diary he writes that nothing really important has been said about the rules of political ethics since Machiavelli. Politics can be 'fair' only in the breathing spaces of history; elsewhere and at other times there is no rule possible other than the old one: that the end justifies the means. To be effective the Party needs its unity, needs the 'solid anchor-chain' of No. 1. (It was no coincidence that Gramsci recognised the Party as the modern 'prince'.[37]) As for himself, Rubashov reflects, 'I no longer believe in my infallibility. That is why I am lost.' Meanwhile a former comrade, Bogrov, is dragged past Rubashov's cell to be shot, his legs hanging limp, feet clanking on the cobbles. Rubashov's mind is invaded by an image of Arlova, the mistress he betrayed, in a similar state, her high-heeled shoes trailing noisily along the corridor. The detail of this vision upsets the equilibrium (the balance of means and ends); the 'unimportant' factor grows to be the absolute, the immeasurable.

Ivanov visits Rubashov's cell and immediately attacks Rubashov for having discovered a conscience, since this 'renders one as unfit for the revolution as a double chin. Conscience eats through the brain like a cancer.'[38] Rubashov asks why Bogrov was shot and is informed that Bogrov, a naval expert, had supported the building of large-tonnage submarines; his preferences in submarine design were Trotskyist by implication: 'You would have done the same thing in our position.' Rubashov's reply challenges the whole means/ends balance: 'you did not hear him whimpering'. Ivanov counters that one had to acknowledge (as Rubashov once had) that ultimately the only rule of political ethics must be that the end justifies the means. He goes on: 'To sell oneself to one's conscience is to abandon mankind'.[39]

By the time of Rubashov's third interrogation, however, Ivanov himself has been shot and his place taken by his immediate junior. Gletkin is not of the revolutionary old guard. He is one of the products of the revolution and is clear about the revolutionary tasks for his own generation. 'For the first time in history', he tells Rubashov, 'a revolution has not only conquered power, but has also kept it ... The bulwark must be held at any price and with any sacrifice ... whoever did not understand this necessity had to be destroyed.'[40] Rubashov's only remaining duty, Gletkin argues, is to die for the Party.

But Rubashov now believes that the Party has forsaken the revolution.[41] The object of revolution had been the abolition of senseless suffering – suffering produced by an 'accidental', social cause. It had proved impossible to alleviate this kind of suffering (if indeed it had been alleviated) without an enormous increase in what Koestler describes as biological fatality – starvation caused by ideologically motivated policies such as large-scale industrialisation, or collectivisation of the land.

The story ends in Rubashov's capitulation. From the beginning of the novel we are aware that he has come to the end of his tether, both physically and emotionally. Moreover Rubashov had committed crimes against ordinary proletarians in the name of the Party; engineered the liquidation of intellectuals in the name of the Party; permitted the torture and execution of his own mistress in the name of the Party. If he were not now, in the name of that same Party, to accept his own death, then all his previous acts would lose their moral coherence, leaving him with only an unbearable guilt. Far better to avoid individual moral judgement just once more, in the name of the Party.

And yet his death hardly touches the central debate over ends and means. Koestler is primarily concerned to examine the success of the revolution in terms of its own aim – indeed, as he claims, the aim of all revolutions – the alleviation of 'accidental' suffering. Yet there is a contradiction in Koestler's argument. Rubashov says: if a revolutionary tells you that to make an omelette you must break eggs, ask to be shown the omelette. You will find revolutionaries always short of omelettes but seldom short of broken eggs. It is nevertheless possible to believe – perhaps Rubashov himself believed – that things could have worked differently. However his second line of argument seems to suggest quite the opposite. If the sound of Arlova's high heels on the cobbles or Bogrov's whimpering (for example) were to become the dominant consideration, then it would be hard to justify any revolutionary politics, including those to which Rubashov once aspired, since they would certainly require violent deaths. This argument implies that all revolutions would destroy their own legitimacy.

In these novels Koestler offers a choice between the infallibility of the 'solid anchor-chain' of No. 1 and the all-too-fallible, ineffectual humanity of Spartacus: two ends of the spectrum of revolutionary leadership. Whatever misgivings we might have concerning the morality of postrevolutionary society, it can hardly offer its citizens anything worse than total defeat and the agony of death on the cross. And Spartacus' deathbed conversion to some noble cause on whose behalf he must hand on the cup unsullied hardly amounts to a row of beans coming from a man marked by an incapacity to discern cause or purpose in the movement which he found himself leading. His mixture of humanitarianism, rank indecision and second-hand, second-class Machiavellism could hardly have been better designed for revolutionary failure. Koestler is right to suggest that a revolutionary credo could have transformed Spartacus' Sun State, but, as Spartacus himself recognised, both the leadership and the people have to believe in it or they will be left with Ivanov's reductionist morality. But is the problem so easily resolved?

The concern with means and ends that pervades these novels was a matter of personal experience for Koestler. The best account of his own career in the German Communist Party is to be found in 'The Initiates', a chapter in the collection edited by Richard Crossman, *The God That Failed*.[42] Koestler writes about the 'necessary lie, the necessary slander, the necessary intimidation of the masses to preserve them from short-sighted errors; the necessary liquidation of oppositional groups and hostile classes; the necessary sacrifice of a whole generation in the interests of the next'.[43] These 'little truths' were accepted because of the faith in the infallibility – the big truths – of the Party and the historical inevitability of its triumph. However Koestler's own faith was shattered by the reversals of party policy and the purges.[44] These left him numbed, but when he saw the swastika hoisted over Moscow airport and heard the Red Army Band strike up the 'Horst Wessel Lied',[45] Koestler saw the big truth for what it was: a big lie.

The prospect of having to come to terms with the Party's fallibility meant, for Koestler as for Rubashov, a complete reassessment of one's past actions. Where now was the justification for the betrayal of Richard? Richard knew that his wife and comrades would die a terrible death in Dachau or Oranienberg, knew that the Soviet Union had betrayed them. And Rubashov, 'knowing' him to be historically wrong, betrayed him to the Nazis. As Koestler wrote, the faithful learned to accept that anyone who disagreed with the party line was in reality an agent of fascism 'even if he happened to have his kidneys smashed to a pulp by the fascists in Dachau'. These, said Koestler, were the polemics of *Alice in Wonderland* in which the Queen of Hearts organised a croquet game with the hoops provided by moving soldiers and the balls by live hedgehogs. But the Party's game was consequential: Salome played the queen and when she called for a player's head, she got it on a bloody platter.

No reading of *The Gladiators* or *Darkness at Noon* can fail to recognise Koestler's ambivalence concerning the relationship of means and ends. Gletkin, with the task of making Soviet factories run efficiently, finds that terror is his only effective weapon; Spartacus' compassion renders him unable to act decisively. In the essay *The Yogi and the Commissar*,[46] Koestler envisages a gamut of political positions between these two apparent extremes. At one, the commissar believes in imposing change, believes that a 'radical reorganisation of the system' will cure all humanity's ills and that, as a consequence, any means, including violence and treachery, is justified. He believes that his position is authenticated by reason and that all who disagree should therefore be classified as enemies of progress. At the other end of the gamut is the yogi. His position is that faith in reason as opposed to personal enlightenment is misplaced and that since ends are almost always unpredictable it is means alone that signify. Since no causal relationship between means and ends can be demonstrated, violence is logically insupportable. Real change, for the yogi, is not possible from without, by any external agency. For the commissar, change from within is a sentimental fiction invented in its own self-interests by the ruling class.

In Koestler's view the commissar's problem is rooted in the law of detours. The road to utopia or to socialism is tortuous and at many points the summit will be out of sight. Often it will be necessary for the travellers to move off at a tangent; indeed it might well prove necessary on occasions to go backwards to avoid some obstacle. At such times, says Koestler, 'the inertia of the mass is converted into a violent centrifugal force'. Only the force Fulvius referred to as the will of the knowing (the commissar) will keep the mass moving, ultimately upwards, towards the summit. Yet this will, though it may seek to 'act the angel', must from time to time 'act the brute', and employ deception, coercion, indeed brutality to keep the mass on the move. Yet faces grow to resemble the masks they wear. One cannot 'employ' brutality: one can only act brutally. The will of the knowing cannot be justified by appeal to some disembodied reason; it must justify itself. And it may well prove to have been wrong.

For his part the yogi's position is equally problematical. As he seeks enlightenment and eschews violence, as he subordinates ends to means, the yogi loses the capacity to respond to events. Had the British Army withdrawn from India, says Koestler, Gandhi's declared policy of non-resistance to the Japanese might very well have led to the death of millions of his fellow citizens. If, on the same upward march to utopia, or enlightenment for all, the yogi is willing to offer no guidance on direction other than that each is the guardian of his own soul, then the Appian Way is always likely to be marked by crosses.

It is disingenuous of Koestler, then, to write in a second essay with the same title, published two years later,[47] that 'neither the saint nor the revolutionary can save us; only a synthesis of the two'. We have already seen, through the example of Huxley's grey eminence, that synthesised saints and revolutionaries offer no guaranteed solution. Indeed Koestler himself acknowledged that the mystic who converts to a 'party man' might become a dangerous, even unhinged, fanatic. Koestler's novels and essays shed a chillingly bright light on the relationship between means and ends but he is too honest and experienced to offer any simple reconciliation of the dichotomy.

I argued earlier that consequentialism as a justification for desperate revolutionary acts or for despotic regimes was unconvincing. If we pursue this argument as a consequence of reading Koestler we might reach another conclusion, that means and ends can be viewed as not qualitatively separate categories at all. The true nature of Koestler's law of detours is that the Final End of revolution (utopia? socialism?) is very soon lost to view and that at many points intermediate strategic targets (new ends) will need to be selected and to attain these, tactical decisions (new means) will need to be taken. The moment a tactical decision is isolated for implementation it, too, can be seen as a new end requiring new means, and so on. The law of detours implies the elision of means and ends, of acts and consequences, suggesting that decisions must be taken in the context not of some potential future good but of some identifiable, visible (or knowable) good, for each decision is in fact a means/end.

Koestler's primary aesthetic achievement is to show us the force of the law of detours. The novels depict a leader who is too fastidious to force the mass of men on against its will (to get his hands dirty) and a leader who, though he would stop at nothing to move the mass on – and has blood up to his elbows – nevertheless gets lost and who, more importantly, firmly believes that the revolution, too, is lost. Through Koestler's narratives we hear Arlova's heels on the cobbles; we understand Gletkin's resort to terror in organising his labour force; we are torn like Spartacus between the conflicting needs to maintain social cohesion and yet to deal justly and humanely with people – a dichotomy that transcends contingent considerations.[48] Imaginative literature shows itself able to convey through graphic illustration a general truth not capable of being stated explicitly. It is the force of Koestler's imagery that carries the argument forward. He confirms Djilas's dictum that 'nothing so well reveals the reality and greatness of ends as the methods used to obtain them'.[49]

The reality of revolution

If imaginative writers can contribute to our understanding of the attempt theoretically to justify revolution and can depict the unravelling of those theories in what might be called the post-revolution, they can also depict the nature of the revolutionary process in the modern industrial state. William Morris attempts to give an account of a Marxist revolution in *News from Nowhere* through the story told by Old Hammond. The central character of this visionary tale, presumably Morris himself, awakes one morning to find himself transported to a futuristic London which has become a communist paradise. Old Hammond is the man who introduces him to the new world, its customs and histories, and it is he who tells the story of the revolution, or civil war, that led to the creation of the socialist utopia. Morris gives over some thirty pages, about a seventh of the whole book, to his story.[50] He explains in detail how the revolution grew naturally out of a general strike, itself the consequence of trade union demands finally pushing a liberal government into resistance – much as Marx had predicted.

In his account of the revolution Hammond does not minimise the bloodshed and destruction, though there is an air of inevitability about the outcome – we know the violence will not be in vain. We are told that if the government had felt able to use the army against the people, as against a foreign enemy, then the revolution would have been lost; but the government had not the stomach for such a business and neither could the army be altogether trusted.[51] Although the revolution had generally benign consequences, Hammond doubted whether 'without this seemingly dreadful civil war, the due talent for administration would have been developed amongst the working men'.[52] It was also fortunate that the former ruling class was either killed in the war or, recognising the error of its ways, able to come to terms with the new system. Not only was the entire structure of capitalist production dismantled but the spirit that had enervated it was also destroyed. Although the workers, in victory, were unskilled in managing the new system of governance, the necessity of rebuilding society after such huge destruction and, of more even immediate importance, of feeding a starving population, obliged them to pull together. As life improved, not simply in terms of material abundance but of self-evident moral quality, so the fear of counter-revolution subsided. No need, then, of a period of dictatorship, for the 'spirit of the new days, of our days, was to be delight in the life of the worlds; intense and overweening love of the very skin and surface of the earth on which man dwells, such as a lover has in the fair flesh of the woman he loves'.[53] A happy outcome!

It would be unfair simply to dismiss Hammond's (Morris's) account as sanitised and unrealistic. He described passages of the revolutionary war in detail: 'deep lanes were mowed amidst the thick crowd; the dead and dying covered the ground, and the shrieks and wails and cries of horror filled the air, till it seemed as if there was nothing else in the world except murder and death'.[54] It was as if, Hammond concluded, 'the earth had opened and hell had come up bodily amongst us'. Yet the outcome is certain. The revolutionary is like a person who has steeled himself for an operation. It will be bloody and painful, and he wishes it was not necessary. But it is, and at the end he knows the body will be cleansed and healed. We are back in the world of means and ends, and for Morris the end seems to have a surgical certitude. And what is the end of revolution? To establish 'that overweening love of the very surface of the earth' which all will enjoy. This optimism is as breathtaking as Jack London's socialist revolutionary leader Everhard in the novel

The Iron Heel[55] whose ambition was simply to bring about 'the abolition of the conflict of interests'. (On the other hand in *his* depiction of the revolution, London unleashes the terrible dogs of war to do their bloody business. No surgical operation here.)

How different a picture is provided by the best-known of all modern writers on revolution, George Orwell. Orwell's attitude towards revolution was, on the face of it, ambivalent. In *Homage to Catalonia*[56] he experienced in Barcelona what he took to be a revolutionary socialist society and whilst he admitted that there were aspects of this society he neither understood nor liked, he 'recognised it immediately as something worth fighting for'. And Orwell is not using the phrase 'fight for' figuratively. Yet at the same time he seems to have realised that revolutionary Barcelona was doomed – indeed we suspect that this was part of its appeal. In Spain Orwell met an Italian volunteer whose compassion and decency inspired him to write the poem 'The Crystal Spirit'. Yet he perceptively commented: 'I knew that to retain my first impression of him I must not see him again.' Revolutions might be intoxicating in the evening but cold sobriety, and worse, awaited the morning after.

Orwell was, or soon became, aware of the tensions within the so-called revolutionary movement in Spain. The communists sought to control and organise all forces centrally and argued that to turn the war into a social revolution would play into the hands of the fascists. The anarchist and Trotskyist forces, on the other hand, were dedicated to achieving the broader aims of the revolution. And Orwell? 'The revolutionary purism of the [Trotskyists] ... seemed to me rather futile. After all, the one thing that mattered was to win the war.' And yet when the communists attacked and persecuted their former allies and Orwell himself was lucky to escape with his life, he recognised the crucial importance not merely of ends but of means. Orwell's attitude towards revolution remained ambivalent; indeed it provides an excellent example of doublethink. On the one hand, he saw revolution as representing the eternal struggle of the working class which he likened to the growth of a plant. The plant is blind and stupid 'but it knows enough to keep pushing towards the light, and it will do this in the face of endless discouragements'.[57] On the other hand, revolutions, as his Spanish experiences taught him, tend to be dominated by the wrong people with the wrong motivation and *Animal Farm* shows clearly how Orwell thinks this happens.

We should be clear from the outset that Orwell did not write *Animal Farm* as a condemnation of revolution: it was a condemnation of the Russian revolution. He wished to disassociate the Russian revolution and its aftermath from 'socialism' in order to save the latter, and he gives enough clues for the reader not to mistake his intention. Marx, Stalin and Trotsky are clearly represented, as are the Kronstadt naval rebellion (1921), the Treaty of Rapallo (1922), the German invasion of Russia (1941) and the Tehran Conference (1944). For all that, it is impossible to tie the fable down to only that period of history, to only that country: *Animal Farm*, for many readers, is a story of revolution any time, anywhere.

This particular revolution takes place on Manor Farm. It follows a speech made by an old boar, Major, modelled upon the concluding section of Marx and Engels's *Communist Manifesto*, in which Major declares that all animals are equal and all men are enemies. The animals must reject all the privileges that humanity assumes, Major tells them: living in houses, sleeping on beds, wearing clothes, drinking, smoking, using money, engaging in trade – or they will come to resemble the hated humans. Major set as the chief task of the days ahead to educate the animals for revolution, and immediately the pigs, the cleverest of the animals, assume a leadership role. Most prominent amongst them were Napoleon, Snowball and Squealer.

Old Major died before the revolution dawned but dawn it did, sooner than anyone had expected, one midsummer's day when Jones the farmer, hung over from the previous night's celebrations, forgot to feed the animals. They broke into the store shed to feed themselves and when Jones and his men tried to evict them the animals drove them off. 'Almost before they knew what was happening', says Orwell, 'the Rebellion had been successfully carried out.' Now to establish the revolution. The majority of the animals were blissfully happy at the departure of their masters but quite childlike in their unconcern about what was to become of them. 'They rolled in the dew, they cropped mouthfuls of the sweet summer grass, they kicked up clods of the black earth and snuffed its rich scent.'

Meanwhile Snowball and Napoleon took effective control. It was revealed that during the past three months the pigs had taught themselves to read and write – not, of course, forbidden by Major – and they wrote on the big barn wall the Seven Commandments incorporating the spirit of animalism. Thereafter they organised the other animals. We should note two developments in these early days of the revolution. First, what happened to the milk and later on to the apples. 'Never mind the milk, comrades', said Napoleon when asked. It was being taken to the pigs for their exclusive use. So were the apples. Squealer explained to the other animals that this was necessary because these particular foods were so important to brain workers, adding convincingly, 'this has been proved by Science, comrades'. The second development is that the pigs did not actually do any work, but directed and supervised the other animals. With their superior knowledge it was natural that they should assume the leadership. From the beginning, then, a division of labour came naturally into being.

Animals are not equal; it is natural for the more intelligent to take control. It is equally natural that they should begin to assume privileges. The commandeering of the apples and the milk was the only issue upon which the two leaders, Napoleon and Snowball, were to agree. The source of the pigs' power was their superior intelligence, and Snowball soon had under way many schemes that, because their success depended upon technological competence (the application of intelligence), were likely to increase the pigs' power. (It was precisely the fear of its propensity to empower the intellectuals that made Morris so dismissive of technology and industrialisation in *Nowhere*.) Thus in the evenings the pigs studied blacksmithing, carpentry, and so on. They also tended to dominate the rather perfunctory but symbolically important weekly meetings of the animals; it was they who put forward all the resolutions that were voted upon.

Technological advance was at once the safeguard and the death knell of the revolution on Animal Farm and if Snowball never fully realised this, Napoleon certainly did. The new lifestyle of the revolution would inevitably be based upon a high degree of technical sophistication, only possible if Snowball could procure dynamos and cables and other commodities which Animal Farm could not itself produce. They would have to be obtained through trade, and only by producing more than they themselves required, considerably more, in the way of eggs and crops and so on, could Animal Farm trade. But Major had specifically warned the animals against engaging in trade.[58] Snowball's plans, we might say, were those of a scientific, not an ethical socialist, and in his society, just as in Napoleon's, there was no place for equality of power. His chief stated concern was to improve the living standards of all the animals: the Shavian maximisation of welfare.

The lynchpin of Snowball's technological society was a windmill, and it was against the building of this windmill that Napoleon took his stand. He offered no alternative plan for increasing agricultural productivity, he did not raise moral or intellectual objections to building the windmill, neither did he attack the plans as a threat to the principles of animalism; he simply urinated on them. The windmill, after all, was Snowball's idea and not his own. This was not the only issue between the two leaders. Snowball wished to send pigeons to other farms to encourage the animals to revolt, but Napoleon clearly recognised that Animal Farm might need the help of its neighbours in the future and was more concerned about the well-being of Animal Farm than about spreading the gospel of animalism.[59] Orwell shows that divisions within the revolutionary leadership are inevitable, and that these differences, whilst they may be presented as doctrinal, here socialism in one country versus world revolution, are also personal and so inevitable.

When the animals held a meeting to decide on whether to go ahead with the building of the windmill, with an affirmative decision almost a foregone conclusion, Napoleon produced his most persuasive argument: nine huge dogs with brass-studded collars, trained in complete obedience to him. Snowball barely escaped their attentions with his life. After the latter's very rapid departure from the farm, Napoleon announced the cessation of Sunday meetings – which had anyway proved a rather farcical attempt at worker control – and the setting up instead of a special committee of pigs to run the farm. Stage two of the revolution had been reached; the struggle for power was over and the 'debate' about the direction of social development had been concluded.

At this point Napoleon decided that the windmill should be built after all (as he explained, it had really been his idea all along) and the animals on the farm began a year of intense effort. Orwell writes: 'all that year the animals worked like slaves'. The choice of simile is tragically significant. What is more, Napoleon actually put into operation his new policy of trading with other farms. Animal Farm began to sell eggs, thus breaking a basic principle of animalism. Around this time the pigs also broke the commandments; they moved into the farmhouse and slept on beds. Squealer, however, took good care to ensure that the principles of animalism were upheld. For example, the injunction written on the barn wall had read not to sleep on beds, now it read not to sleep on beds *with sheets*. The natural leadership which the pigs had assumed from the earliest days of the revolution began to assume a character similar to that of Jones; it clothed itself in the same kinds of privileges.

We begin to realise that Animal Farm's success will not be measured by its ability to establish a new, egalitarian way of life but by its technical and managerial efficiency. Yet this very efficiency was in question, for the windmill was blown down in a gale because its walls were too thin, and the potato harvest was lost because the clamps failed to keep the frost out over winter. The only clear measure of increased efficiency was to be found in the area of the techniques of social control. Whereas Jones had been intermittently cruel and careless, Napoleon and the pigs were systematically savage. Their assumption of forbidden privilege continued and Squealer's task of changing the commandments surreptitiously, so that the legitimacy of the revolution cannot be questioned, kept him busy. So when the pigs discover the pleasures of alcohol, the commandment originally forbidding animals to drink was surreptitiously amended to become an injunction against drinking *to excess*.

At the first sign of revolt, when the hens refused to lay the increased number of eggs required as a basis for trade with the other farms, Napoleon acted with great brutality. This ushered in the period of show-trials in which animals confessed to crimes that they had almost certainly not committed and which were always acknowledged by the 'criminals' to have been organised by the banished Snowball.

There seems to be an inevitability about the sequence of events on Animal Farm. Only occasionally do we catch a glimpse of possible alternative developments. One such possibility presented itself when Boxer the carthorse expressed publicly some slight doubts about Napoleon's policies and was attacked by the dogs. He beat them off easily and could have killed them. It was within his power at that point to challenge Napoleon's leadership. But Boxer was, in fact, one of the latter's strongest supporters and unaware that the animalism to which he wholeheartedly subscribed had been betrayed. Orwell believed in the latent political power of the active working class (excluding its 'sheep') but clearly also believed that the workers would be duped by revolutionary leaders skilled enough to appeal to their instinctive loyalties. He had seen working-class audiences swayed by the rhetoric of Oswald Mosley. At any rate, Boxer did not seize his chance and his subsequent fate at the hands of the duplicitous Napoleon becomes all the more poignant.

The revolution on Animal Farm, then, was a failure. The animals worked as hard and probably harder than under Jones and had as hard a life generally. True, in the early stages they believed that they were working for themselves and this made a great difference, but the feeling did not last. The moral principles according to which the doctrines of animalism had been formulated were slowly perverted, as each proved either impracticable or a hindrance to the aspirations of the pigs. Now, it could be argued that failure was chiefly a consequence of the fact that the animals had been catapulted into revolution before they had become sufficiently politically conscious; because, in Marxist terms, history was not ready, the bourgeois revolution not yet completed. But Marx had also said that the violence of revolution would accelerate the growth of consciousness, yet the most numerous of the animals on the farm were sheep. Who could have roused their political consciousness?

Moreover we should remember in whose 'hands' the task of political education (consciousness-raising) was placed: the pigs. No doubt Animal Farm is not a sound analogy for human society, yet the leader of the Marxist Social Democratic Federation, Hyndman, wrote: 'a slave class cannot free itself. The leadership, the initiative, the teaching, the organisation, must come from those comrades who are in a different position and who are trained to use their faculties in early life.'[60] Leadership must always come from the pigs.

It might alternatively be argued that the revolution on Animal Farm failed because the leadership forsook the principles of the revolution and lost contact with the mass movement. This is to assume that the pigs did at one stage subscribe to the principles of animalism, which is itself open to question. It is to suggest that as leaders of the revolution the pigs might have worked closer with the mass movement. Yet in the early days of the revolution the only aspiration that the mass movement could put into effect was to crop mouthfuls of the sweet summer grass and snuff the rich scent of the black earth. The animals needed to be organised by their natural leaders; this much seems unarguable. In other words the objectification of the principles of animalism was the task of a leadership which would, apparently inevitably, become divided but which collectively would be unlikely to countenance the canvassing of alternatives. Control of Animal Farm passed from a social caste – the farmer and his family – to a political caste – the pigs. The gains in this transfer for the other animals were minimal. In fact since the tyranny of pigs was more efficient the animals could be said to be worse off than before. Benjamin the donkey was the only animal, apart from the pigs, who could claim to have any insight. He had no illusions about a time when all animals would be free and equal. After all, the choice for the animals on the farm was rule by a drunkard or a pig; Orwell could hardly have presented his view of the choice more forcefully.

Richard Rorty was unstinting in his praise of *Animal Farm*. In depicting the events of the failed revolution Orwell 'attacks the incredibly complicated and sophisticated character of leftist political discussion ... by retelling the history of the [twentieth] century in terms suitable for children'.[61]

Conclusions

Revolution seems at first sight to offer socialists a prompt and effective way of redressing the many profound ills of their unequal society. Writers such as Koestler, Morris, London and Orwell, as well as many who wrote from a post-colonial perspective, were initially drawn towards the apparent certainties of the barricades. However, as we remember, Bernard Shaw pointed to an assumption that is both hidden and unwarranted: that the forces of revolution would inevitably be victorious. He went on to suggest the contrary: 'demolishing a Bastille with seven prisoners is one thing; demolishing one with fourteen million prisoners is quite another'.[62] Shaw is right: to manage a successful socialist revolution in a modern industrial state would be immeasurably difficult. To some revolutionaries this hardly signifies: they were concerned with (more correctly consumed by) vengeance. Hemmelreich, for example, in André Malraux's *Man's Estate*, wished only 'to requite by no matter what violence, to avenge with bombs the unspeakable horror of the existence which had poisoned him since the day of his birth, and which would poison his children in the same way'.[63] Yet for the socialist concerned with victory, not vengeance, the storming of the barricades is the easier part. It is the establishing of the post-revolutionary society that provides the real problem. Huxley's revolutionary Mark Staithes explains: 'Revolution's delightful in the preliminary stages. So long as it's a question of getting rid of the people at the top. But afterwards, if the thing's a success – what then? More wireless sets, more chocolates, more beauty parlours, more girls with better contraceptives ... the moment you give the people the chance to be piggish, they take it thankfully.'[64] We might add that just as the successful revolution gives the people the chance to be piggish, so, as Orwell shows, it gives the pigs the chance to be people-ish. Indeed the excesses of the Russian revolution graphically depicted by Koestler and Orwell and also by others, notably Victor Serge and Mikhail Bulgakov, were all invoked by implicit or explicit reference to Machiavelli's consequentialist mantra.

The power of these vivid narratives of revolution brings the reader face to face with the possible consequences of revolutionary ideology. Concepts become icons: the revolutionary potential of the working class, for example, is the chanting of the sheep or the fate of Boxer; socialism in one country becomes Loewy, hanging; historical inevitability is the dragging off of Richard's pregnant young wife. What gives these narratives greater force is that the authors so often had actual experience of what they wrote about. (Even Morris, after all, had been present at the Trafalgar Square riots of 1887.) For all of these reasons means and ends, revolution and its aftermath, become for the reader a set of experiences and not simply concepts.

5
Narrative and the Law

Much is made of the distinction between evolution and (violent) revolution in political discourse. Those who opt for what Shaw apologetically described as 'the slow, sordid, cowardly path to justice',[1] the piecemeal accretion over the years of legislative and behavioural change leading to a more socially and economically just society, imagine that they are copying the ways of nature. What better imprimatur could there be for a programme of political change? Indeed President of the European Commission Romano Prodi used exactly the analogy of nature's slow, steady but ineluctable evolution when accounting for the development of the Commission and its powers.[2] No surprise then that were we to compare those who supported violent revolutionary change with those who supported non-violent evolutionary change in Britain, we should find the latter a more numerous and on the whole more celebrated group. But we ought not to forget that, unlike violent revolution, which is usually understood in quite a specific way, a characteristic of evolutionary politics is its very diverse nature: we probably would not recognise it if it trod on our toes. It might be more appropriate, in fact, were we to present the initial comparison as between revolution and 'not-revolution', for we can be confident of only one piece of common ground as far as the evolutionists are concerned: they do not believe in violent revolution. But what *do* they believe in? Some support the notion of a paternalistic, Platonic type of government run by an authoritarian but welfare-conscious elite; others look to create a weak 'federal' system permitting the maximum amount of freedom for citizens to evolve as individuals within their own self-governing communities (what once might once have been innocently called soviets). In other words there may be as many, and indeed as distinct, differences between various kinds of evolutionists as between evolutionists and revolutionists.

In order to make sense of these many and conflicting evolutionary theories it will be necessary to categorise them, and the most appropriate way to do so, initially at any rate, is to consider separately the writing of three major exponents of contrasting evolutionary theories. The first of the three is the scientific socialist, Bernard Shaw, and we shall consider separately two strands of Shavian evolutionary theory. We shall then pass on to the theories of another scientific socialist, H.G. Wells, whose views differed markedly from Shaw's, and finally, having dealt with what might be called the mainstream of socialist evolutionary thought, we shall be turning briefly to the writing of Aldous Huxley, who might properly, background and training notwithstanding, be considered as an ethical and not a scientific socialist. His work provides an example of individualistic evolutionary theories.

Before we go on to discuss these three evolutionary theories, however, it will be helpful to return briefly to the distinction between evolution and revolution. I mentioned that the evolutionary way was considered by many of its exponents to be the natural way. However the evidence of natural evolution, such as we are able to interpret it, indicates that far from exhibiting slow, steady progress at a fairly even rate, evolution is characterised by lengthy periods of stasis followed by sudden and (dare one say it?) revolutionary, often violent revolutionary change. Species adapt to very sudden changes or they die out; *that* is the evolutionary process. Evolutionists like Shaw and Wells reacted to this apparent inconvenient contradiction to their theories in different ways: for Shaw it was necessary for men to take control of the evolutionary process, to direct it and to speed it up. Nothing natural here. Wells, who was himself a biologist, believed Shaw to be entirely mistaken. His own evolutionary theories mirrored natural evolution much more accurately and envisaged the same kind of sudden changes – indeed disasters – and looked to man's capacity subsequently to rebuild, adapt, and perhaps anticipate the next change. But what unified both writers, and indeed ethical socialist writers like Huxley, was, as we shall see, a strong belief that violent revolution was brutal, hugely wasteful and entirely counterproductive: they believed, that is to say, in the efficacy of the law.

Shaw: the inevitability of gradualness

One of the difficulties in analysing Shaw's work is that he concerned himself with issues at a number of levels more or less simultaneously. He declared himself, for example, to be a man of practical wisdom, talking in everyday language about the world we know and offering (sometimes) practical advice, as in *Everybody's Political What's What* (1944) and *The Plain Woman's Guide to Socialism, Capitalism, Sovietism and Fascism* (1929); he sought in other words, to make our known world a better place. Second, he declared himself to be an advocate of wholesale social reorganisation, undertaken by far-sighted leaders whose virtues his plays so often sought to extol: an advocate, that is, of a totally new kind of society, highly disciplined, and based upon a rigidly managed economic equality which would optimise the deployment of talented people. Third, Shaw wrote as a philosopher whose ultimate goal was to coax into existence a new kind of 'man' as different, he said, from bourgeois man as bourgeois man is from Neanderthal man.[3] This three-staged evolutionism makes Shaw appear even more inconsistent than he is. Reading him, as one critic said, is like 'looking through a pair of field glasses where the focus is always equally sharp and clear but where the range may be changed without warning'.[4] Moreover such a diverse approach presents problems for the author himself. As the same critic pointed out: 'The Socialist [Shaw] takes sword in hand to battle for a sounder society based upon a redistribution of income; and the long-term philosopher-poet [Shaw] comes to sap the socialist's faith with misgivings as to the capacity for righteousness and soundness of the material of common humanity as contrasted with philosopher-poets.'[5] In this chapter we shall be more concerned with Shaw the practical man and Shaw the advocate of wholesale social reorganisation than with Shaw the philosopher, though it will be helpful briefly to consider Shaw's ultimate project. We shall begin, in fact, by training the field glasses exclusively on Shaw the advocate of constitutional change – on Shaw the Fabian.

In the 1908 reprint of *Essays in Fabian Socialism* Shaw wrote: 'We set ourselves two definite tasks: first to provide a parliamentary programme for a prime minister converted to Socialism as Peel was converted to Free Trade: and second, to make it as easy and matter-of-course for the ordinary respectable Englishman to be a Socialist as to be a Liberal or a Conservative.'[6] Shaw wanted the Fabian Society to remain a small elitist group which might hope to persuade leaders of any political party of the wisdom of Fabian policies. It was on these grounds that Shaw successfully opposed Wells's attempt in 1907 to make the Fabian Society a mass movement bent upon propaganda among the mass of the voters.[7] Although Shaw frequently showed some sympathy to the aspirations of revolutionary socialists he nevertheless continually sought to emphasise the advantages to be gained through piecemeal reform. In *Essays in Fabian Socialism*, for example, he wrote:[8]

> Let me, in conclusion, disavow all admiration for this inevitable, but sordid, slow, reluctant, cowardly path to justice. I venture to claim your respect for those enthusiasts who still refuse to believe that millions of their fellow creatures must be left to sweat and suffer in hopeless toil and degradation, whilst parliaments and vestries grudgingly muddle and grope towards paltry instalments of betterment.

'Sordid' and 'cowardly', yes – but the slower way to progress is 'inevitable', according to Shaw. Moreover, he will venture to claim our 'respect' for revolutionary socialists, but not our support. Parliament may move towards small-scale measures of progress in a half-hearted and ill-considered way, but move towards progress it does. And Shaw would claim that history was his witness. The Fabian Society, along with other like-minded socialists in the Labour movement, had a noticeable impact upon the policies of Liberal governments in the two decades leading up to the First World War, especially in the labour and trade union legislation of the 1906–14 government.[9] When Labour governments took office their influence was even more direct. In 1929, for example, the government of Ramsay MacDonald (himself an ex-member of the Fabian executive) contained twenty Fabians, of whom no fewer than eight sat in the Cabinet. Whether any of the measures passed by these ministries justified the Fabian policy of persuasion is quite another matter.

Nevertheless Shaw had mounted a strong defence of gradual, evolutionary change in a short story entitled 'Death of an Old Revolutionary Hero'.[10] The story concerns the demise of one Jo Budgett of Balwick at the age of ninety. In the story Shaw explains that the newspapers had reported that Budgett's wife had tried to prevent Shaw from attending the funeral on the grounds that he had once actually tried to kill her husband.

Jo Budgett, it seems, had become seriously ill at the age of seventy-five and the then young Bernard Shaw had gone to visit this old lion of revolutionary socialism. Jo spoke at length to his young admirer about his apprenticeship in the revolutionary cause, served, he said, in the struggle against the 1832 Reform Bill. *Against?* asks the bewildered young Shaw. 'Aye, against it', he said:

> Old as I am, my blood still boils when I think of the way in which a capitalist tailor named Place – one of the half-hearted Radical vermin – worked the infamous conspiracy to enfranchise the middle classes

and deny the vote to the working man. I spoke against it on every platform in England ...

History records that 1832 was the first step only, and that the vote was further extended to industrial and then agricultural workers in 1867 and 1884, and eventually to women in 1928. We are immediately struck, as Shaw wants us to be, by the short-sightedness of Budgett's argument. (On the other hand we might note that 1832 itself, in increasing the electorate from 435,000 to 652,000, still left nineteen in every twenty men without the vote.)

Jo's indictment of piecemeal reformism continued in the same vein. He criticised Chartism with its five (*sic*) points to fool the people and keep them from going to the real root of their distress. Then Budgett took Bright and Cobden to task for trailing the red herring of Free Trade across the track of the emancipation of the working classes. 'I exposed them and their silly lies about cheap bread; and if I'd been listened to, no Englishman need ever have wanted bread again.' Next came those 'black blots on our statute books', the Factory Acts, which regulated and thereby perpetuated in legislation the 'accursed exploitation' of working-class women and children in the factory hells. Then came a 'worse swindle', the Reform Bill of 1867, which only served to give a 'handful of votes to a few workmen' so as to bolster the lie that Parliament represented the people and not 'the vampires that live by plundering them'. After a sally against the Education Act of 1870, Jo went on to deprecate the International, Karl Marx, the Paris Commune and the whole socialist movement in Britain, with its 'half-hearted Chartist palliatives', claiming that he had soon seen through Hyndman and that William Morris was 'just as bad'. By this time the youthful Shaw's image of the Revolutionary Lion had been shattered.

Budgett did not demur when Shaw concluded that his guiding principle had always been 'all or nothing'. Shaw went on to suggest to his erstwhile hero that since 'all' was out of the question, Jo's revolutionary socialism stood for nothing: it was, in effect, a primitive form of nihilism. By the end of his interview, Shaw had become quite convinced that Budgett was the sworn enemy of steady progress and so attempted to bring about Jo's death. Jo had said that the slightest noise would be enough to kill him and so Shaw contrived to bring down a grandfather clock, making his escape out of the open window. But to no effect: fifteen years of agitation were left to the Revolutionary Lion. When he finally died it was chiefly as a result of his apoplexy regarding a bill to enfranchise women – because it contained a property qualification.

He had remained true to his ideal of 'all or nothing' with the fervour of Ibsen's Brand. The moral of the story is that whereas Budgett's absolutist principles bound him 'tighter than ... a hooligan with a set of handcuffs' to an ineluctable nihilism, others less ambitious, who pursued the 'sordid, slow, reluctant, cowardly path to justice', actually achieved, in the fullness of time, very substantial progress.

What Shaw does in the course of this short story, then, is to indicate how much piecemeal change has affected the political and social contours of the lives of the majority of people, and, conversely, how the policies of revolutionary change would have made such steady improvement impossible.

'Death of an Old Revolutionary Hero' is remarkable for the fact that it manages, in a subtle and humorous way, to establish in the reader's mind a criticism of revolutionary politics which is likely to stay there. It is the opinionated, self-righteous, narrow-minded nature of Budgett as much as the long-term aggregation of measures of reform which convinces us that he is wrong. Not only has he managed to turn the admiration of his young visitor to unremitting scorn but he remains oblivious of this fact. Can we even begin to imagine what a society reconstructed after a violent revolution led by the likes of this man would look like? Yet Shaw is clever enough to let us feel the moral force of Jo's argument and sympathise with his impatience.

For Shaw, though, the immediate way forward was to forget about revolution and instead to concentrate on permeating the existing political structure with socialist ideas. 'In the first place', he wrote, socialism 'must be a continuing policy for developing our existing institutions into socialistic ones, and not a catastrophic policy for simultaneously destroying existing institutions and replacing them with a ready-made Utopia.'[11] But his involvement in practical politics led Shaw to the conclusion that, after all, swapping capitalism for socialism by changing the machinery of government was not likely to be very successful, especially bearing in mind the advent of mass democracy. As we have seen, Shaw had no faith in the working class, declaring that 'they make greater sacrifices to support legions of publicans and sporting bookmakers than free political institutions would cost them; and there is no escaping the inference that they care more for drinking and gambling than for freedom'.[12] But if democracy was incapable of administering a socialist society, great leaders were not.

Shaw believed in the existence of naturally dominant people, and his plays contain many: Andrew Undershaft in *Major Barbara*, Magnus in *The Apple Cart*, the millionairess in the play of that name, Caesar in

Caesar and Cleopatra, and so on. These men and women were society's natural leaders 'in whom the "great abstractions" and a genius for practical affairs combine to make a natural monarch'.[13] Like Carlyle's heroes their power lay 'in their transcendence of the ethical codes and spiritual limitations of ordinary human beings'.[14] Although Shaw recognised the need to exercise some democratic control over these natural leaders, indeed he devised an elaborate hierarchical system of elected 'panels' to perform such a function, he placed his faith in the superior wisdom of the natural rulers to act in the interests of all. It will come as no surprise that Shaw cast himself and his fellow Fabians in the role of natural leaders whose task was to organise the whole of society along socialist lines and for its own good. He argued: 'socialism without experts is as impossible as shipbuilding without experts or dentistry without experts'.[15]

The criterion according to which these 'experts' would make their decisions was simply wisdom, which by definition they possessed to a greater extent than their fellow citizens; thus when they acted they did so in the interests of all. Widespread dissatisfaction with their rule would therefore be unlikely, revolt unthinkable. After all, 'When a railway porter directs me to No. 10 platform I do not strike him to the earth with a shout of "Down with Tyranny" and rush violently to No. 1 platform.'[16] A compelling picture but not entirely a convincing one. Whilst the great majority of people would willingly accept the railway porter's expertise in deciding which is the best train for them, they are not so likely to accept the political scientist's expertise in deciding what constitutes the wisest course of action in any given event. It is the travellers after all who decide on their destination; they merely consult the porter on travel options. In politics no such agreements exist in terms of destinations (ends) so the travel arrangements (means) remain contentious. And we have already considered the interrelation of means and ends. Hannah Arendt argued that Plato's Republic was an escape from politics altogether and into notions of ruling. Some are naturally entitled to command and others obliged to obey: that is really all there is to it, and Shaw was always ready to acknowledge Plato's influence on his own thinking. But the notion of suitability to rule is not exclusively Platonic. Aristotle too spoke of some men 'so far superior ... in virtue and political capacity' that they should not be constrained by law or government. The men, he continues, 'we take not to be part of the state but to transcend it'.[17]

A second aspect of Shaw's attitude to great people – and the change from 'men' to 'people' is, as we shall see, an important one about which we should be clear – is that whilst they currently constitute only a small proportion of society – between 5 and 10 per cent – they need not always be so few. Indeed one of the chief arguments with which Shaw underpinned his faith in gradual change was that if society's leaders could be persuaded to enact policies leading towards equality of income and greater gender equality as well as other socialist measures of amelioration, the social and political system would be transformed as the proportion of unusually talented people increased. No more flowers would be 'born to blush unseen / And waste their sweetness on the desert air'. In his most active years as a socialist Shaw argued continuously for equality of income, stating that it was the only thing about human beings which could be equalised. To those who argued that, given equality of income, nobody would wish to take up either the most demanding or the most unpleasant occupations, Shaw countered that the most demanding jobs were invariably the most inherently rewarding, and that the most unpleasant jobs were generally the least well-paid anyway. For the younger Shaw equality of income was a necessary condition for the naturally superior to assume their rightful places in the political hierarchy and to multiply.[18] He retreated from the position of complete equality later on.[19] In an open letter in 1943 he told the philosopher Joad that to give everyone an equal share in the nation's income would reduce us all to poverty and the cultivation of science, art and philosophy would become impossible. 'Civilisation would perish, and with it most of the people.'[20] Despite this retreat, Shaw's ideal society was always meritocratic and always far more equal than existing capitalist society; and so it would encourage the emergence of a gifted leadership.

By dint of permeating existing political parties and institutions with socialist ideas, then, Shaw hoped to make possible the advent of a planned, socialist society in which naturally gifted leaders would dominate and people of action would provide the maximisation of welfare for all. By means of equalising income (almost) they would then make possible the emergence and eventual growth of groups of previously socially deprived men and women of natural talent until society as a whole would be able to aspire to a totally new kind of lifestyle.

The clearest picture that Shaw left of a gifted leader operating within the constraints of a democratic polity is that of King Magnus in *The Apple Cart*. The play received a cool reception in many quarters, being perceived as an attack on democracy: indeed it was prohibited from being staged in Dresden, the author admitted, because it was considered a 'blasphemy against democracy'.[21] Although Shaw pleads not guilty to this charge he does go on to ask us to consider democracy as 'a big balloon...sent up so that you shall be kept looking up at the sky whilst other people are picking your pockets'.[22] People have no more aptitude for governing, for writing laws, than for writing plays. So much for the judgement of the common people. And yet Magnus's most powerful weapon in his struggle against the Cabinet is his threat to abdicate and fight an election, to 'go to the people', and the threat resides precisely in the certainty that those much maligned people will recognise Magnus's superior political talents and elect him.

Whilst it is true that Magnus enjoys the best lines, his opponents, the representatives of modern democracy, are themselves monarchs of sorts. Take the trade union leader and President of the Board of Trade Boanerges: 'No king on earth is as safe in his job as a Trade Union official. There is only one thing that can get him sacked; and that is drink. Not even then, as long as he doesn't actually fall down.' His relationship with his members, 'the people', is sharply depicted: 'I say to them "You are supreme. Exercise your power". They say "That's right. Tell us what to do".' Just the kind of natural development in a democracy that Kierkegaard had warned against.[23] What Magnus offers, however, is an example of the old Tory principle of kingship: a leader trained for his duties from an early age, above faction, able to act on behalf of all of his people. Most of the democratically elected Cabinet by contrast are in the pocket of the multinational company Breakages Limited.

Although Magnus is a good example of a Shavian ruler he is far from the only one. Epifania (the heroine of *The Millionairess*), Saint Joan and Mrs Warren are women of action, and Ann Whitefield in *Man and Superman* and the eponymous Candida are both masterful women who choose to act through their men. These are all dominant women with a capacity for wise and decisive action and serve to illustrate Shaw's argument for greater equality, in this case gender equality. In banishing women to the drawing rooms, or worse to the kitchens *à la Coming Up for Air*, society wilfully deprives itself of half of its potential leadership cadre.

By removing social barriers, by allowing natural leaders to assume responsibility for society, Shaw believed that we could make possible a fundamental change in human nature. Having dismissed the mass of mankind out of hand as a potential evolutionary force – recognising, like Kant, that nothing straight was ever made from the 'crooked timber of humanity' – he recognised also the long-term limitations even of his men of action.[24]

History teaches, Shaw argues, the limits of even the great rulers. Indeed it advises us to give up any idea that 'man as he exists is capable of net progress'. But as G.K. Chesterton pointed out, Shaw's passion for socialism was so strong that he did not wash his hands of progress: he washed his hands of man. 'Our only hope, then, is in evolution. We must replace the man with the superman.' By the turn of the century Shaw had come to accept the central importance of genetics, after reading Blake, Bunyan, Samuel Butler and Schopenhauer, especially the last's *The World as Will and Representation* (1819). It has been said that his evolutionary theories 'gave him simultaneously a fresh sense of individual significance and a cosmic sanction for his socialism'.[25] Indeed, as far as Shaw was concerned socialism became 'the embodiment and forefront of the upward struggle of the Life Force'.[26]

What was this Life Force? 'Unless we believe', said Shaw, 'that the life in us is a divine spark that can be nursed into a steady flame and finally into an illuminating fire, then there is really no sense in belonging to a Fabian Society or indeed in taking the trouble to feed ourselves.'[27] This force within us naturally aspires to what Don Juan in *Man and Superman* calls a 'higher organisation, wider, deeper, intenser self-consciousness, and clearer understanding'. By making himself the servant of the Life Force, by willing what it wills, mankind has developed and will develop much further. Shaw rejected Darwin's theory of natural selection, with its emphasis on pure chance, and held to Lamarck's view that a species evolved through the exercise of will, with the characteristics thus acquired by one generation being transmitted to the next. Shaw associated himself with the French philosopher Bergson who in *L'Evolution Créatrice* (1907) spoke of the *élan vital*, a creative life force which dominated evolution. But what Shaw proposed, however, was nothing less than the taking in hand of evolution (and no doubt slinging it in the way it should go). It is one thing to recognise the reality and supreme importance of evolutionary change, as, for example, a Christian palaeontologist such as Teilhard does in *The Phenomenon of Man*: it is quite another to offer practical proposals for speeding evolution up by means of deliberately devised programmes. Shaw suggests, in the Preface to *Back to Methuselah*, that since a weightlifter can, by training harder, 'put up' a muscle, an earnest and convinced philosopher ought, with similar dedication, to be able to 'put up' a brain. That Shaw was in earnest should not be doubted. For him 'the only fundamental and possible Socialism is the socialisation of the selective breeding of man; in other terms, of human evolution. We must eliminate the Yahoo, or his vote will wreck the commonwealth.'[28]

Shaw examined themes of creative evolution in a number of plays, but it is in *Man and Superman*, one of his major works, that they are most fully dealt with. Shaw begins with an Epistle Dedicatory in which he outlines the reasons behind his belief in progress through evolution.

'I do not know whether you have any illusions left on the subject of education, progress, and so forth. I have none. Any pamphleteer can show the way to better things; but when there is no will there is no way.' The only answer, says Shaw, is to 'breed political capacity', and the way to do that is to maximise the natural leadership and talent existing in society. He uses the analogy of a domestic electrical system to explain the role of the natural leader. Think, he says, of all the copper wire that 'gorges itself with electricity' yet gives out no light. But then think of those scraps of resistant material that will not allow the current to pass until it has made itself useful to us by providing light and heat.

This illumination provided for the benefit of all by the 'self-consciousness of certain abnormal people' is a source of great satisfaction for those involved. Shaw's naturally talented elite includes not only political leaders but also men of letters. Both in this play and in *Candida* Shaw deals with the place of artists in general in his social scheme. The artist is a man apart, not to be inhibited or restricted by enduring emotional attachments or humdrum domestic arrangements. Shaw's artist is a close relation to Nietzsche's artist–philosopher, the overman who must be so far removed from ordinary men that he can shape them. Yet both Eugene in *Candida* and Tavy in *Man and Superman* are, to some extent, figures of fun. They are essentially romantics who, in the rough-and-tumble of the world, are no match for the realists such as Candida herself and Tanner, not to mention the predatory Ann Whitefield.

Tanner can be assumed to personify Shaw's idea of the natural leader, a man with two responsibilities, one of which he is aware of from the beginning of the play and one of which he is slowly made aware of as the play progresses. The first is the responsibility of assuming a political role. It is made clear to us that Tanner will naturally enter Parliament, besides which he has a reputation for radical politics, having just written a book entitled *The Revolutionist's Handbook*. The second responsibility Tanner owes to the Life Force. He has to marry Ann and, we may assume, join her in the making of superchildren. He is, in short, a physical embodiment of Shavian evolutionary theory.

Tanner is a modern Don Juan whose self-awareness causes him to reject the primrose path of dalliance so as to pursue the purposes of the Life Force. The importance of the Don Juan myth to understanding the play is underlined by the dream sequence in Hell in which Don Juan, amid sundry interruptions, conducts a dialogue with the Devil on the relative merits of Heaven and Hell. The latter place is depicted as pleasant enough: man can do what he pleases but he must accept the limitation that there is nothing for him to strive after. Don Juan is bored in

Hell. 'As long as I can conceive something better than myself', he complains, 'I cannot be easy unless I am striving to bring it into existence.' The Devil argues the necessity of accepting the impossibility of genuine progress towards a higher form of humanity. 'Beware of the pursuit of the superman', he warns: 'it leads to an indiscriminate contempt for the human.' Critics who argue that this quotation indicates Shaw's awareness of the possible inhumanity of his evolutionary theories[29] would do well to remember that it is the Devil who speaks these lines; in fact they suggest a philosophy totally alien to Don Juan and, of course, to Shaw.

The central theme, then, of Shavian socialism, is evolution, an ever-continuing, upward thrust towards, at the social level, a higher form of social structure, scientifically organised, and at the individual level, eventually, a higher form of life altogether. For Shaw man was, to use Nietzsche's expression, 'a rope tied between beast and overman'.[30] Until comparatively recently Shaw's ideas were considered fanciful in the extreme and even today Lamarckian theories of evolution continue to be generally disparaged, relegating notions of the life force to the margins of history. And yet through the exercise of our political will we have already impacted upon man's development. Most people in the West live almost unimaginably longer and healthier lives than was the case when Shaw was born. These changes, dramatic though they appear in a historical context, will seem almost insignificant as man's knowledge of the human genome increases. We shall return to this point later, in a different context. Our capacity to alter life forms through cloning and genetic engineering means that, in theory at least, by application of the human will, man can indeed impact indirectly upon his own development. Forward to Methuselah!

Wells: science and the future

Unlike Shaw, H.G. Wells was by training and by inclination a scientist. Both were elitists, both believed that if it were to be 'improved' society would have to depend upon the farsightedness and organising abilities of its political leaders and its men of ideas. But for Wells the problems which beset men were, in the strictest sense, technical and technological, and mankind's response would be to evolve a higher technology, superior social organisation and so forth, to overcome these problems. Only scientists – not political scientists or social scientists like the Fabians, but physical scientists – possessed the necessary training and disinterested philosophy to succeed. This is borne out by the Wellsian utopias we shall be considering later: they are based upon some great scientific breakthrough, not a social one. Yet, like Shaw, Wells rejected revolution as an agent of real change.

It is necessary to grasp what Wells had in mind as an objective when he tried to appropriate science to the cause of social progress. Wells speaks of a garden planned overall with a view to symmetry, of the juxtaposition of colours and shapes, of a whole which is something more than the sum total of its constituent parts. Wells's future, as we shall see later, was a utopia for the creative imagination, but if reason, *à la* Hobbes, was the servant of the passions, it was nevertheless a *sine qua non* of successful development:

> In the future, it is at least conceivable, that men with a trained reason and a sounder science, both of matter and psychology, may … at last attain and preserve a social organisation so cunningly balanced against exterior necessities on the one hand, and the artificial factor in the individual on the other, that the life of every human being, and indeed, through man, of every sentient creature in earth, may be generally happy.[31]

To what extent Alfred Polly, that most human of Wells's creations, would have been happy in such a well-ordered environment is open to question. Dostoevsky too would argue that, living in the reign of universal common sense, man would want only to 'send all this common sense to the devil'.[32]

The fundamental difference between Wells's evolutionary theories and Shaw's was precisely this emphasis which the former placed upon mankind's integrated well-being. Man's survival, according to Wells, depended upon his developing a species-consciousness, and from his historical studies Wells discerned just such a trend. In *Boon* (1915) Wells referred to species-consciousness as 'the Mind of the Race' and commented that: 'It [the human race] begins to live as a conscious being, and as it does so, the individual too begins to live in a new way, a greater, more understanding and more satisfying way. His thoughts apprehend interests beyond himself and beyond his particular life.'[33] For Wells, then, the man of the future would be a completely integrated species being, not a Shavian, still less Nietzschean, superman.

The task of the new species being was, to quote Masterman in *Kipps*, to build the imagination to use socialism to 'create and direct the public will'.[34] Man's progress has always depended on the ability 'to evolve the extrinsic, cumulative, transmissible mental environment of civilisation'.[35] Civilisation being a 'fabric of ideas and habits', it tends to grow 'through the agency of eccentric and innovating people, playwrights, novelists, preachers, poets, journalists, and political reasoners and speakers, the modern equivalents of the prophets who struggled against the priests – against the social order that is of the barbaric age'.[36] In other words Wells assigns a special role to the artist in general in helping to create a species-consciousness. This makes Wells's artist far more important in the process of evolution than Shaw's. Wells was aware of the scope of his claim. He himself was prepared to sacrifice his standing as a novelist in order to promote his political ideas; selling his birthright, it was said, for a pot of message.

Wells was adamant about the need to prepare people for socialism. He was willing to invest a great deal of time on works such as *The Outline of History* (1920), *The Work, Wealth and Happiness of Mankind* (1932) and *A Short History of the World* (1922). Nevertheless, like Shaw, he did not for a moment believe that socialism would be brought into being by popular acclaim. Building a socialist world state was a task for elites. He saw members of these elites forming themselves into an 'open conspiracy' aimed at securing world government based upon rational social and economic planning. The elites he envisaged included professional groups, trade unions, transport and communications authorities, manufacturers and so on. In 1933 Wells set out his ideas in a polemic entitled *The Open Conspiracy*. He had himself paid earlier visits to both Stalin and Roosevelt to discuss his 'open conspiracy' theories. He was later to claim to have had some influence over President Woodrow Wilson's move to establish the League of Nations. Yet he was not entirely optimistic about its success. He had criticised Foreign Secretary Grey, declaring: 'For him, a League of Nations was necessarily a League of Foreign Offices': not at all what Wells had hoped for.[37] Governments would be generally sympathetic to cooperative international developments because of three growing pressures. First, ever-increasing international cooperation would oblige national leaders to recognise the limitations of any national or even purely regional solution to their problems. Second, overpopulation would cause global problems requiring global cooperation in the effort to solve them. Third, the enormously destructive capacity of modern warfare would oblige major nations to cooperate in order to limit or even eliminate it. As in so many things Wells's anticipation of the decline of the nation state was prescient.

Wells was sanguine, however, when discussing the possibilities for his socialist world state. He believed that one would come into being eventually but probably only after mankind had failed to respond to the worldwide problems he outlined, thus bringing about some major but not fatal catastrophe. From the ashes, as of necessity, would arise the phoenix of world socialism. Wells pursued these theories relentlessly; together with his scheme for mass propaganda, they are part and parcel of his general concept of the growth of species-consciousness (the Mind of the Race). Catastrophe as a catalyst became part of the theory only after the 1914–18 war, an event so damaging to the growth of species-consciousness that it had to be accommodated somehow into the general theory. In *Boon* Wells coined the phrase that it had been the war to end war, and in this sense catastrophe was given a positive role in Wells's evolutionary theories. Indeed, we might note that in his earlier novels it is only through catastrophes that Kipps, Polly and George Ponderevo are able truly to discover themselves.

For the story of the advent of world socialism, however, we are best served by turning to a later work, *The Shape of Things to Come* (1933). Here the diplomat, Dr Philip Raven, sets out the details of dreams he was having about the future before his death in 1930. Wells, a friend of this fictitious diplomat, undertakes the task of editing the notes Raven has made of his dreams and the book is supposed to be the outcome of his efforts. It tells of the inevitable collapse of competitive capitalism, 'absolutely incapable of controlling the unemployment it had evoked and the belligerence it had stimulated', and of the emergence of the World State.[38]

> It has been a chronicle of disaster, wherein particular miseries, the torment and frustration of thousands of millions, are more than overshadowed by its appalling general aimlessness. We have seen the urge towards unity and order, appearing and being frustrated, reappearing and again being defeated. At last it reappeared – and won. The problem had been solved …
>
> It was no great moral impulse turned mankind from its drift towards chaos. It was an intellectual recovery. Essentially what happened was this: social and political science overtook the march of catastrophe.

Wells's attitude to the social sciences has mellowed. He now believes that the response of social scientists to catastrophe would be more truly 'scientific' than some of their earlier analyses. Yet he remained convinced that the central concern of 'the so-called science of sociology' ought to be what he referred to as 'utopography'.[39]

George Orwell once parodied Wells's philosophy as representing a simple struggle between the scientific and the romantic mind. He wrote: 'On the one side science, order, progress, internationalism, aeroplanes, steel, concrete, hygiene: on the other side war, nationalism, religion,

monarchy, peasants, Greek professors, poets, horses. History as he sees it
is a series of victories won by the scientific man over the romantic man.'[40]

Orwell is correct in so far as when in his best fiction Wells tries to present us with the contrast between the kind of man he admires and the
kind he despairs of, the contrast often takes the form of a scientific man
against a romantic man. A clear example of this is in *Tono Bungay*; when
George Ponderevo sails down the Thames in his new destroyer, past the
bastion of 'legalism' (as Wells uses the word), the Houses of Parliament,
he stands as an exemplar of the creative person's concern for the future.
But he is a scientist. Edward Ponderevo, who represents a world concerned with custom, tradition and the past, is a romantic. True, Edward
is finally brought down by the forces of 'legalism' but he gives them a
run for their money. Moreover, whilst Wells provides a sympathetic
treatment for some of his scientific heroes like George, we have only to
remember Griffin (the invisible man), and Dr Moreau, to realise that
despite his often stated view that a scientific training, with its emphasis
on the discovery of verifiable 'truths', was the best training for political
leadership, Wells clearly became aware that science in itself was by no
means a value system. In short, Wells did see the future of man as
depending upon a successful scientific response to problems of an essentially technological character, but he also understood that science itself
could not provide an answer: it provided only the means to an answer.

Wells's earlier work included a number of brilliant allegories of his theories of progress. We observed earlier that the nature of evolution itself
contains the idea of revolutionary change and Wells accommodated this
via his notion of catastrophe and response. Perhaps the most vivid picture of a more general idea of the nature of progress, however, is provided by the novel *Food of the Gods*, for it allows a role to science and to
catastrophe and illustrates Wells's belief that progress, though inevitable,
is uncompromisingly difficult. The story concerns the development of
herakleophorbia, a wonder food that produces stupendous growth in all
living things that eat it. The scientists who make the discovery are hardly
heroic – they are described as exemplifying 'the unfaltering littleness of
men'. They decide to set up a farm in order to experiment with the food
and their lack of wordly wisdom immediately becomes apparent when
they appoint to run the farm a reprobate and his wife whose misman-
agement and general laziness add new dimensions to the story. They
allow the food to be scattered, so it becomes consumed not only by the
chicks in the experiment but by wasps and rats. Wells's descriptive powers are used to best advantage here, the advent of the huge rats being
particularly harrowing. As one of the scientists remarks: 'We ... scientific

men ... work always for a theoretical result ... but incidentally we do set forces into operation.'[41] Progress is in for a bumpy ride.

Wells shows how all the forces of established society combine against their work. The expense to the state of accommodating the increasing number of giant children is formidable and public opinion – the 'inevitable inertia of the great mass of people' – becomes fixed against them.[42] And where the people go, there the politicians follow. One up-and-coming demagogue, Caterham, becomes the champion of 'little-ness' and claims the sobriquet 'Jack the Giant Killer'. For their part the giants come to understand that the future is theirs: 'a time will come when littleness will have passed altogether out of the world', leaving the world to the giants who will be continually doing 'greater and more splendid things'.[43] Meanwhile Caterham decides to act. Opposition to the giants has (miraculously) united the Liberal Party behind him. Caterham is not concerned about abstract principles of progress, that 'invincible tide of growth that flowed and flowed', but only about 'gatherings and caucuses and votes – above all votes'. He is in short a 'vote-monster'.[44] He uses military force to attack the giants, with con-siderable loss of life. But Caterham is 'yesterday' and cannot stand against 'the full preponderance of the future'. Caterham attempts to force the giants to move away to some deserted part of the globe and to agree neither to create more of their food nor to procreate. They refuse and declare themselves ready to fight. Their stand is not for themselves, says one of the giants, but 'for the greatness ... in the purpose of things ... to grow and still to grow' until finally they achieve at last '"the fellowship and understanding of God. Growing ... till the earth is no more than a footstool ... till the spirit shall have driven fear into noth-ingness, and spread ..." He swung his arms heavenwards – "*There*".'[45]

This imaginative *tour de force* shows Wells at his best, giving an iden-tity to evolution and indicating clearly its quasi-revolutionary nature. Wells uncompromisingly shows the incapacity of capitalist democracy to come to terms with the future. Yet if he thought that his labelling of the arch politician, the vote-monster, as Jack the Giant Killer would win the sympathy of readers for progress he was to be mistaken. As we have seen, Orwell was later to claim that Wells's theories of progress extolled the virtues of Giant the Jack Killer.

We cannot fully understand the sudden burgeoning of species-consciousness, however, unless we grasp the central role that Wells had set aside for himself in the process. He was to be the great sage and prophet who would rescue mankind from catastrophe. This is why Wells, as he got older, became less optimistic; his pessimism grew in direct proportion to his own apparent failure to arouse mankind. Perhaps, though, the world will not be faced with the simple choice of catastrophe or rapid transition to world socialism; perhaps world government will come, much as Wells suggested, but more gradually; perhaps mankind will muddle through, as often before. But if it does, then maybe the evolutionary theories popularised by Wells in the first half of the twentieth-century will have played no small part. Orwell, a perceptive critic who developed a personal distaste for Wells, nevertheless wrote: 'The minds of us all, and therefore the physical world, would be perceptibly different if Wells had never existed.'[46] Wells was wrong to accuse humanity of not allowing him to save it. The epitaph he is said to have considered for himself, 'God damn you all. I told you so', would have been inappropriate, belittling his significant achievement in the growth of what he called the mind of the race.

The case for moral evolution

There remains one last theory of evolutionary change to be considered and it is, unlike the preceding ones, essentially ethical rather than scientific. That is to say, it anticipates a change in the character of man as we know him being the product of moral choice, not evolutionary genetics or taking herakleophorbia. Unlike the scientists, proponents of this theory hold that change can only be internally and not externally induced. Change comes about as a response to a new understanding of the relationship between man and his environment, an understanding of religious or quasi-religious dimensions. The exemplar of moralistic evolutionary theory we shall consider is Aldous Huxley, and the novel in which he sets out his theory most concisely and pertinently is *Eyeless in Gaza*.[47] The leading character, Anthony Beavis, in stating his own personal problem, states mankind's: 'The problem is: how to love?';[48] how to feel a persistent affectionate interest in people? If the individual can learn to solve this problem, his relationship with his environment, and hence the environment itself, will be transformed. Miller, an anthropologist, reinforces the closeness of the connection between individual man and society at large:[49]

> States and nations don't exist as such. They are only people. Sets of people, living in certain areas, having certain allegiances. Nations won't change their national policies unless and until people change their private policies. All governments, even Hitler's, even Stalin's, even Mussolini's, are representative. Today's national behaviour – a

large-scale projection of today's individual behaviour ... Or rather, to be more accurate, a large-scale projection of the individual's secret wishes and intentions.

For Miller, as for Huxley, the important fact in the relationship between man and society is that the former plays the dominant role: 'society' is simply a representational image of men in the particular. For society to change, men must change. Miller is not without hope of such change because of what he takes to be four observable facts. We are all capable of love; we impose limitations upon our love; we can transcend these limitations if we choose; love when expressed is returned. If men acted on these facts, society could be transformed. The only alternative to this is a kind of hell, which Miller goes on to describe as 'the incapacity to be other than the creature one finds oneself ordinarily behaving as', a definition which would have appealed to Shaw's Don Juan.

Later in the book, Miller analyses English politics, suggesting that most reforms have been made without the principles underlying them ever being accepted. 'There are no large-scale plans in English politics, and hardly any thinking in terms of first principles.' This absence, he continues, has resulted in a tolerant and good-natured political system.[50]

> Deal with practical problems as they arise and without reference to first principles; politics are a matter of higgling. Now higglers lose tempers but don't normally regard one another as fiends in human form. But this is precisely what men of principle and systematic planners can't help doing. A principle is, by definition, right; a plan for the good of the people. Axioms from which it logically follows that those who disagree with you and won't help you realise your plan are enemies of goodness and humanity.

This analysis is completed by the indictment that a government with a comprehensive plan for the betterment of society is a government that uses torture. But Miller goes on to argue that, whether it wills it or no, a government today is obliged to plan, at least to some degree, because of the constantly accelerating speed of technological advances and because of the universal ability to prevent conception. In such circumstances, the lack of broad planning would, says Miller, simply lead to breakdown. But in devising plans, governments must think in concrete and not ideological terms, 'For if you begin by considering concrete people, you see at once that freedom from coercion is a necessary condition of their full development into full-grown human beings.'[51]

But most modern governments fail to realise that economic prosperity based on the possession of 'unnecessary objects' does not lead to individual well-being; that a leisure filled with only passive amusements is not a blessing; that the urban lifestyle which people are encouraged to strive for can only be gained at a high psychological price; that an education system which 'allows you to use yourself wrongly' has no real value. Yet modern man accepts readily all these undesirable aspects of planning as natural and unavoidable. Why?[52]

> Because he is so little aware of his own interests as a human being that he feels irresistibly tempted to sacrifice himself to these idols. There is no remedy except to become aware of one's interests as a human being, and, having become aware, to learn to act on that awareness. *Which means learning to use the self and learning to direct the mind.*

Miller's argument, then, accepts the inevitability of planning but wishes planning to be merely skeletal, allowing as much scope as possible to the individual. The individual, however, must make a response, must learn to become a complete individual, acting out of love for his fellow men. Only then will society be transformed. 'Wouldn't it be nice', says Miller, '... if there were another way out of our difficulties.' But of course there is no 'salvation from outside, like a dose of calomel [or perhaps Fabian malt extract!].'

One who wrote more explicitly about the importance of love, and who tended to emphasise Eros at the expense of agape, was Huxley's mentor during his early years as a writer, D.H. Lawrence. Lawrence's politics were clearly not socialist in any normally accepted sense. Yet just as Lawrence shared (indeed helped to form) many of Huxley's views on the ills of capitalist society,[53] so he also shared Huxley's view on the nature of political and social change. For Lawrence, too, men had to change the nature of their relationships with each other. He wrote:[54]

> If our civilisation had taught us how to let sex appeal flow properly and subtly, how to keep the fire of sex clear and alive, flickering or glowing or blazing in all its varying degrees of strength and communication, we might, all of us, have lived all our lives in love, which means we should be kindled and full of zest in all kinds of ways and for all kinds of things.

Democracy, as far as Lawrence was concerned, had to concern itself not so much with redistributing property as with allowing each man to be spontaneously himself. Man would then rediscover his wholeness. Only then would he be moved by a new impulse to free himself from[55]

> the extraneous load of possession, and walk naked and light. Every attempt at pre-ordaining a new material world only adds another last straw to the load that has already broken so many backs. If we are to keep our backs unbroken, we must deposit all property on the ground and learn to walk without it. We must stand aside. And when men stand aside, they stand in a new world; a new world of man has come to pass. This is the Democracy; the new order.

Those, like Huxley, who argue that society can only change as individuals change, cannot provide a plan of action for us: they have none. But what they have to say, though we deal with it briefly here, is nonetheless important. George Woodock the anarchist set out Huxley's political philosophy as advocating 'not only military resistance to war, but also a policy of general social reorganisation aimed at replacing the institution of the state ... by a libertarian society in which ... economics would be decentralist and Henry-Georgian and politics Kropotkinesque and cooperative'.[56] Well, it can resist war but how can pacifism create such a society? Ethical socialists advance a very different view of evolutionary change to those of the scientific socialists. Huxley's theory puts him in direct opposition to Shaw, who argues that only the natural leaders in society are capable of achieving progress, and to Wells, who emphasises communality at the expense of individuality. But for all three, as indeed for all who believe in evolutionary change, the process is inevitably gradual. 'A change is a slow flux, which must happen bit by bit', wrote Lawrence. 'And it must happen. You can't drive it like a steam engine.'[57]

Conclusions

So much for the evolutionists. Yet for all their hopes for mankind, their literary powers let them down. Shaw is conspicuously unable to paint a convincing picture of a great man, one who might lead a socialist state for the benefit of all. Which of his heroes would inspire our confidence? Certainly not the irascible Higgins. For his part Undershaft is favoured with most of the good lines in *Major Barbara* but he fails to convince us that his philosophy is consistent or practicable. Perhaps King Magnus in *The Apple Cart* shows the skills of a consummate politician but he is no visionary leader nor indeed is he interested in leading. Morrell in *Candida*, the paradigmatic muscular Christian, seems to have all the leadership qualities one would expect from a Fabian philosopher king. His bookshelves are full of the great works of socialist literature, he has a dominating presence, he is politically active on behalf of the poor, he has a capacity to inspire loyalty, and yet by the end of the play he is undermined by an effeminate young poet and exposed as weak and vulnerable, neurotically dependent upon his wife Candida. Indeed if we were to nominate Shavian leading characters for their inspirational qualities it would be women who would come to the fore. Barbara, Candida, Vivie (or indeed Mrs Warren) and Ann Whitefield of *Man and Superman*. None of these, however, with the arguable exception of Barbara, has political ambitions or indeed is much interested in public affairs and Shaw makes no attempt to portray the warrior leader Joan of Arc as anything but a tragic ingénue.

For his part Wells's portrayal of the inevitable triumph of the future over the past leaves us hankering nostalgically after the past. We cannot help but imagine what Artie Kipps or Alfred Polly would have made of 'the Mind of the Race' and even if Wells was right to claim that Orwell deliberately misrepresented him, the Orwellian characterisation of Wells's progressivism as the embodiment of Giant the Jack Killer strikes us as unerringly apt. As for the ethical socialism of Aldous Huxley, it depends on we humans reforming ourselves, so we can legitimately quote the phrase which the author himself declares to sum up every account of human life: '*video meliora proboque; deteriora sequor*',[58] roughly 'I know which is the better course but I choose the worse'.

6
The New Jerusalem

'A map of the world that does not include Utopia', said Oscar Wilde memorably, 'is not worth even glancing at, for it leaves out the one country at which humanity is always landing.'[1] Wilde was not using the word utopia in its classical sense; dreams of a classical utopia had ceased to exercise imaginations long before. Classical utopia had represented, in Judith Schklar's words, an 'expression of the craftsman's desire for perfection and permanence'[2] and was not so much emblematic of faith in the future as of contempt for the present. For St Thomas More, for example, the utopian enterprise was concerned to contrast the crudeness and dissolution of contemporary Europe with the unity and virtue of classical antiquity. To heighten the contrast between the indicative and the normative, More gave no indication of how utopia was to be arrived at.[3] Classical utopia, inspired by a belief in a universal, rational morality, failed to survive the age of reason ushered in by the French revolution. Thereafter classical utopia gave way to progress and science, and political philosophers who wanted to change the world instead of only writing about it eschewed classical utopianism. Marx and Engels, for example, believed that they understood fully the course of history and could predict future developments with scientific accuracy:[4] what need did they have of utopia? 'It was ideology', Schklar noted, 'that undid utopia after the French Revolution.'

Yet if nineteenth- and twentieth-century socialist writers were not utopian in the classical sense, they did paint pictures of the kind of society they hoped to achieve, and they intended these pictures to be understood both as criticisms of contemporary society and as inspiration for reformers and revolutionaries. 'The Golden Age lies before us and not behind', said the scientific socialist Edward Bellamy, 'and it is not far away.'[5] Like their classical predecessors, too, socialist 'utopians' took for granted a faith in man's capacity for justice and rationality. As Walsh wrote: 'the hope of an earthly utopia can exist … only because the dreamer assumes that he and his neighbours are good enough and rational enough to sit down and plan a better world. Not merely plan it, but build it.'[6] So the new 'utopians' did more than paint a picture of what their new worlds would be like; they told us how to get there.

The task of providing a picture of a future society that is worth striving after is a crucial one and so merits our detailed consideration. So far in this work we have sought to establish and sustain a distinction between ethical and scientific socialists and will continue to do so, despite the acknowledged variety of utopian visions, in the discussion that follows. We shall consider one example each of 'ethical' and 'scientific' utopias, those painted by William Morris and H.G. Wells. At the end of each we shall consider works of imaginative literature which offer a comment on and critique of ethical and scientific utopias, those of Aldous Huxley and George Orwell.

The utopia of the individual

William Morris believed men to be 'artists' by nature, by which he meant that their most basic instincts were creative and not, for example, political, in the Aristotelian sense. The most fulfilling thing a person could do was to create, and the job of society was to maximise the opportunities for creativity. In many respects this is as fundamental a statement of ethical socialism as we are likely to meet. Morris himself resorted to politics chiefly because he believed that bourgeois society was structured in such a way as to restrain these creative instincts and thus prevent man from becoming whole. Morris was persuaded to become a socialist precisely because the men he saw about him were stunted and incomplete – alienated (in the Rousseauian sense) – and in no way comparable to his vision of the full man. 'In the times when art was abundant and healthy', he wrote, 'all men were more or less artists; that is to say, the instinct for beauty which is inborn in every complete man had such force that the whole body of craftsmen habitually and without conscious effort made beautiful things … and the audience was nothing short of the whole people.'[7] Potentially we are all artists. But what exactly is art?

'Art', says Morris, echoing Ruskin, 'is man's expression of his joy in labour.'[8] Morris identifies art not as a specific category of human activity but as a frame of mind in which most activities may be undertaken. If one takes pleasure in doing a particular task it becomes art.[9] Our pleasure should be twofold: pleasure in the making and pleasure in the using.[10] Yet certain important preconditions inhere in this pleasure. First, for people to take pleasure from making an object they must know that its use is beneficial to society. Much of what was made in Morris's day was 'embarrassing or superfluous to the daily life of a serious man'.[11] Morris was also opposed to the mass manufacture of 'shoddy' goods, and not only because their abundance implied the existence in capitalist society of a large underprivileged class who could afford nothing better. No pleasure can be had from making shoddy goods. So for people to be creative – to be whole – they must live in a society in which only the true needs of a whole people are met. 'No one would make plush breeches', Morris concluded, 'when there were no flunkies to wear them.'[12]

Morris's second precondition was that men must work under agreeable conditions. He believed that those factories which continued to operate in a just society – the majority, being currently given over to the production of either shoddy or luxury goods, would be unnecessary – should become 'centres of intellectual activity' providing a wide range of social and recreational facilities.[13] Finally, Morris argued for variety of work. Under the capitalist system men are educated to play a certain role in the system. But this is not 'due' education, which should enable young people to become proficient in a variety of handicrafts. In Morris's just society these conditions would be fulfilled, so that it would be possible to envisage labour becoming 'a real tangible blessing in itself to the working man, a pleasure even as sleep and strong drink are to him now'.[14] Such a society would be very different to Morris's own, and he shows us how different in the influential novel *News from Nowhere*.

The central character in *News from Nowhere* is referred to as the guest. We shall call him Morris. Morris awakes one morning to find himself transported to a London quite different from the one with which he is so familiar; he has travelled forwards in time. Only slowly does Morris begin to realise what has happened, and so his first reactions give us some good clues as to the enormity of the changes that have taken place. First, Morris notices how clean and bright the Thames looks. When he sees an oarsman on the river he is immediately seized by the man's physical appearance. Dick is described as being of berry-brown skin with well-knit muscles, a 'specially manly and refined young gentleman'. Indeed, 'almost everybody was gaily dressed [including a multicoloured dustman called Boffin] but especially the women, who were so well-looking, or even so handsome that I could scarcely refrain my tongue from calling my companion's attention to the fact'.[15]

The presence of such beauty and abundance is the more pleasing to Morris since he finds, on his journey into the centre of London, no contrasting poverty. When he tackles Dick on the subject, the latter does not understand the meaning of the phrase 'poor people' and can only imagine that his guest is alluding to sick people. Morris's journey provides a source of constant visual pleasure. The urban landscape was 'not only exquisitely beautiful in itself, but it bore upon it the expression of such generosity and abundance of life that I was exhilarated'.[16] Yet the architecture did not dominate so much as integrate into a generous and noble popular lifestyle.

This lifestyle, Morris soon discovers, values spontaneity and encourages inspiration in all its aspects. In education, for example, he learns that Nowhere's children educate themselves and at their own pace. Formal education, though it scarcely merits the description, concerns the acquisition of life skills in, for example, carpentry. The more traditional skills, such as reading, seem to be the product of cultural osmosis: 'Most children, seeing books lying about, manage to read by the time they are four years old.' Foreign languages are acquired from the children of 'guests from oversea', and along with these, in some secret manner we never discover, Latin and Greek.[17]

The journey ends at the house of Dick's kinsman, Old Hammond, the sage of Bloomsbury, a historian of considerable repute in Nowhere. Hammond's task is to explain to Morris – and thus to the reader – how the ugly, brutal and divided society of Victorian Britain transformed itself into the colourful pleasant and completely egalitarian society of Nowhere. Moreover he will explain how social and political arrangements are organised. The discussions that Morris has with Hammond form the central core of the book.

The revolution that destroyed capitalism occurred in the middle of the twentieth-century. The first great post-revolutionary change was the movement of population from town to country. Agriculture had been badly neglected prior to this. Now people found what they were fit for and did it. The consequence was that although the population remained much the same size as it had been in Victorian times it became far more evenly spread and the differences between town and country became increasingly few, thus avoiding the dangerous fault-line that emerged in late twentieth-century British social and political life. The style of life became more simplified everywhere and differences of status and function fell off society like dead scales. We have already observed that 'education' has been socialised, but the general mistrust of book learning as elitist has led to the demise of all seats of learning. No great loss, these, says Hammond: these were merely 'breeding places of peculiar kinds of parasites, who called themselves cultivated people'. No education system, then, for Nowhere.

And no legal system either. With the abolition of private property and the hierarchy that a Lockean system of ownership implied, the whole structure of civil law and the court system has become redundant. In marriage, for example, the absence of property permits the establishment of relationships based upon love and not law, affection and not ownership. In a society free of unnatural constraints the only crimes to remain are crimes of passion. These, Hammond suggests, will defy any legal system. In Nowhere they are regarded not so much as the actions of habitual enemies of society as the occasional transgressions of friends. They are not punished, since punishment achieves nothing in such cases. Within the atmosphere of Nowhere's 'true communities' such transgressions are never repeated because remorse overtakes the transgressor.

As with law so with government: the egalitarian, communitarian society has no need of it. The Houses of Parliament, the centre of a government of a mighty empire in Morris's day, has become the Dung Market: 'fertility may come of that', jokes Hammond, 'whereas mere dearth came of the other kind.' Hammond, *à la* Marx, continues that in reality Parliament had represented nothing but a sort of watch committee 'sitting to see that the interests of the upper classes took no hurt'.[18] Parliament had been nothing more than 'a sort of a blind to delude the people into supposing that they had some share in the management of their own affairs'. Hammond habitually uses his knowledge of Victorian capitalism to illustrate by comparison how much better things are arranged in Nowhere. He suggests to Morris that the Victorian two-party system was simply a game. How else could politicians have 'eaten together, bought and sold together, gambled together, cheated other people together'? In Nowhere, by comparison, differences of opinion are real enough, yet they never provide a foundation for a partisanship that might crystallise into permanently hostile parties. 'We are very well off as to politics', Hammond concludes 'because we have none.' In Nowhere, by contrast, local community councils take decisions after each neighbour has voiced an opinion and, since all are equal, the verdicts of the majority of their peers are accepted by each.[19]

The citizens of Nowhere lead a simplified life. There is no buying and selling, only a system of barter and exchange, which is self-regulating and guided by general custom. Everything that is produced in Nowhere is either for the direct use of the citizens or else for bartering. The fear of foreign domination is unknown, since the world is full of equally peaceful neighbours, and the pressures of international and domestic competitive capitalism are entirely absent. This is a world in which creative man can lead a full and unalienated life, making only the things that he and his neighbours need and value.

These discussions with Old Hammond concluded, Morris and his party make a trip up the river Thames (in fact Morris here describes his home territory and includes a picture of his own house at Lechlade). After their first day on the river, relished by Morris because of the beauty and abundance of the countryside through which they pass and the pleasure of the company, they stay overnight with a 'grumbler' (one who hankers after the old ways of capitalism) and his beautiful grand-daughter Ellen. The grumbler praises competition, believing it to produce a brisker and more alive society, more notable than their own in terms of the great works of art it produces, and so on. Ellen argues that for the ordinary citizen, herself for example, the world of competitive capitalism would be far harsher, reducing her rapidly to a grey middle age, whereas she now is at the height of her beauty. As for the cultural achievements of competitive capitalism, she declares: 'Books, books! Always books, grandfather! When will you understand that after all it is the world we live in which interests us; the world of which we are a part, and which we can never love too much?'[20] Ellen is not only an assertive young woman but is exceptionally beautiful even by the standards of Nowhere. She later explains to Morris that her beauty has been the cause of frequent problems. This is why she has been living in seclusion.

As Morris's party progresses up the Thames the reader is struck by several features. The first is the absence of machinery. The railway has disappeared, and the lock gates have been minimally maintained but not significantly improved. 'You see, guest,' Morris is told, 'this is not an age of inventions.'[21] The second is that even Morris is surprised, and despite himself not pleasantly surprised, that the talk of those he meets is all about country matters. At one stage he finds himself commenting that they talk about the weather like children. Third, shortage of useful work is a worry for Nowhere. Morris's party come upon a group who are decorating the interior of a fine house. One of the sculptresses remarks to another: 'Now, Philippa, if you gobble up your work like that, you will soon have none to do; and what will become of you then?'[22] This is said in jest but it carries a note of earnest.

Not long after, the story ends as it began, as Morris is spirited away from Nowhere as mysteriously as he arrived. The depth of his remorse at leaving behind this utopian vision is palpable.

But are we readers as sad to leave? The country is full of buxom girls and broad-shouldered youths, beautiful, strong and healthy. The consolations of life for the citizens of Nowhere might be summarised as freedom, happiness, energy, beauty of body and artistic environment. The supposition is that art – joy in labour – would consume all equally. But the demise of learning, the dismissal of activities such as contemplative philosophy or indeed invention in favour of 'life', the absence of institutionalised religion, presumably because each of these might lead to the establishment of elitist structures, leaves Nowhere a one-dimensional society not so remarkably different, I will try to show, from Huxley's brave new world: 'I demand a free and unfettered animal life for man first of all'.[23] Much the same ambition as Huxley's World Controller. As Maurice Hewlett commented:[24]

> A race of fleshy perfection, worshipping phenomena, relying on appearance, arguing from sensation; a nation of strong men and fair women, conscious of their own growth and of their country's, owning an art which springs from and is directed to Nature, Simplicity, Truth, which yet sees no significance, no shadow behind these comely forms, dreams no future, owns no standard, accepts no explanation, needs no justifying.

Nowhere's citizens have no private property. Utopus, the designer and founder of St Thomas More's commonwealth, had also designed a society in which private property as such did not exist. More wrote of 'private' houses: 'who so will may go in, for there is nothing within the houses that is private of anie man's owne'.[25] Things are much the same in Nowhere. Yet unlike in More's utopia there seems to be no corresponding gain in community consciousness. The community contributes little to their way of life beyond providing the most effective environment for each to explore the limits of their individuality and creativity. Moreover, although the people we meet are sharply defined as individuals, especially by their clothing, there is a superficiality about them. We do not feel that we know them, or indeed that there is anything about them we need to know. Real communities comprise people who come together because they have needs which they cannot fulfil individually or in small groups. Community implies specialisation of function and usually of status, and often hierarchy results. Morris's communities, by contrast, appear to be mere shells and their members disappointingly superficial. Ellen points to her beauty as an example of how much better things are in Nowhere than they were in nineteenth-century Britain. 'It is as if', Hewlett muses (only a little unfairly), 'a pheasant were endowed with sensibility and lamented the moulting season.'[26] E.P. Thompson wrote of William Morris that his private life had been a failure largely because of his inability to pass 'from romantic illusion to human intimacy'. Applied to his novel, this criticism could hardly be more apposite.[27]

Morris believed passionately in the creative vitality of what we might call folk art and culture; all the citizens of Nowhere would be suffused with the beauty of nature and seek to express it in their lives. In emphasising the spontaneity and naturalness of this process, however, he seems willing to sacrifice the entire cultural heritage of a people because to absorb and transmit it would involve not only communion with nature but communion with art galleries, libraries and concert halls, and with conservatoires, art schools and the like.

Morris's utopia is characterised by Hewlett as a stagnant society with no 'dreams of the future' to sustain it. Wells depicted Nowhere's citizens in *The Time Machine* as the Eloi.[28] The Eloi have magnificent buildings but have long since lost the skills to make use of or maintain them; fine libraries, but the books have decayed through lack of use. The Eloi are concerned with beauty, but almost exclusively physical beauty; concerned with the arts, but almost exclusively with singing and dancing in the river. The Eloi represent a people who live together in communities but who lack the drive and purpose that breathes life into a community; a people who sing and dance in the sunlight; a people whom Wells characterises finally as 'mere fatted cattle',[29] representatives of a human intellect that had set stability, comfort and ease as its principal objectives and in the process had 'committed suicide'.

Is it unfair to accept such a prognosis for the future of the citizens of Nowhere? Neal Ascherson clearly thinks not, for he finds the prognosis relevant to modern man as well. In time, he warns, without the stimulus of necessity, 'we, like the Eloi, will grow soft and defenceless and lose [our] memory of any skill but eating and giggling. Then, at last begins the hour of the hungry Morlocks.'[30]

In his stirring account of the Peasants' Revolt of 1381, Morris's John Ball, the hedge-priest, asks the peasants: 'What shall ye lack when ye lack masters? Ye shall not lack for the fields ye have tilled, nor the houses ye have built, nor the cloth ye have woven; all these things shall be yours, and whatso ye will of all that the earth beareth.'[31] Taking Nowhere all in all, and with a glance over our shoulders at the Eloi, we might conclude that in the long run, though the fruits of the earth might be more equally shared in a fundamental egalitarian world,[32] if we lack masters we might soon also come to lack everything by which an advanced civilisation sets store.

The utopia of the individual subverted

The primary task of ethical socialism is to create a society in which all may be happy. This is a simplification but surely not a distortion. Marx's whole thesis was that if the misery of the working class were to be alleviated – and he was concerned in *Capital* and elsewhere as much with general spiritual impoverishment as with the more obvious social and economic kind – then people would lead fuller, happier lives. It is true that for the socialist happiness entailed clear social and moral prerequisites, but nonetheless the expectation was that in a socialist system men and women would choose to act in a social rather than a selfish manner precisely because this was the way to happiness. Morris says as much in *News From Nowhere*. What was the purpose of the bloody revolution, Old Hammond asks, if not to make people happy?[33] For Morris, as for Marx, it would be impossible for a people to be happy if they were not all equal. Indeed Old Hammond says: 'Looking back now, we can see that the great motive-power of the change was a longing for freedom and equality ... that rejected with loathing the aimless solitary life of the well-to-do.'[34]

But what if people could act socially in an unequal society? Morris attempted to depict a society in which people were free to do the things they like doing. But what if instead a society were able to provide its citizens with 'the secret of happiness and virtue – liking what you've got to do'?[35] In *Brave New World* Huxley describes a political and social system that seeks to produce people who act socially and are happy. The objective of the state, according to the Director of the Central London Hatchery and Conditioning Centre, is to maintain social stability – impossible, he claims, without individual stability. The way to keep an individual stable is to keep him happy. Thus the objective of the brave new world is much the same as that of socialist societies such as Nowhere's: to oblige the people to act socially and thus to be happy and stable (two sides of the same coin). Whilst no self-respecting utopian or Marxist (or indeed any other socialist) would recognise their desired society in this brave new world and whilst Karl Marx would have been more fearful of it than even Bernard Marx, others, less sanguine about the triumph of socialism through reason, might see some similarities between the ends and indeed the means of an imagined socialist society and this brave new world.

Huxley introduces us to a world of genetic and social conditions, the objective of which is to produce a stable society. 'No civilisation without social stability. No social stability without individual stability.' In the 'old days',[36] we discover, children were brought up by parents. The home and family of the 'pre-moderns' made them 'mad and wicked and miserable'. Theirs was a life of prohibitions, temptations and remorse, disease, uncertainty and poverty – and consequently strong emotions.

'And feeling strongly (and strongly, what was more, in solitude, in hopelessly individual isolation), how could they be stable?' In the brave new world, by contrast, as one of the World Controllers explains:[37]

> The world's stable now. People are happy; they get what they want and they never want what they can't get. They're well off; they're safe; they're never ill; they're not afraid of death; they're blissfully ignorant of passion and old age; they're plagued with no mothers or fathers; they've no wives, or children, or loves to feel strongly about; they're so conditioned that they practically can't help behaving as they ought to behave.

And although society is even more rigidly ordered than Wells's technology-based utopias, people feel themselves to be equal in the most fundamental sense. As a puff of white smoke emerges from the crematorium one new worlder remarks: 'whoever he may have been, he was happy when he was alive. Everybody's happy now.'[38] And everyone belongs to everyone else and works for everyone else. In the most fundamental of senses the good citizens of the brave new world love one another.

Boredom and depression are not unknown, but the citizens can relieve severe cases with the drug soma. Soma helps people live only for the present: 'Was and will make me ill, I take a gramme and only am'.[39] Opium has become the religion of the masses. Moreover whilst the new world has no Church Militant the 'religious' experience can be formalised. Ford's Day Solidarity Services take place at which six males and six females drink from the Loving Cup, swallow their soma tablets and try to achieve Oneness.[40]

The intellectual elite readily concedes that happiness may appear squalid in comparison with the glamour of a good fight against misfortune, but it provides a far more stable basis for social arrangements. There are sacrifices to be made: art, science (except that which deals with 'the most immediate problems of the moment', which is to say, technology) and history are forbidden to the citizens of the new world, just as they are discouraged in Nowhere: each can lead to discontent with the present and thus unhappiness. Moreover God has become redundant. After all, religion traditionally provided people with a refuge when the world turned against them but in the new world 'there aren't any losses for us to compensate; religious sentiment is superfluous'.[41] As for the Christian virtues such as compassion and charity, they are simply no longer needed: 'these things are symptoms of political inefficiency'.[42] The rights claimed on behalf of individuals by the liberal entail other 'rights', according to the new world elite:[43]

> the right to grow old and ugly and impotent; the right to have syphilis and cancer; the right to have too little to eat; the right to be lousy; the right to live in constant apprehension of what may happen tomorrow; the right to catch typhoid; the right to be tortured by unspeakable pains of every kind.

Their guardians had denied the citizens of the new world all these rights; just like the citizens of Nowhere they are beautiful and healthy and whole.

In short what Huxley does in *Brave New World* is to remove as far as possible all the hindrances, all the pressures, which alienate people. The technological base of the new world allows the Controllers to condition people to like the environment in which they live, whereas socialists like Morris would have people create the kind of environment they like. But in both cases a congenial environment exists and the people of both worlds live contentedly in it. In short, although superficially Morris's and Huxley's are worlds apart, in important ways they are very similar.

When the Savage in *Brave New World* claims the right to be an individual, to have an identity, he wittingly phrases his claim as the right to be unhappy. He thereby raises a challenge to progressive political ideologies such as socialism: that the equal and unalienated individual who constitutes their objective may not be a complete person at all. 'The pursuit of happiness', as the Science Editor of *The Times* wrote when discussing Huxley's novel recently, 'leads instead to a spiritual emptiness: stability, however earnestly we may desire it, is a denial of human potential. Welfare is ill-fare. These lessons are as true today as they were when Huxley wrote them.'[44]

Surely they are truer. Huxley dreamed of a world where conception could take place outside the womb, dreamed of a world in which embryos could be genetically engineered to avoid sickness and disease, where all the problems of child-rearing which may disrupt the professional careers of approximately half of the population are taken care of by society, where the social pressures that destroyed Rousseau's individual are simply diffused, and where all the social and economic goods that we may aspire to are attainable. We have not yet achieved such a society but are much, much closer to it than even the hedonistic California of the 1920s which inspired Huxley's novel. Indeed in his recent novel *Atomised* Michel Houllebecq writes: 'The society Huxley describes in *Brave New World* is happy: tragedy and extremes of human emotions have disappeared. Sexual liberation has come to stay – everything favours instant gratification ... This is exactly the kind of world we are trying to create, the world we want to live in.'[45] As the mynah bird in Huxley's *Island* chirps: 'It's here and now, boys!'[46]

For Huxley individual identity is the product of unhappiness, of alienation. To the extent that we are successful in creating a society that eliminates such dehumanising pressures, as a consequence of Morris's ideology or Huxley's technology, we lose the very humanity or individual identity that we are motivated to enhance.

Those who control the brave new world are Platonic philosopher kings. Their chief joy is in sustaining a stable order and like Plato's rulers they recognise that the state and the individual are one. There is no social stability without individual stability. In the manner of Dostoevsky's inquisitor they seek only to save people from the doubts and insecurities that would destroy them. Nobody who truly loves the people could do less. That most of us squirm at the prospect of a brave new world that has such people in it should not obscure the fact that modern scientists are beginning to acquire the technology to realise much of that vision; and what drives that technology is popular demand.

It goes without saying that Huxley's novel is ironical and yet perhaps the chief irony is this: whilst we recognise that the 'prisoners' of the brave new world show us that the absence of alienation does not necessarily equate with wholeness – indeed may even be inimical to it – we ought also to reflect that many people in the twenty-first century would have reason to prefer the new world, even with its lack of freedom, to their own fractious world of pain and scarcity – and freedom. As one critic argued, '"going right in chains instead of wrong in freedom" does not seem so bad after all'.[47] After man's fall from grace, we are told, God left him the freedom to act antisocially and he took it. As Anthony Burgess demonstrated in *A Clockwork Orange*, society can hope to correct antisocial behaviour and restore stability but only at the expense of individual identity. As Burgess says, the state succeeds in its primary aim (through aversion therapy) but only by denying Alex free moral choice.[48] Is this the price of an equal, happy, sociable society?

The scientific utopia

For the scientific socialist it is not enough that man should be happy; he must have a sense of purpose. In Shaw's *Man and Superman* Don Juan leaves Hell because of its 'tedious, vulgar pursuit of happiness'. The essence of the scientific socialist's utopia is that it never ceases to develop; it represents not a 'permanent state but a hopeful stage, lead-ing to a long ascent of stages'.[49] The most appropriate metaphor for the scientific socialist's ambition is not the citadel but the ship of state.[50] On the SS *New Jerusalem* the importance of individuals resides only in their specific functions as crew-members, though, of course, it is advan-tageous to have a robust, contented crew, for they will be all the better sailors. The voyage on which the ship is embarked is no pleasure cruise; it is a journey through dangers and discomforts towards a way of life quite different from that with which we are familiar.

Nothing more clearly distinguishes the scientific socialist than this species-consciousness: the belief that society is organic and that it ought to think and act as a whole. That is why scientific socialists such as Shaw and Wells continually underlined the importance of elite leadership, for at the early stages of the development of a socialist society, only the most politically conscious elements would be capable of deciding the direction in which society ought to be heading. Orwell was partly right when he suggested that Shaw and the Fabians wanted to turn the world into 'a sort of super garden city'.[51] But he was completely right to point out that scientists like Wells assumed that a 'reasonable', planned form of society run by 'scientists rather than witch doctors' will come about sooner or later,[52] though equally right to add that such a society was not just around the corner. The models which scientific socialist writers like Wells and Shaw used for their politically conscious elite were, as we have seen, none other than themselves and their friends; they were tak-ing their own (self-perceived) political and species-consciousness, their own reasonableness, their own common sense, as being general. Yet even were we to grant these scientific socialists as much as they granted themselves, they would still have to convince us that the rest of society would be equally reasonable and commonsensical in recognising the benefits of their rule. We may feel a little better qualified to exercise judgement on these issues after a detailed consideration of Wells's scien-tific society in some detail. We shall be considering *A Modern Utopia*.

Wells begins by telling us that this book is 'neither the set drama of the work of fiction you are accustomed to read, nor the set lecturing of the essay you are accustomed to evade, but a hybrid of these two'.[53] In fact it is an unsuccessful attempt to weld together political commen-tary and fiction, though one cannot deny that the fictional element provides an extra dimension.[54] Wells and a botanist friend are on a walking tour in the Swiss Alps.[55] They have just had a pleasant lunch, and Wells is turning his mind to consider various aspects of the perfect world when: 'And behold! in the twinkling of an eye we are in that other world.' Wells and his companion have slipped mysteriously into a parallel universe.

This Utopia is a replica of Earth down to the smallest feature, but in manner, custom and social arrangements, it is quite different. Wells wants us believe that his Utopia is not simply a dream; he claims to be dealing with realities in a way that Morris never did.[56] He takes Morris to task for changing the nature of man altogether, making 'the whole race wise, tolerant, noble, perfect... every man doing as it pleases him, and none pleased to do evil, in a world as good in its essential nature, as ripe and sunny, as the world before the fall'. Wells, on the other hand, builds his Utopia upon man as we know him: 'We are going to accept this world of conflict, to adopt no attitude of renunciation towards it, to face it in no ascetic spirit, but in the mood of the Western peoples, whose purpose is to survive and overcome.' Indeed, when he wakes up on his first morning in Utopia poor Wells has had a nightmare in which he had to converse with an unavoidable dustman in green and gold called Boffin.[57] No: Wells's is a world of real men.

The Utopian world exudes an atmosphere of calm and order, the foundation of which is the subordination of nature to technology. Inter-city communications, with high-speed trains and a system of motorways, make travel cheap and efficient. Utopian industries are set in clearly defined geographical areas, other areas remaining unpolluted. Yet Wells's Utopians are like Schopenhauer's people – hedgehogs clustering together for warmth but not wishing to become too closely packed; so the Utopians retain their own castles – their private houses. In addition the Utopians may, if they choose, 'own' some small business enterprise, though proprietary rights will be circumscribed.

All this contrasts with Nowhere but in nothing is the contrast stronger than in the attitudes to work. For Morris, it will be remembered, work was to be a joy, a form of art. For Wells this is 'bold make-believe'. If work were a blessing, 'never was blessing so effectively disguised... It needed the Olympian unworldliness of an irresponsible rich man of the shareholding type, a Ruskin or a Morris playing at life, to imagine as much.'[58] Each Utopian is required to undertake a certain minimum workload and anyone undertaking more than this minimum is entitled to more privileges. 'The modern Utopia will... exercise the minimum of compulsions to toil, but it will offer some acutely desirable prizes.'

Another important characteristic of the Utopian lifestyle is that women are no longer in any sense inferior. Marriage continues, though with ample provision for divorce without disgrace, but it is based upon a far greater degree of independence for women. A housewife receives a wage and, in addition, a family benefit which increases with each child who attains more than the minimum state requirements in terms of health and physical and mental development. All the citizens of Utopia impress Wells with their physical well-being. 'Everyone one meets seems to be not only in good health but in training; one rarely meets fat people, bald people, or bent or gray. People who would be obese or bent on Earth are here in good repair, and as a consequence the whole effect of a crowd is livelier and more invigorating than on Earth.'[59]

Wells's earlier descriptive passages concern the countryside, but when he comes to describe Utopian London he interests us especially, for his London is as different from the actual London as it is from Morris's. It contains 'a mighty University' with 'great journals of thought and speculation, mature and splendid books of philosophy and science, and a glorious fabric of literature. There are huge libraries and magnificent museums.'[60] Wells then goes on to give us an inkling of the atmosphere of this mighty and beautiful capital city: 'Great multitudes of people will pass softly to and fro in this central space [rich with palms and flowering bushes and statuary], beautiful girls and youths ... grave and capable men and women going to their business, children meandering along to their schools, holiday makers, lovers, setting out upon a hundred quests.'[61]

The sense of order and cleanliness which pervades the public and private space of Utopia reminds us of Orwell's comment that intellectuals are often drawn to socialism by a desire to create a clean, orderly society. Indeed when Wells wakes up in Utopia for the first time a discreet notice indicates the price of the room, and points out that the price is doubled if you do not leave the toilet as clean as you found it.[62]

As we might expect in a scientific socialist state, the 'collective spirit', as Wells calls it, is the driving characteristic, but Wells leaves scope for initiative. In Utopia, as in Bacon's House of Saloman[63] (so mercilessly put to the satirical sword in Swift's Laputia), scientific discovery is encouraged at every level of society so that Utopian research will progress 'like an eagle's swoop in comparison with the blind man's fumbling of our terrestrial way'.

The most significant difference between terrestrial social and political arrangements and those of Utopia, however, are to be found in the administration. Not only does science provide Utopians with a government as beneficent as it is strong but it also makes possible the creation of an extensive bureaucracy celebrated for its efficiency and humanity.[64] Science has made possible the blossoming of the paraphernalia of government in Utopia in much the same proportion as it had withered in Nowhere. The World State is the only landowner of any size, though local authorities hold land feudally, as landlords. Much of industry is run by the state, and all energy resources are vested in public ownership.

Wells believes that competition is not merely inevitable but enormously valuable, and Utopian social arrangements do not seek to abolish competition but to make endurable the margin of failure.[65] Thus every citizen who agrees to fulfil the minimum quota of labour imposed by the state will be guaranteed good housing, a sufficiency of food and clothing, good health and sanitation. Every citizen will be educated and trained by the state, and insured against ill health and accidents. The application of scientific management principles will make it possible always to balance the 'presence of disengaged labour' with the pressures of unemployment. Thus poverty would be abolished for all but the idle.

Population control is central to the continued success of Utopia's social arrangements; like other features, it is a scientifically applied scheme of control aimed at preventing the birth of 'weaklings'. Where this control is not successful the state will give itself the power to take the lives of the deformed and diseased – though these are the only lives the state may take.[66] Scientific birth control is also preemptive; only certain kinds of people – the 'personally efficient' – may reproduce. Personal efficiency is defined as being self-supporting, mature, physically fit and free of transmissible disease. Wells does not discuss these criteria more precisely nor does he suggest who would be responsible for enforcing the regulations or how. More fundamentally the morality of this programme is open to question and some might sympathise with Joseph Conrad who wrote to his friend: 'The difference between us, Wells, is fundamental. You don't care for humanity but think they are to be improved. I love humanity and know they are not.'[67]

The keystone of governance in Wells's scientific Utopia is its hierarchical social structure. One of the book's more interesting sections is the encounter between 'Earth-Wells' and his Utopian alter ego. 'Utopian-Wells' explains that whilst Utopians do not believe that all men are equal, neither do they believe in the accidental categorisation of people into social classes. Instead, Utopians are classified according to temperament.[68] There are four classes: the poietic, the kinetic, the dull and the base. The first two classes are thought to constitute the 'living tissue of the state'. None of these classes is hereditary; people may drift in and out of their own accord – much as the dead may commute between Heaven and Hell in Shaw's *Man and Superman* – though naturally they will tend to stay in the class to which they are temperamentally best suited.

The characteristics of these classes are as follows. The poietic possess creative imagination: they are the artists and the truly creative scientific minds, the great philosophers and the moralists. The kinetic class comprises very capable but conventional people. Utopian-Wells explains that there are two kinetic types, the mainly intellectual, who comprise, for example, judges and administrators, and the mainly emotional, including great actors, popular politicians and preachers. The dull class is made up of men and women of 'altogether inadequate imaginations' described by Utopian-Wells as incompetent, formal and imitative and as counting 'neither for work nor direction in the State'. Lastly the base comprises men and women with no moral sense. They might be described as the criminal class of Utopia. In Utopia criminals are banished to isolated islands and left to their own devices, for they are seen as a threat to society (unlike Huxley's brave new world where the threat to society is posed by poietics and it is they who are banished to the islands).

The political structure of Utopia, however, is not based upon these social divisions. Power lies in the hands of a voluntary nobility known as the samurai, of which, as we might guess, Utopian-Wells is a member. The samurai fulfil functions similar to those of Plato's guardian class. They are not a hereditary class: in fact any intelligent, healthy and efficient adult over twenty-five may elect to follow the Common Rule. First they must follow a course of instruction at college and pass an examination. Having then elected to follow the Common Rule they are required to keep themselves in peak physical and mental condition in order to serve the state. Although the samurai are forbidden all the trappings of public worship, religion plays a large if totally mysterious part in their lives: their god is transcendental and mystical. Wells concludes: 'I saw more clearly now something... in the bearing and faces of this Utopian chivalry, a faint persistent tinge of detachment from the immediate heats and hurries... of the daily world. It pleases me strangely to think... how near men might come then to the high distances of God.'[69] (Godliness is, after all, next to cleanliness.)

Practically all responsible positions in Utopia are held by samurai. Although the Order occupies power, indeed you have to be a samurai to vote, at least one-tenth of the supreme legislative assembly must be elected from outside the Order because it is believed that 'a sort of wisdom... comes from sin and laxness'.[70] Earth-Wells might have argued for the retention of an unreformed House of Lords in the United Kingdom on similar grounds. Wells's depiction of the duties and way of life of the samurai is inconsistent: although we know that the samurai take a cold bath every morning we have not the least idea of the nature of the legislative and administrative machine in which they work, nor how the Order allocates tasks of varying status among themselves.

Wells's Utopia does contrive to capture the flavour of an efficiently organised state in which life appears to be more orderly and vigorous than it is in the twenty-first century. His book was enormously influential in its day. But a question shapes in our minds as the discussion progresses: what is the purpose of it all? What is the dream that drives? We are told that those who comprise the 'living tissue' of the state, the poietics and the kinetics, appear to be 'not only in good health but in training'. In training for what? Could it be that, like virtue, training is its own reward, regimen itself the most enduring benefit of regimen?

The scientific utopia subvested

One of two basic assumptions underpins the socialist's project: the politically conscious scientific elite who direct the project will act for the good of all citizens, as they do for example in *A Modern Utopia*, or they will voluntarily dismantle the sophisticated, centrally organised machinery of power which they built up when the socialist victory was won, as they do for example in Morris's Nowhere. No writer treated these assumptions more contemptuously than George Orwell did in his novel *Nineteen Eighty-Four*. Here Orwell turns his attention to an elitist socialist society forged in the revolution and hammered into shape in the post-revolution.[71] Oceania represents a society that sees itself as an organic whole with no place for individual aspirations; a society that calls into question the whole idea of individuality. It represents a perverted form of Wellsian scientific socialism. Orwell writes:[72]

> The ideal set up by the Party was something huge, terrible and glittering – a world of steel and concrete, of monstrous machines and terrifying weapons – a nation of warriors and fanatics, marching forward in perfect unity, all thinking the same thoughts and shouting the same slogans, perpetually working, fighting, triumphing, persecuting – three hundred million people all with the same face.

Regimentation has the purpose not of achieving stability *pace* Huxley but of maximising the powers of the elite. Technology harnessed to psychological control mechanisms of great sophistication makes this feasible. 'The possibility of enforcing not only complete obedience to the will of the State, but complete uniformity of opinion on all subjects, now existed for the first time', says Orwell.

In Oceania, with its population of 300 million, the Party comprises only 15 per cent. Of this 15 per cent, 6 million (2 per cent of the whole) belong to the 'brains' of the state, the Inner Party, and 39 million (13 per cent of the whole) belong to its 'hands', the Outer Party. The remaining 85 per cent of the population belong to the proletariat, left very much to their own devices – indeed one of the Party mottoes claims that animals and proles are free.[73] Winston Smith, the central character of the book, conveys the nature of Oceanian society by means of reading aloud from a copy of Goldstein's subversive *Theory and Practice of Oligarchical Collectivism* (modelled on Trotsky's *The Revolution Betrayed*). Goldstein points out that it had always been assumed that if the capitalist class were expropriated, socialism would follow. But in the event what happened was quite different. 'The so-called "abolition of private property" which took place in the middle years of the century meant, in effect, the concentration of property in far fewer hands than before: but with this difference, that the new owners were a group instead of a mass of individuals.' But once established in power the elite showed no inclination whatever to share that power with the people or to improve their living and working conditions.

Winston's tormentor O'Brien, a member of the Inner Party, regards the purpose of scientific 'socialism' in Oceania as being to maximise the power of the Inner Party and he has a precise idea of what constitutes power. 'Power is in inflicting pain and humiliation. Power is in tearing human minds to pieces and putting them together again in a new shape of your own choosing', and the power of the Inner Party is growing steadily. The picture of the future that emerges is of 'a boot stamping on a human face – for ever'.[74] The scientific socialist dream has become a nightmare.

Orwell seeks to strip power to its essence. Power can only be measured in terms of the inflicting of pain: that is the only certain expression of one individual or group exercising control over another. Power is not a means, to achieve some ideological end for example, it is itself an end. Orwell suggests not simply that power tends to corrupt but that the exercise of power inevitably attracts not those who want to make the world better nor indeed those who want to enjoy power's attendant privileges, but sadists: this is a picture of power as psychosis. It is natural to assume that Stalin was the model for the sadistic ruler of Oceania but Orwell's unease was generated a little nearer home. It is well-known that when at Eton Orwell liked to be regarded as the new Bernard Shaw.[75] As we have seen, these early Fabians saw themselves as exponents of what might now be called tough love and Shaw's ready support for fascist and Soviet dictatorships convinced Orwell that his heroes were drawn to socialism precisely because it enabled them to break society down and recreate it in their own image. Orwell believed that he lived in an age that worshipped power and even his heroes – no, especially his heroes – were susceptible to its attractions.

Orwell also recognised that a totalitarian society must subsume the individual entirely and he elucidates a set of conditions which he takes to form the basis of individual identity and which must be controlled by the state to secure its stability.

First and crucially, Orwell claims for the individual the right to be his own judge of reality. The Party stands against this claim, demanding of the individual that he reject the evidence of his own reason and senses. 'But I tell you, Winston,' says O'Brien, 'that reality is not external. Reality exists in the human mind and nowhere else. Not in the individual mind: only in the mind of the Party, which is collective and immortal. Whatever the Party hold to be truth is truth.' It is precisely the Party's ability to pronounce *ex cathedra* on the nature of reality that destroys individual identity, and this explains why, according to Orwell, 'the heresy of heresies was common sense'. This bears further investigation. That common sense is a heresy can be seen as an expression of Orwell's intrinsic Protestant belief in the 'priesthood of all believers'. There is reality and we all know what it is. Symbolically two plus two equals four and we do not need to turn to the scientist or the priest to know this: this certainty is what gives us our fundamental identity as individuals. Yet reality is not so straightforward. Relativity theory tells us, for example, that under certain conditions two plus two does not equal four. Quantum physicists tell us that under certain circumstances particles of matter may be in two places at the same time. Common sense tells us that neither of these is possible. Time was when all people *knew* what their senses told them: that the world was flat, stationary and the centre of the universe. Dostoevsky uses the notion of common sense not as a safeguard of individual identity at all but as a threat to it. His denizen of *The Underworld* likes occasionally to believe that two plus two equals five.[76] Dostoevsky believes that it is man's right to irrationality, not to common sense, that sustains his individual identity.[77] Moreover, when Orwell equates our grasp of common-sense 'reality' with a grasp of historical 'truth' he makes a giant leap. Walter Lippman tells us that 'truth' or reality is the product of 'the habits of our eyes'. Only by controlling early-life experiences as the state does in Huxley's brave new world could individuals be deprived of Orwellian common sense (or indeed his Dostoevskian flight of fancy).

Orwell's second claim for the individual is for family life.[78] In Oceania family life among Party members had broken down entirely. 'The family had become in effect an extension of the Thought Police. It was a device by means of which everyone could be surrounded night and day by informers who knew them intimately.'[79] The importance of family life for Orwell cannot be underestimated. We know that he believed that it was the strength of working-class family life that gave working-class communities their sense of solidarity and equality: this was the basis of Orwellian socialism. What was important about the working class, he said, was that their loyalty was not to a set of ideas but to each other.

Third, Orwell claims a cultural tradition for individual identity. The individual must feel himself a part of that tradition and be able to pass it on to his children. As far as Orwell is concerned the most important component of that cultural tradition is language. In Oceania the Party sought to control behaviour by systematically controlling vocabulary through Newspeak. 'Don't you see', Syme explains to Winston, 'that the whole aim of Newspeak is to narrow the range of thought? In the end we shall make thought crime literally impossible, because there will be no words in which to express it.'[80] So much has been written since about the general manipulation of language by political regimes that the continued importance of Orwell's argument hardly needs emphasising.[81]

Another component of the cultural tradition is history. Winston was always trying to bring the past to life as a cordon sanitaire around his individual identity. The book he bought for his diary was an attractive old one, with smooth creamy paper. He bought it in Charrington's junk shop, to which he was instinctively drawn. Then he bought a paperweight, a beautiful but useless object. 'If it [the past] survives anywhere, it's in a few solid objects with no words attached to them, like that lump of glass there',[82] Winston remarks. Predictably, when the Thought Police finally broke into the room which Winston and his lover Julia used, one of them picked the paperweight up and smashed it to pieces on the hearth-stone, thus obliterating the past. It is not so much the truth-value of the past as its symbolic value that signifies. What is important to identity, national as well as individual, is a story. If our story can be changed then our identity comes immediately under threat.

Orwell's fourth claim for individual identity is that of a full emotional life. Julia's great strength, as far as Winston was concerned, was her love of carnal pleasure. He prized her vaunted promiscuity because her 'simple undifferentiated desire [constituted] the force that would tear the Party to pieces'.[83]

Fifth, Orwell claims material sufficiency as a precondition for living a decent life. Winston possessed some ancestral memory that caused him to reject as unnatural the discomfort, the dirt and the scarcity of

Oceania.[84] Goldstein argues that it is deliberate Party policy to maintain scarcity for all Outer Party members, so as to enhance the importance of even minor privileges. Competition for vital day-to-day necessities, overall scarcity and shoddiness, Orwell suggests, breaks down the human spirit and renders a truly individual life impossible.

Last but by no means least, Orwell demonstrates the importance of privacy to the individual. In Oceania he had none. He was constantly watched by the telescreens and was obliged to walk about with what Winston described as an expression of quiet optimism; any other visible emotion might condemn him. Privacy, Orwell claims, and here he is at odds with many socialists and utopians (though not Wells), is the *sine qua non* of a fully individual life.[85]

For Orwell power is inevitably a malevolent force whose aim is to crush individual identity.[86] He presents a picture of a scientific socialist society in which all the aspirations of scientific socialists have been perverted by a malevolent elite that has consistently used the powers gained during the revolution and the post-revolution entirely for its own ends. *Nineteen Eighty-Four* is the ultimate warning against entrusting the monopoly of technological or managerial expertise to an elite, and yet this is largely what Shaw and Wells proposed. Orwell's final picture shows a man at one with himself, his fellows and, above all, with the Party. Winston is sitting at a table in the Chestnut Tree Café, alone and yet part of the great corporate identity: 'He had won a victory over himself. He loved Big Brother.'[87]

Conclusions

Narratives offer an especially appropriate form for exploring the strengths and inconsistencies of the 'utopian' project. Morris and Wells provide us with broad pictures of the kind of society they considered to be worth striving for, visions not blueprints, and if they seem to most readers to contain important contradictions they nevertheless invite us to reflect on the way we live now and the ways we might live. Huxley, by contrast, casts some fundamental doubts upon the very desirability of 'improving' man, and Orwell, for his part, warns against any kind of political project that requires strong leadership. And none would require this more than the reconstruction of society.

We have mapped the ambitions for mankind that prompted Morris and Wells to construct their utopias. The demons that drove Huxley's and Orwell's dystopian warnings have also been discussed. Since the general decline in the West first of religious practice and belief and then of socialism, no encompassing social or political philosophy has been developed to give people a sense both of what they are and what they might be. Fukuyama has argued that Western liberal values have won a final global victory: we have no need of visions any more. Even those persuaded of this might reflect on what this demand-led victory might mean. In his novel *Atomised*,[88] Houllebecq compares Huxley's new world and our own. Man's control of the processes of reproduction, he points out, is now even more precise than Huxley suggested and we can foresee a time when reproduction will become a managed social process, dissociated altogether from sex; a time when procreation will be controlled to avoid the inheritance of disease and disability. With these developments the family will disappear and the formative ties associated with it such as father–son relationships will become redundant, with all the psychosocial consequences these developments imply. The pharmaceutical application of genetic information will erase the distinction between youth and age, and voluntary euthanasia will bring a quick, discreet and utterly painless end to life. The standard objection to *Brave New World*, says Houllebecq's Bruno, is that it represented a totalitarian nightmare but that is 'hypocritical bullshit' because it really comes close to 'our idea of heaven',[89] and thus in a real sense is emblematic of the triumph of liberalism. It gives individuals what they want.

Bruno's lifestyle, depicted so vividly in the novel, itself represents a considerable triumph of individual choice. Houllebecq depicts a society in which, stripped of their link with reproduction, lust and greed still exist 'not as pleasure principles but as forms of egotism'.[90] These forces, bent on sexual gratification, are shown to be self-destructive and the central character of the novel makes his life's work the salvation of the world through biological discoveries that make possible a world populated by Shavian supermen and -women created rational and eternal as a consequence of man's mastery of the human genome. It represents the final stage in the evolutionary process, much along the lines that Shaw predicted: at last the Yahoo has been eliminated. It is a world marginally more frightful than that which it replaces in Houllebecq's novel. This novel gives an admittedly jaundiced picture of what we are and what we might be; it makes the reader long for an alternative philosophical vision, and to appreciate more fully perhaps the role of the utopian writers whose work we have discussed here.

7
The Power of Narrative

A good book...is a force a tool a weapon to make the dreams of
today become the reality of tomorrow.
(Roger Garaudy, quoted in David Caute, *The Illusion*, 1971)

'So this is the little lady who made this big war!' said President Abraham
Lincoln when introduced to the author Harriet Beecher Stowe. Her
Uncle Tom's Cabin had reached a massive readership, including those
who normally read very little. It sold more than 300,000 copies in the
USA in the year 1852–3; in the English-speaking world only the Bible
exceeded it in sales at that time. The book, said Frederick Douglas, the
black anti-slavery campaigner, 'lit a million campfires in the front of
the embattled hosts of slavery'.[1] Lincoln was exaggerating for effect,
Douglas too engaging in hyperbole, but it cannot seriously be con-
tended that Beecher Stowe's book was anything other than highly influential in helping to create the kind of public opinion that enabled
Lincoln to change the Civil War from a constitutional dispute to a
moral crusade, to sustain the struggle and thus finally to win it.

In this final substantive chapter we shall return to the theme with
which we began, the nature of the general relationship between narrative
in the form of imaginative literature and politics, this time by considering
specific examples, and Beecher Stowe's book is an obvious starting
point. In *The Power of the Story, Fiction and Political Change*,[2] Michael
Hanne provides a full account of the central themes and the reception
of Beecher Stowe's *Uncle Tom's Cabin*. He examines four other books
which, he claims, had a similar impact upon the world: Ivan Turgenev's
A Sportsman's Notebook, Ignazio Silone's *Fontamara*, Solzhenitzyn's *One Day
in the Life of Ivan Denisovitch* and Salman Rushdie's *Satanic Verses*. We shall
examine and build on Hanne's discussion of these examples in sequence.

Hanne contends that Turgenev's *A Sportsman's Notebook*, which was published in 1852, was an instrumental factor in the framing of the decision to abolish serfdom in Russia, thereby liberating fifty million people. Published originally as a set of individual stories between 1847 and 1851, each was read by the future Alexander II whilst his father was still on the throne. Alexander succeeded to the throne in 1855 and almost immediately set about the necessary preparatory work for abolition. Serfdom was in fact abolished throughout the Russian Empire in 1861.

The *Notebook* was warmly received by a whole gamut of influential readers and this may have been because the writer was wise enough not to attack serfdom as a system or indeed landowners as a class. We observe, for example, that when landowners mistreat their peasants the author presents this not as the inevitable consequence of an iniquitous social and economic relationship but as an instance of that particular owner's inhumanity. All the same, the government banned the book in 1853 but not before the whole of the first edition had sold out. The official fear was not that the landowners would feel that Turgenev had undermined their own position morally but that literate serfs might get hold of copies and be confirmed, indeed encouraged, in their opposition to serfdom as a system. The main effect of the book, however, was to exercise influence in an entirely different direction: on Alexander himself, the future Czar. Few would want to argue that without Beecher Stowe's or Turgenev's work slavery and serfdom would not have been abolished, yet as Hanne shows, their influence was clearly profound.

Just over a century later, in 1962 to be precise, there appeared in the USSR another book that was to play its part in the destruction of a system, Alexander Solzhenitsyn's *One Day in the Life of Ivan Denisovitch*. Entirely coincidentally the publication of this book fitted in with Khrushchev's recently adopted policy of de-Stalinisation, which began with his 'secret speech' to the Twentieth Congress in 1956.[3] Khrushchev had personally authorised the publication of *One Day in the Life* in 1962. It had got into Khrushchev's hands via his secretary Lebedev, and the narrative is reported to have moved him to tears. It is no exaggeration to say that subsequently Khrushchev used the novel to help make policy. Solzhenitsyn, like Turgenev, skilfully identified his targets. Ivan Denisovitch was working-class and a good communist; so he was a role model for, not an opponent of the regime. Moreover Solzhenitsyn the author carefully avoided all contact with the Western press, so that he could defend himself, and be defended by his supporters, against charges of treason. 'He who controls the record of the past', so Khrushchev must have consoled himself, 'legitimates his authority to command the present and define the future.'[4] Nevertheless the book could be used by critics to indict not just Stalin and his works but 'the authorities' generally and before long people began publicly to ask questions, notably in the press, that the leadership did not want asked. Khrushchev found that he had 'unleashed a tiger that neither he nor his successors in the leadership could control'.[5] When Khrushchev's own power began to wane so did Solzhenitsyn's standing. Though recognition from the West followed (he was awarded the Nobel Prize in 1970), Solzhenitsyn was exiled in 1974. After his subsequent return to Russia in 1994 he was afforded a platform from which to publicise his social and political philosophy. His comments on the government, however, were seen to have played into the hands of its enemies, especially the ultras and the communists. Though he has generally been seen as 'bigger than any politician', a kind of a Tolstoy figure,[6] Hanne is right to conclude that, all in all, Solzhenitsyn 'turned out to be, like many creative writers who have taken up a political position before him, infinitely less persuasive at proposing political arrangements for the future than at opposing the status quo'.[7] Many – but not all.

Bearing this in mind, and bearing in mind too that Khrushchev's championing of the book gave it immediate prominence, we should not forget that it was the literary quality of the text and thus the strength of its message that made it and its author so influential. Once again we find ample grounds for believing that narrative, in the form of imaginative literature, has had a direct impact upon politics. When Cyril Connolly reviewed it, he declared that *One Day in the Life* was a blow 'struck for human freedom all over the world'. A reader in the Ukraine, says Hanne was more prosaic. He wrote to Solzhenitsyn: 'In Kharkov I have seen all kinds of queues – for the film *Tarzan*, butter, women's drawers, chicken giblets and horsemeat sausages. But I cannot remember a queue as long as the one for your book in the libraries.'[8]

Hanne refers to two other texts that, he assures us, have been very influential, Ignazio Silone's *Fontamara* and Salman Rushdie's *Satanic Verses*. However, although the former is a brilliant fable at the expense of Italian fascism, analysing its nature with formidable forensic skill, it is hard to depict the book as having enjoyed political influence in any way equal to that of the three other texts of which we have been speaking. Dario Fo admiringly commented that Silone had used the comic form to dismantle the structures of fascist power. He did not: the Allied war machine did. Rushdie's book *Satanic Verses*, on the other hand, had a political impact but not its intended one. According to Rushdie the target was not Islam but fanaticism, yet it was perceived as a gratuitous attack upon the Islamic faith and not as a criticism of any political system. The consequences of its publication in 1988 were grave: there were public demonstrations in Britain and Canada; demands for the book's banning by a number of Islamic governments; riots in India and Pakistan in which some twenty people were killed; the issuing of a fatwa against the author; the subsequent withdrawal of the ambassadors of all EU countries from Iran; the killing in Brussels of two who had spoken out against the fatwa; the murder of a translator and serious attacks on two others and a number of other atrocities. All in all the book had a political impact even if it was not the intended one. And as Rushdie himself said, 'if a work is capable of being misread or misunderstood, it is the artist's fault'.[9]

We have concentrated on three of the five works that Hanne considered. Although his analysis demonstrates their formidable influence they are no more than examples. Upton Sinclair's *The Jungle*[10] is another such example. Written in 1905 this book offered an account of the living and working conditions (especially in the meat industry) of immigrant workers. Edmund Wilson commented that the book raised fundamental questions about the nature of capitalism so powerfully that Americans could not ignore them. It had a very direct consequence: the passage of federal legislation (the Pure Food and Drug Act) *within a year* which transformed working practices in the food industry.

A book of greater but longer-term influence was Alan Paton's *Cry the Beloved Country*.[11] Considered the most important novel in South African history it did not, unlike *The Jungle*, have an impact on legislation. In fact the opposite: the National government introduced Apartheid within the year (1948). Paton's novel became an immediate worldwide best seller and its influence on white liberal opinion inside and outside South Africa was both continuing and enormous. In 1995 Miramax produced a film based on the novel. The book is almost Orwellian in tone, arguing that if white South Africans would be true to their Christian ideals a more caring and more equal society would result. Both of these books were acknowledged to be novels of great literary power as well as being politically influential.

Moving to twentieth- and twenty-first-century Britain, on the basis of the criterion established in Chapter 1 of long-term critical acclaim, we would surely be obliged to conclude that there are no modern examples of novels or plays written since the 1960s that are likely to be politically influential in years to come. There are no Bernard Shaws or H.G. Wellses, George Orwells or Aldous Huxleys. The plays of David Hare and Tom Stoppard, though they are good examples of modern works that have an interest for the student of politics, are intentionally limited in their sweep and ambition. Perhaps this should come as no surprise for, as we have already seen, if Kuhn is to be believed, modes of explaining the world change from time to time; paradigms shift.[12]

The postmodernists insist there was just such a shift since the 'revolutionary year' of 1968 from a mode 'which proclaimed the availability of "truth" towards one which proclaims instead the much more modest "pragmatic usefulness"'.[13] Knowledge becomes, as a consequence, local and contingent (*à la* Rorty), or even relativist. It appears to be true that the days of the grand narrative are over: compare the sweep and ambition of the depiction of the 'working class' in the novels of Dickens or Galsworthy, or Zola or Tolstoy, with those of John Braine, Lynn Reid Banks or Alan Sillitoe, for example. In the United Kingdom, though, 1968 was more a symptom than an instrument of change, and that change had begun earlier, as the imaginative literature of the 1960s shows. Indeed some critics might want to date the change from 1956 and the production of John Osborne's *Look Back in Anger* when Jimmy Porter singlehandedly laid waste a number of established grand narratives.

Narratives and politicians

If we accept the importance to politics of narrative forms, especially imaginative literature, is it possible to say anything at all about how this influence works? Can it be analysed or even measured, for example? In 1963 a short article entitled 'What Influences Labour MPs?' appeared in a prominent journal.[14] It comprised a brief survey in which the vast majority of the 110 respondents agreed that literature had influenced their political thinking considerably. Most influential among imaginative writers, the survey revealed, were Bernard Shaw and H.G. Wells, with writers like Orwell and Koestler also enjoying some favour, especially with 'rightist' MPs. The survey further indicated, not surprisingly bearing in mind what has been said above, the absence of any modern writer of comparable status or influence. All in all some important issues were raised. Ten years or so later I attempted to follow up some of the issues raised by conducting another survey of Labour MPs. I had a more limited objective in mind, however: I proposed to examine the manner in which an imaginative writer might seek to influence politics. More precisely I concentrated on three of the writers whom Alexander and Hobbs had discovered to have been influential: Shaw, Wells and Orwell. Each, we know, wrote consciously to bring into being a socialist society, though their views of what that was differed. I wished to explore, as thoroughly as possible in so sensitive an area, how and with what success such writers may promote their cause. Difficult though the task obviously was, it proved to be by no means an impossible one. After all, Shaw once said that 'fine art is the subtlest, the most effective means of propaganda in the world, except only the example of personal conduct'.[15] If he was right it would prove possible to substantiate the extent and analyse the nature of the influence of imaginative writers.

It goes without saying that it is impossible to isolate the various factors which go towards making a particular policy, but if it could be shown that a significant number of Labour MPs had read and claimed to have been influenced by imaginative writers, we might reasonably confidently conclude that the politics of the party must have been affected in some measure. And what is more, we might be able to say something about how this influence had been established.

A questionnaire was sent out to every Labour MP and a series of lengthy follow-up interviews with twenty Labour members was conducted. Ninety-six members returned completed questionnaires, a response rate of just over 30 per cent. Although in normal survey conditions this would represent a fairly low response rate, it has to be remembered that our figure represents a percentage not of a sample but of a total population, and this puts the matter in a different perspective. An introductory letter was sent with the questionnaire, which stressed the importance of members replying even if they were unfamiliar with the authors and felt their own political beliefs to have been little affected by imaginative literature. Not surprisingly, however, the great majority of respondents indicated that they were familiar with these authors. So we may conclude that the political views of at least some 30 per cent of the party had been influenced to some degree by imaginative literature. Whilst it is impossible to be certain that the percentage is not higher, two factors indicate 30 per cent to be a reasonably realistic figure. First, Alexander and Hobbs, at a time when questionnaires to MPs were less numerous, received replies from a slightly larger number of members of whom the bulk claimed to have been influenced by imaginative literature. Second, by the time of my own survey over ten years later, when questionnaires were more prevalent, members had become far more selective about the kind of surveys to which they would contribute: they tended to cooperate only in areas in which they were interested.

The object of the questionnaire was principally to discover the extent of the influence of imaginative literature upon politicians and also the nature of that influence. Quantitative analysis provided no more than an indication of the numbers of members influenced by imaginative literature and told us something about their background. But the questionnaire returns also provided the possibility of qualitative analysis through the answers to several open-ended questions. As regards the extent to which MPs felt their politics to have been influenced by what they had read, 52 per cent thought that their political thinking had been influenced at least 'quite a lot'. Two open-ended questions sought to discover whether any other writer had been widely read or influential. In fact none had. Occasional references were made to the works of William Morris, Jack London and Arthur Koestler, and several members mentioned specifically Tressell's *Ragged Trousered Philanthropists*. No postwar British writer was mentioned by more than two respondents. It was noteworthy that older respondents claimed to have read more than younger respondents, and certainly to have been influenced more. This also appeared to be true for those who were generally regarded as being on the left of the party. The latter category was also more prepared to accept the importance of imaginative literature in the formulation of their political thinking. Moreover it appeared to be the case that those who had held some position of responsibility within the party, such as members of the Cabinet and Shadow Cabinet, junior ministers and so on, were better-read and more influenced by what they had read than were the rank-and-file members.

The broad contours of this enquiry, then, lent support to the findings of Alexander and Hobbs's study: a significant number of Labour MPs had read and been influenced by imaginative writers. But the questionnaire returns also showed that older and left-wing MPs appeared to be both wider-read and more influenced. No British socialist writer appears to have matched the influence of Shaw, Wells and Orwell, and no modern writer of anything like comparable powers of persuasion appeared to be at hand. Imaginative writers, then, can – or at least could – hope to influence political events by influencing political actors. But how? Three quotations from questionnaire returns provided a useful guide for further enquiry:

> Imaginative writers can help to create ... a general climate of opinion.

> These writers were able to appeal to the politically sophisticated, the activists, much more so than the heavy, turgid writings of 'serious' writers.

> They added to the intellectual background against which highly influential men made political and social decisions.

Taken together these statements claim that imaginative writers are seen to influence politically aware members of the general public, thus creating a climate of opinion; that they are able to influence political activists, such as MPs; and finally that they are able to exert influence over the decision-makers. Critics who attempt to analyse the source of particular policies assess differentially the contributions of public opinion, the party rank and file and the leadership. The imaginative writer, however, is in a position to influence all levels. Let us explore these three statements in a little more detail.

In what sense could writers be said to create a climate of opinion? Bernard Shaw once claimed: 'I write plays with the deliberate objective of converting the nation to my opinions … I have no other effectual incentive to write plays.'[16] Now what did Shaw mean by 'the nation', or, to put the question more generally, in what sense can authors be said to influence the public? Obviously they can only be writing for the better-off sections of the public, since it is chiefly the latter who attend the theatre or buy serious novels – though this was much less the case in the past. But writers are surely more selective even than this. After all, Shaw also described theatre-goers as 'crowds of unobservant unreflecting people to whom real life means nothing'.[17] No, writers have somebody quite specific in mind when they try to influence 'public opinion'. Richard Hoggart identified the target reader by the phrase 'the intelligent layman' which, though it appears unhelpfully simplistic at first, turns out when closely examined to identify the true nature of the author–reader relationship. The concept of the 'intelligent layman' is symbolic: it represents, so to speak, a projection of the writer himself or herself back into the 'state of innocence'. That is to say, writers must believe that those for whom they are writing (which is not the same as saying those who read them) will, when led out of their innocence by the information the writer has to offer, follow their argument to their conclusions. They will be as convinced as the writer was. The celebrated TV naturalist David Attenborough, when speaking of his own ability to communicate, put this notion much more pithily: 'I think of myself as talking to myself. As if I didn't know what I was talking about.' This is surely the supposition that a writer makes who wishes to communicate political or social values.

The three writers under consideration in this survey were clearly successful in leading wide sections of the thinking public out of their innocence. A quotation from one MP typifies many statements made about Shaw and Wells: 'They influenced changes in the attitude of a whole generation.'[18] But some MPs argued that Orwell achieved the widest measure of public reaction when his *Nineteen Eighty-Four* appeared on BBC television. Indeed the phrase 'Big Brother is watching you' immediately gained and still retains wide currency. Such a general public reaction is a bonus but, as we have seen, it is principally the intelligent layman for whom such works are written. It is the intelligent layman whose generalised support creates the climate of opinion in which reform becomes possible. Some MPs offered the specific example of Shaw's *The Doctor's Dilemma* as being, to quote one, 'good spadework for the National Health Service'. Another made a similar point: 'Shaw and Wells, with Dickens, were the catalysts who made possible the welfare state.' Similar arguments were advanced in more general terms by a number of other MPs. 'Shaw and Wells made people think deeply about the whole subject of social class', said one. He went on to explain that writers gave specific form to a vague social awareness among politically uncommitted or weakly committed people. 'All three of these writers made the middle class think!' said another.

More pertinent to the second level of political activists, it is nonetheless true that imaginative writers also serve to strengthen the convictions of the already committed member of the public. For the intelligent (but no longer innocent) layman this function of reinforcement is an important one. Additionally the destructive element of the imaginative writers' influence needs to be noted. By their critical, often satirical, always iconoclastic view of society they may assist dramatically in promoting the public questioning of accepted attitudes. This is a function that seems to come naturally to many imaginative writers, and one that all three in the present study performed remarkably well. One MP claimed that Shaw and Wells in such works as *Pygmalion* and *Tono Bungay* 'created the iconoclastic view of bourgeois society upon which so many of our generation were brought up'. In these ways then the imaginative writer may influence the general 'climate of opinion'.

Considerable though the writers' influence may be with the general public, or at least the intelligent layman, it is probably at the second level, the level of the party activist, that their influence is at its most marked. Here the writers possesses a captive audience. They do not create opinions here so much as give them definition and focus. 'Political attitudes', said one MP, 'are seldom the outcome of reading – a person has the tendency to read the kind of stuff which supports his own political attitudes, and these are the result of his own observations and are conditioned by his own mode of life.' What the writer does then is to lend specific shape to strongly held, and in the case of many, especially older working-class MPs, poorly structured ideas. 'They are seldom if ever innovators', said one, 'they give a higher degree of articulation to what is already being thought.'

This function of articulation appears to have been most significant for older working-class activists. It is clear both from the questionnaire returns and from interviews that older MPs, typically from working-class backgrounds, held either of two distinctive attitudes. First, a deprecatory attitude held by a minority: 'The influence of these men has been greatly exaggerated by themselves ... their contribution in working-class areas of the country was negligible.' Again: 'All they did was to modify the genuinely revolutionary aspirations of the working people.' But the second and more prominent view was one of gratitude and respect. These MPs had enjoyed few of the benefits of formal education. Their education had been the result of private reading, WEA classes and so on. So it grew up unsystematised but rich. Moreover for a variety of reasons these MPs possessed a ready respect for intellectuals. One such MP suggested that to discover that a writer of world repute was arguing in a similar manner to oneself was to feel that one's ideas had received a kind of imprimatur. Not only did these writers give authenticity and intellectual respectability to ideas that had wide currency among working-class activists but also they helped to systematise those ideas.

It would be unreasonable to suggest that imaginative writers did not perform a similar function for middle-class activists, but for obvious reasons the process was a more dramatic one for the working class. In short, they added substance and roundness to beliefs for numbers of activists from all social backgrounds, as perhaps the following examples will help to substantiate:

Although I would have said that I was in favour of toleration and free speech I don't think I ever fully realised what that implied until I read *Saint Joan*.

I don't think I had any clear idea of the possibilities of the classless society until I read Shaw.

Tono Bungay seemed to put in sharp definition all one had wanted to say about the evils of the capitalist system.

Wells's imaginative survey of man's place in the universe and the hopeful assessment of his potentialities gave sustenance and clarity to my own views.

My attitude towards the Soviet system had been equivocal and generally muddled. Orwell opened my eyes and purged me of Stalinism forever.

Orwell showed so clearly why one ought to be a socialist and yet at the same time showed the pitfalls.

This is the function which imaginative writers have performed for Labour Party activists. Naturally enough their critical and iconoclastic attitudes have also been widely influential at this level but it is the more positive function that appears to have been the most important.

Bernard Shaw and his Fabian friends set great store by the influence they believed themselves to enjoy with the political establishment. As is well-known, for a long time the Fabian leaders were reluctant to support an independent pro-labour party in Parliament and instead argued for a policy of 'permeating' the major parties. Indeed Fabian leaders, Shaw included, expressly advised Fabians to go out and join their local Liberal and Conservative associations, so as to influence the policies of the major parties. Indeed Shaw once said: 'We want to send Fabians into the Unionist party to make the Unionists intelligent.'[19] But we know that the path of history was to lie in a different direction and when the Labour Party was finally formed, it received support at all levels from the Fabians. Yet we still find the movement bitterly divided over whether its primary aim should be to influence men of power or to broaden the supportive base of socialism. This issue was to take the form of a personal confrontation between Shaw and Wells – both Fabian elitists but the first attempting to win the ear of the mighty and the second seeking to lead a mass movement trying to win socialist converts through education. Shaw and his allies carried the day.

It has already been pointed out that those with positions of responsibility within the Labour Party appear to have read more and been influenced more than the party rank and file; in both cases not just more but substantially more. It would be impossible to take this line of argument any further. We could not substantiate any example of a specific policy emanating from a Labour Cabinet that was the direct product of an imaginative writer's influence, though when Shaw's close friends and colleagues Sydney Webb and Lord Olivier sat in the first Labour Cabinet the relationship was direct enough. On the other hand it is difficult not to believe that policies promoted and put into effect by a group of individuals, several of whom owed much to imaginative literature for the shape of their politics, would not reflect these influences in some measure.

In conclusion imaginative writers have good reason to believe that, in principle, they may exert an influence in politics at three levels. They may indeed convert the 'intelligent laymen', who may be instrumental in helping to form a general climate of opinion; they may also add definition and focus to the broad views of activists within the Labour movement; and finally they may affect significantly the policy preferences of decision-makers.

But what is it that enables imaginative writers to exert political influence? Is it the strength and cogency of argument or is it the vividness of a particular image which forms the most common vehicle of influence? This poses a problem: is it possible after all to separate the two and if so, is it possible to assess their influences separately? From replies to the questionnaire a certain general pattern did indeed appear to emerge, and in the course of interviewing it was possible to test this pattern to some extent. The pattern suggested that MPs with a working-class background in particular, but also the majority of MPs who claimed to have been influenced 'quite a lot', seem to have been influenced principally by certain images which writers created. This is an important consideration, because although writers cannot choose their audience they can choose their method of proselytising. Wells gave up the brilliantly imaginative literature of his earlier period to write overtly didactic novels, encyclopaedic histories and general biology texts in order, he said, to win over the masses to his brand of socialism. This approach provoked the comment from Lytton Strachey that he had ceased to think about Wells when Wells became a thinker. Judging by the evidence of this study such misgivings were well-merited.

The imaginative writer's ability to capture in miniature a whole landscape of political and social commitment was, it seems, what gave them influence, especially over MPs with a working-class background. In questionnaire replies and in interviews numbers of examples from the works of all three authors were provided. Among them were Orwell's short story 'Shooting an Elephant', which one MP referred to as 'a consummate condemnation of imperialism in a nutshell'. Another Orwell short story, 'A Hanging', was referred to by a second MP as 'the great unanswerable indictment of capital punishment'. The key word here is 'unanswerable', and a third example shows precisely why. Bernard Shaw frequently argued publicly the case for equality of opportunity. It would result, he said, in a break-up of social stratification and thus make possible a humane and just society that was the prerequisite of socialism. Many could and did take issue with Shaw but nobody could argue the point with Eliza Doolittle.

The nub of the argument then is that the imaginative instinct of a writer can enable them to make concrete in an unforgettable character or situation a whole ideology. This image, once having influenced a person's thinking, is likely to prove highly resilient. The survey found many examples to illustrate this point and again one of the best was from Orwell. Many MPs referred to *Animal Farm* and its leading characters. One wrote: 'How I hated those damned pigs; and when I look around I still see them sitting there in the House of Commons.' A later interview elicited the fact that he was referring to colleagues in his own party.

It seems reasonable to conclude then that imaginative writers have enjoyed influence principally as a result of their ability to create symbols which certain people could identify with their own experience and value system, and which therefore served them as a valuable means of synthesis and reinforcement. This influence appears to have been particularly important for working-class MPs short of formal education and for other chiefly left-wing MPs whose commitment to socialism was rooted as much in emotion as anything else.

A second general statement arises as a corollary to this: that middle-class MPs, especially of the centre and right-of-centre, with an extensive formal education, tended to be more influenced by the argument contained in an author's work than by any images they create. Numbers of such MPs were able to quote from the prefaces of Shaw's plays and from Shaw's and Wells's non-fictional work, such as *The Intelligent Woman's Guide*, and Wells's world histories. These works were read simply because the majority of intelligent, well-educated people read Shaw and Wells. In fact one MP admitted to having bought his wife *The Intelligent Woman's Guide* as a birthday present. What they looked for was intellectual nourishment rather than an ideological reinforcement, but a cameo character, scene or incident which could be carried around like a locket or medallian would be a bonus for these MPs too.

It appears generally true that those for whom political activity was the result of personal and often emotional motivation rather than a natural career choice tended to retain the symbols they acquired from their reading of imaginative literature. Generally speaking those most influenced were older, further to the left, and came from a working-class background.

We observed that the older MPs appear to be more widely read than the younger.[20] Prima facie it might seem only logical that the older the MP the more he would have read. But in fact the great majority of MPs undertook their reading whilst they were still young.[21] This discrepancy in reading among the age categories highlights an important paradox which can only have grown; these days the Labour Party in Parliament has a far higher level of formal educational attainment than it has ever had in the past, yet it seems to be less widely read.[22]

This contradiction was pointed out to those MPs who were interviewed. Their consensus explanation took the following lines. In the days before the improvements in the education system began to have an effect upon the education of working-class children, the Labour movement was more respectful of ideas and of men of ideas. It was prepared to be led and influenced by men of intellectual and social standing, such as Cripps, Dalton, Cole and Laski. But in the postwar period a significant number of working-class and lower-middle-class young people 'proved' themselves through the machinery of formal education. They had no feelings of deference, so the argument runs, towards their social and intellectual 'betters'. But the education which these men and women received was largely instrumental; it eschewed the more traditional, rounded education of the public schools and their imitators, it lacked the undisciplined broad sweeps of knowledge of their self-educated senior colleagues; it taught them to distrust the latter's respect for visionary notions. For these younger MPs the men of 'ideas' to whom they listened tended to be academic specialists – especially economists and sociologists. 'General reading isn't as important as it once was', said one. 'There is a preoccupation with events today... our time is taken up with reading journalists, social scientists and economists.'

There is, however, another and quite different argument to explain the diminishing influence of imaginative writers: after all, the party had completed much of its mission, so what need had it of visionaries? Labour had put together the basic structure of a more just society, and what remained to be done amounted to little more than social engineering. Poverty and other forms of acute social distress seemed, for a number of respondents, to be absolute rather than relative. Christopher Mayhew put this argument neatly: although he had been prepared to fight during the 1930s to secure the basics of life for the poor, he felt under no compunction to increase the GNP in the modern era so as to 'lever up' housing and education programmes. Poverty was not, after all, relative.[23] In brief: the socialist vision of earlier years, which imaginative writers helped to shape, has become realised in part and has thus been made otiose.

Finally it was argued that, no doubt partly because of the two reasons given but also for reasons discussed earlier, imaginative writers with a political bent of the stature of a Shaw, Wells or Orwell were simply not around any more. Neither in answering the open-ended questions in the questionnaire nor in interview did any MP suggest the name of any postwar British writer whom he thought to have had a comparable influence on the development of his own political thinking.

Taken together, the argument concludes, these three factors have produced a Labour Party with a vision that is now essentially instrumental and not utopian, as is well-exemplified by the party's campaign in the 1964 general election when socialist utopianism was symbolically burned up in the white heat of the Wilsonian technological revolution.

Now finally to a brief summary of the part played by the imaginative writer in the development of the British Labour Party. The imaginative writer may influence reflective members of the general public (thus affecting the climate of opinion, and hence party policy indirectly), any member of the Labour movement or any decision-maker (thus having a more direct influence). Those in the past who have used that potential seem to have fulfilled two important functions for the movement. First, imaginative writers have acted as unifying agents. Because they have held the attention of many throughout the movement their ideas have been common currency for a great number at all levels. Socialism we have seen, is a coalition of fairly disparate elements. It has needed the unifying force of a vision of the good society to sustain it; or at the very least it needed such a vision to establish itself as a political force. The vision of the socialist society was compounded of many elements; but the contribution of imaginative writers to this utopian exercise was considerable, just as were the highly critical pictures they painted of contemporary society. By Appointment: Corrosive Social Critics and Purveyors of Visions – these were the major roles of imaginative writers in the history of the Labour Party. Through their critiques and through the visions they created, such writers helped to provide the movement with a sense of unity and purpose.

A second important function arises out of this. The imaginative writer has the opportunity to present vividly the problems and aspirations of ordinary people to senior politicians whose job by its very nature leads them to lose contact with the people. The parliamentary party as a whole, especially as it became more professionalised, tended to become increasingly concerned with day-to-day party-political matters. Imaginative writers kept MPs in touch with the ordinary people whom they claimed to represent by presenting vivid images of the lives those people lead and the problems they encountered. In short the writer's second function has been to transmit social values in a form which politicians, artificially separated from the people, would recognise and act upon.

Yet the role of the visionary in an age of non-visionary politics, that of the critic in a reasonably successful but disillusioned liberal democracy, is to say the least limited, and the findings of the survey tend to support the generally accepted view that we live in such an age. The survey endorsed the conclusion of the earlier study by Alexander and Hobbs: the contribution that imaginative writers made to the development of the British Labour Party was considerable. But we have been able to go further; we saw not only that the influence of imaginative writers was significant, but that it was becoming far less so. In the past imaginative writers offered a moving criticism of contemporary society, an indication of the problems confronting socialist movements and a vision of what the socialist society might be like. Nowadays visionaries are an endangered species.

It would not be appropriate, however, to ignore the possibility that film, at least in part, may have taken the place of imaginative literature and we shall be turning our attention to film in the Postscript. Although no comparably detailed study has been undertaken we can be confident, as we shall see shortly, that many Labour MPs will have seen and been moved by films by directors like Ken Loach. But for all the reasons discussed above they will not have had the same impact as the imaginative writers: times have changed, paradigms have shifted.

Twenty years after my own survey Platt and Gallagher conducted a similar though broader-based survey, 'From Bevan to the Bible',[24] on what influences Labour MPs. Eighty-five MPs responded to the questionnaire – 31 per cent of the contemporary parliamentary party. Their findings tended to confirm the assumptions made earlier. Bernard Shaw, so influential during an earlier age, was cited by 14 per cent of MPs born before 1945 but by only 2 per cent of those born later. Only Robert Tressell's work stood the test of time for these MPs, 20 per cent of whom claimed to have read and been influenced by *The Ragged Trousered Philanthropists*. Surprisingly Tressell was more influential by far with the younger MPs. As in previous surveys a scattering of MPs referred to William Morris and Jack London, and Wells by now had slipped into this 'occasional' category. Alice Walker's *Color Purple* was also mentioned by three MPs. Platt and Gallagher also explored the impact of film and theatre and found that 21 per cent claimed to have been influenced by films and 43 per cent by the theatre. All in all, the conclusion reached earlier – that narrative forms such as imaginative literature and film can in principle hope to exert some influence over political thought and indeed political events – can be said still to stand. No fewer than 86 per cent of respondents agreed that books had played a significant part in influencing their 'political beliefs and actions'. Nevertheless, whereas only 5 per cent in the earlier surveys felt that intellectuals had not made a significant contribution to Labour thinking, that figure rose to 21 per cent in 1994 while a further 8 per cent answered 'not enough' and an additional 8 per cent 'not recently'.

Conclusions

We began this study by examining the relationship between politics and literature in general and by considering the factors that have traditionally tended to limit the extent to which students of political thought have analysed their discipline through the work of imaginative writers. It is important to acknowledge, however, that in recent years political philosophers have been much more inclined to seek elucidation from imaginative literature. In questioning the nature of reality, philosophers like Rorty and more so Foucault have cast doubt on the supremacy of reasoning, and by extension of philosophy itself. Foucault's vision of all discourse as a network of power relations[25] undermined the notion of 'truth' as something to be discovered and explained by the application of reason. For him there was no neutral and superior form of truth. This movement away from philosophy has done much to establish the credentials of imaginative literature as a mode of explanation – by default, as it were. For Rorty to say there is no such thing as truth is to imply that 'where there are no sentences there is no truth ... only descriptions of the world can be true or false – the world itself, undescribed, cannot'.[26] Rorty suggests that when the great figures of the Romantic movement had argued that imagination and not reason was the central human faculty they were telling us that the catalyst for social change was not so much being able to argue well as to see things differently. This opened the way for imaginative literature to claim a 'truth' as valid as any other.

So philosophy is dethroned and the 'poet–exile', the imaginative writer – the storyteller – returns. Deprived of their haloes, words like truth, science and knowledge become little more than badges identifying literary genres. Let us be clear: Rorty's point is not so much that literature is suddenly discovered to be 'cognitive, powerful and responsible' but that philosophy itself and other 'superior' forms of discourse are exposed as 'imprecise, capricious and methodologically dishevelled'.[27] It is not necessary to accept Rorty's arguments about the subjectivity or contingency of truth to feel their force. Consider as an example that essay of Orwell's, 'A Hanging':[28] through it the writer claims the moral superiority of the condemned criminal to any 'hanging judge'. We discussed Bernard Crick's attempt to verify the essay's authenticity in an earlier chapter,[29] yet it is clear that the whole issue of authenticity is secondary to the argument about criminals and judges. Through his experientially 'true' story (whatever the facts), Orwell confronts us with a judgement about the nature of the judicial system that cannot usefully be assigned a label 'true' or 'false' but which nonetheless demands our attention. This is the force of imaginative literature's army of metaphors. Rorty, whose main objective appears to have been to demolish philosophy's claim to explain the world, does all the same go so far as to suggest that imaginative literature might indeed provide a superior form of explanation if only through the power of its wit and imagination.[30] He is right: story-telling – narrative – in imaginative writing engages us emotionally in a way that no other form of explanation does: it requires us to take sides.

Some writers have always been convinced that their work had no political impact: W.H. Auden was one, though he certainly wrote with the intention of influencing others in the 1930s, as his coruscatingly bitter attack on capitalism in the poem 'A Communist to Others' vividly demonstrates.[31] The current MP and former television satirist John O'Farrell sums up succinctly the argument of those who deem literature ineffectual as a source of political influence when he said apropos of his own art of political satire: 'whoever said that the pen was mightier than the sword must have had a pretty crappy sword'.[32] Well, not all writers who seek to influence thinking are successful, and some, as Rushdie's case illustrates, may be influential in a way quite unlike the one intended, but none can seriously deny the impact of many of the books discussed in these chapters. Indeed O'Farrell's modesty even regarding his own art is not universally accepted. Hanne, for example, argues that 'even … political cartoons, satire … have … undermined the credibility of their targets to quite a devastating degree'.[33] There is another, more insidious line of argument aimed at imaginative writers. It acknowledges their influence but as a negative force. In the words of one respondent in my own survey of Labour MPs: 'All they did was to modify the genuinely revolutionary aspirations of the working people.' As intellectuals they are, according to this argument, paid-up members of the establishment with a vested interest in maintaining the social and political status quo. They only play at being rebels. There is another sense in which their influence may be seen as negative: that what they provide through their work is some kind of Aristotelian catharsis. Narratives do our crying for us and, feeling cleansed after the experience, we can get on with life in the real world. The books we have discussed in this chapter can be taken to expose the limitations of both of these lines of argument: they are far from the whole story. There can be no doubt that narratives shape our perception of political issues: who, for example, having read *Brave New World*, could look on detached at recent discoveries in the field of genetics?

And it is not just our perceptions of issues that may be shaped by our narrative experiences. The BBC's Political Commentator Andrew Marr wrote of Orwell's important influence on British political thinking. 'Thought corrupts language and language corrupts thought, and to reform the language [as he believed Orwell had] is to reform politics.'[34] Many who have read Orwell have changed their habits of speaking and writing and thinking, he goes on. They 'have had, cumulatively, a great influence, helping the language fight back against elitism, abstraction and the rule of experts ... Because of that, Orwell is not just a great writer: he is one of the great political reformers of the century.' Conor Cruise O'Brien called Orwell the Voltaire of his age. His impact on the British political class was to have 'weakened their belief in their own ideology, made them ashamed of their clichés, left them intellectually more scrupulous and defenceless'.[35] But another commentator, Libby Purves, warned: 'We still need Orwell', only 'more than ever.'[36] Although Orwell's special interest in the relationship between language and politics singles him out to some extent in this regard, we observed that one of the chief reasons for studying all imaginative literature with long-term impact was precisely that the quality of writing was a politically significant factor in their influence.

We have examined the relationship between politics and imaginative literature as narrative form in general and theoretical terms and also in detail through the specific example of the development and decline of socialism in Britain. We have analysed and commented on the contribution that narrative, through its experiental understanding of the world, can make to the development of political ideas, and we have examined empirically how narrative forms might exert their influence. The principal role of the imaginative writers was characterised earlier as social critics, as purveyors of vision, as guardians of the language. Our survey of the relevant literature suggests that the writers we have studied were all of them prone to inconsistencies and confusion as critics of society. Moreover none left us an entirely convincing vision of a future society that people would strive to bring into being. Perhaps we should have expected as much: it is part of the enterprise in which they were engaged. What they undeniably did, however, was to illuminate these issues for all who read or saw their work and to provide an experiential understanding of them.

It is no coincidence that we speak nowadays of the implosion of traditional socialism in Britain and also of the decline of the grand narrative. David Marquand, whilst not pessimistic about the possibility of 'new paradigms' for Labour and quite dismissive of the old paradigms which are 'taking an unconscionable time to leave the stage', nevertheless concedes that the new ones have not yet emerged.[37] He might be waiting for Godot, for as Platt and Gallagher conclude in their survey: 'Today's generation of Labour MPs seems to have replaced the search for grand historical narratives or overall philosophies of social organisation with ... practical down-to-earth humanism.' Yet the more reflective members of the party, like the more reflective members of society at large, mourn the loss of narratives and narrators. In the words of one: 'we need to [re]establish our intellectual self-confidence. This is our greatest lack at the moment.' More pithy, perhaps, was the *cri de cœur* of an MP whom I interviewed as part of my own earlier research: 'Shaw, Wells, Orwell – and one or two others – did more to influence and encourage socialism [in Britain] than all the textbooks. God, I wish we had their equal today!'

Postscript: The Implosion of Values

Socialism in Britain developed as an intellectual critique of nineteenth-century capitalism. As we have seen, it possessed an ethical dimension, which was rooted in basic Judaeo-Christian values, and a scientific dimension, which attacks capitalism's perceived inefficiencies and inhumanities. Some socialists sought a revolutionary transformation of society and others a more gradual and controlled change. Many had a clear idea of the kind of society they believed would replace capitalism. The Labour government of 1945–50, described by one knowledgeable American critic as presiding over a collectivist state,[1] represented the apogee of scientific – and some would argue ethical – socialist achievement. But for the next half-century Labour governments won the right to manage 'socialism' for only a decade or so. In fact from the late 1950s onwards Labour itself, or at any rate its leaders, sought to retreat from 'socialism' and finally, under the leadership of Tony Blair, they managed it.

So far we have been considering the portrayal in literature of some of the key elements of these developments in British socialism. We have now reached the stage at which we must address the collapse of socialism and the implosion of its values. In accepting the demise of socialism as established fact (but not necessarily a permanent one), I am not attempting to signal complicity with Fukuyama's global 'end of history' thesis but simply to make a comment on the recent history of organised socialism in the United Kingdom. Since the Labour Party revised Clause Four of its constitution, which party members had traditionally carried on the inside cover of their membership cards (next to their hearts), committing the party to: 'Secure for the producers by hand and by brain the full fruits of their industry, and the most equitable distribution thereof that may be possible, upon the common ownership of the means of production', no major political party in the United Kingdom has championed a set of policy objectives that could even be loosely defined as socialist.[2]

Now, we have seen that narrative literature provides us with a very clear account of socialists' views on capitalism, their hopes for change and their expectations for the future. We might reasonably expect narratives of equal insight describing the demise of socialism. In this Postscript we shall indeed consider some narratives that show the collapse of socialist community values in their heartland, but not strictly speaking literary narratives. I want to suggest that the narrative form most suited to the more immediate and relativist aims of modern writers are not literary so much as visual: film and television. There is a focused directness and immediacy about these visual media. Of course they encourage consideration and interpretation but like photography they are essentially realistic, leaving significantly less to the imagination and therefore less scope to the screenwriter. And they have potentially a huge audience. Arguably no book written in or since the 1960s has had the same impact upon the British public as the documentary TV film on homelessness *Cathy Come Home*, which was shown on television in 1966. It stunned the public and undermined the Labour government, who began to look for communist infiltrators in the BBC.

However there are limitations to film narrative. First, because of its visual nature it can show poverty (for example) but not discuss its economic causes – those 'socio-economic forces that, though not immediately perceptible in phenomenal appearances, are responsible for [its] production'.[3] On the other hand we might think that this medium is particularly well-suited to our postmodernist age, which is said to adjure all metanarratives. We are told that we live in an age of contingency. Second, as Walter Benjamin argued, potentially disturbing images can be 'rendered safe by assimilation into asceticism'.[4] But then, as we have discussed, imaginative writers too have been charged with providing their readers or audience with catharsis rather than incitement to action: they have done our crying for us. Nevertheless the kinds of film made by the realist film-makers of the 1960s could and did bring the grimness, the dirt, the abrasive realities of class distinctions and hostilities, the limited horizons of the lives of ordinary people to mass audiences, and critics like Raymond Williams warmly applauded their achievements.[5] A number of the more successful of the 1960s realist films were in fact based upon novels and so the decision to look at film rather than literary narrative should be seen not as an inevitable step but more as an expression of preference. Though it is likely that more saw the films than read the books it is unarguable that both media were influential – especially since many would been drawn to see the films after having read the books and vice versa.

Working-class values: the 1960s

Let us turn, then, to two films of the 1960s, which show the effect that greater disposable income had upon traditional working-class values. Let us see how socialist values stood up to the depredations of affluence. The affluence of which we speak, though relative was real enough. It was based upon an increase in wages between 1951 and 1963 of 73 per cent (in comparison prices rose by 45 per cent); unemployment was minimal; for the first time consumer goods such as TVs, fridges, washing machines and record players became common and the British working-class began its love affair with the holiday resorts of Spain's Costa Blanca. In the longer term the transformation of the state education system through the implementation of the Butler Education Act of 1944 meant that working-class children with intellectual ability could reasonably expect, if they wished, to gain a middle-class lifestyle. They could build upon the bridgehead established by young working-class men who had been 'educated' in His Majesty's armed forces.

The first film we shall be considering is *Room at the Top*. The film is based upon a novel of the same name by the Yorkshire writer John Braine and concerns an ambitious young man from a solidly working-class background, Joe Lambton, who aspires to wealth and social prominence. Joe's working-class background is quickly sketched in for us by means of a visit that he makes to his home town. His former house has been demolished and amongst the ruins a small girl whom he happens to meet shows him her 'garden'; we can hardly help contrasting her few weeds in the patch of wasteland amidst the debris of bombing and rebuilding with the magnificent grounds of the house owned by the Browns, whose daughter Joe is pursuing. He visits an aunt and uncle who are delighted to discover that Joe is considering taking a job in the locality, returning to his community and his roots. We glimpse a picture of the kind of working-class interior that Orwell eulogised but we see it through Joe's eyes and we know instinctively that he will never return to these roots. 'Community' for Joe is not the life-enhancing environment that it was for Orwell; rather it is a prison of low social expectations and of values that are too confining. When Joe tells his aunt and uncle that he is pursuing the daughter of a wealthy industrialist they warn him against it: his aunt because she divines that it is not Susan herself but her social status that Joe loves; his uncle because he believes in his bones that no good can come from forsaking one's own people. Joe pugnaciously rejects this Orwellian advice because he recognises how cribbed working-class communal life would be for a man with his ambitions. These ambitions have been revolutionised by the 1939–45 war. Joe has met the 'officer class' and has come to understand its weaknesses as well as its strengths. Unlike Hardy's Jude, Joe both knows what it takes to get to 'the top' and is prepared to do it, whatever is necessary, and he knows too that this will certainly mean offending the strict Orwellian moral values which governed working-class life in the north of England.

Joe sets his stall out to win Susan Brown. Susan's mother, like Shaw's Lady Brittomart, knowing exactly the value of the 'right' marriage and the disasters of a wrong one, recognises Joe's social unsuitability for her daughter. Her father too, a worldlier-wise and less class-conscious character, has other plans for his daughter. Despite the opposition of both, Joe manages to infatuate Susan. We should note in parenthesis, though it is not something to which Joe gives even the slightest attention, that Susan is already engaged. To save their daughter from this undesirable (but desired) suitor her mother promptly whisks Susan off on a long continental holiday. Meanwhile Joe has been heating other irons. He encounters an older, infinitely wiser woman, Alice Aisgill, unhappily married, lonely and French. They meet at the local drama club, to which Susan and her fiancé also belong. In Orwell's Yorkshire no young working-class male would have ventured into such hostile middle-class territory: times are changing. Although initially conspiratorial – they discuss his plans to ensnare Susan – Joe's relationship with Alice soon flourishes into romance, a romance that increasingly affects Joe.

At first he is pleased with himself to be balancing several balls in the air at once: pursuing Susan, refusing to be bought off by Brown, and enjoying a highly charged sensual relationship with Alice. Slowly, inconveniently, this relationship strengthens. Alice knows that her age and Joe's ambitions constitute impossible barriers to a permanent relationship, but she becomes able to convince herself, with Joe's help, that this is not so; and anyway Joe will not accept that their relationship has no future. They go away together – a daring enough act in those days – and enjoy a blissful few days in a cottage in the Dorset countryside.[6] But a dreadful argument ensues on their return to Yorkshire. Alice admits that she has posed in the nude as an artist's model. For all his middle-class aspirations Joe's response is instinctive: his working-class value system in all its small-minded, puritanical self-righteousness explodes and Alice has grounds to fear for her personal safety. The writing is on the wall, but their love appears to survive and eventually the affair develops to the point where Alice is hopelessly lost and Joe has convinced himself that he is willing to give up on Susan and all his social ambitions.

Whether he could have stuck to this conviction is debatable but Aisgill, Alice's influential husband, warns Joe that he will never divorce his wife and that he will do whatever is necessary to put a stop to the relationship. Alice confirms to Joe that this is a threat to be taken very seriously. Worse follows when Joe discovers that, before the relationship with Alice had fully flowered, he had made Susan pregnant. Perhaps with Aisgill's threats at the back of his mind he is unable to resist Brown's offer of a senior position in the family firm if he were to marry Susan. Joe goes personally to break with Alice but is unable to carry it off with any sensitivity. Like Gissing's Richard Mutimer he exposes a crass working-class social ineptitude. Alice, devastated, becomes hopelessly drunk and dies in a truly gruesome car accident, almost certainly intentionally. Joe makes it to the top, then, unencumbered by any embarrassing liaisons.

This is a story about the naked ambition of an individual but it is also a story about class in Yorkshire; about a man who confronts and eventually surmounts the barriers surrounding talented working-class people. Unlike Mutimer and those other stock characters in Gissing's novels[7] who try to escape from their working-class prisons and whom fate skewers before depositing them back inside, Joe makes it and on his own terms. On the other hand, in rejecting his origins for wealth and influence he rejects, too, those Orwellian socialist values which bound the working-class together, and a close-up of Joe's stony face as he sets out on honeymoon with an effusively affectionate Susan shows us unmistakably that he fully realises the extent of his loss; whatever their wealth and social prestige there will be no epithalamium in their nuptial chamber.

Finally, if we despise Joe for what he has done we can still sympathise with his absolute refusal to be imprisoned by his working-class origins; still support him when he refuses to be browbeaten by Susan's fiancé, an ex-officer who snidely refers to him as 'sergeant': a decent, reliable chap, that is to say, but not for the officers' mess. Far more hard-nosed than Wells's Arty Kipps, Joe Lambton will not be put down by the class he despises. In some important ways Joe symbolises a social movement triggered by the war and, as I have suggested, soon to be reinforced by the effects of the 1944 Education Act, which was responsible for the great escape of the young working-class, especially men. Yet we realise at the same time that their social success will cut them off for ever from their cultural values in just the way that Orwell predicted. And if we think that Joe Lambton got all he deserved, did he have any realistic alternative to social ambition? Would we have been sympathetic towards him if he had gone back Gissing-like to his roots?

If Joe Lambton was exceptional so too was Frank Machin, the central figure in Lindsay Anderson's adaptation of the David Storey novel *This Sporting Life*. Like Joe, Frank was a working-class male consumed by ambition and equally prepared to act ruthlessly to be successful. There is a fundamental difference between the two, however: whilst Joe is intellectually sharp, Frank Machin's brains are, to coin a phrase, mostly in his football boots. Frank's ambition is to become a great rugby league player. We need to bear in mind that unlike rugby union (in England at least) rugby league is a working-class sport played at the highest level by professionals chiefly from the north of England. The Rugby League was established towards the end of the nineteenth century to make it possible for northern working-class men to play the game of rugby. Because of work commitments they were not able to play on the traditional Saturday afternoon and so sought permission to play on Sundays. When this was denied by the Rugby Football Union (RFU), clubs sought permission to pay their players what they would have earned at work. When this too was denied them by the RFU they set up their own association which permitted payments. They also reformed the rules of the game, changing it from a fifteen-man to a thirteen-man sport. So the game of rugby league has very clear connotations to British people: it is understood to be northern and working-class, and for decades the game was despised by the RFU: whilst, that is, the union game remained formally shut to professionalism.[8] Traditionally, too, rugby league has remained much closer to its roots, unlike soccer, and so when called a 'star' by a fan Frank replies tellingly that only soccer players are stars. His ambition is different: he wants to be a hero. He wants to be a champion of the values of his own class, not someone whose status takes him out of that class. Frank's philosophy is frighteningly direct. 'You see something and you go out and get it. It's as simple as that.' But what he wants is to be a sporting hero, not a star, and he wants to stay within his class. And that ambition turns out to be by no means simple and direct.

Although Frank has no compunction about acting outside of the rules of the game on the field of play – he surreptitiously poleaxes one of his own team during a trial game because this player is intentionally keeping the ball from him – he is not prepared to cheat off the field. Unlike Joe who benefited from his experience in the armed forces, Frank has not been able to observe the social 'enemy' in action and would have no chance of surviving amidst the intrigues of his social betters. Although tempted, for example, he rebuffs the sexual advances of Mrs Weaver, the club owner's wife, because to succumb would be 'unfair' to his own woman, as well as to Weaver. Neither Weaver nor Mrs Weaver will forgive this. Neither share Frank's moral sensitivities.

Machin achieves his ambition on the field, but off the field his social ineptitude continually frustrates him. He is a big, uneducated working-class man who cherishes wealth and what it can bring but has no subtlety, no social skills, and worse still no realisation of his shortcomings. Unlike Joe Lambton he simply cannot manage without the ballast of family and class, where he knows what's what; values of which his wealth and prestige as a hero will inevitably deprive him. He wants to be part of the community and yet to be idolised by it. He is fixated by a need to stand above (but not outside) the herd, and at one point flings open the doors of his lodgings in a working-class estate and hurls abuse at the neighbouring houses, haranguing his widowed landlady, who is his lover: 'you want me to crawl about, just like the rest', he accuses. But no, he isn't like the rest, who only want somebody to 'act big for them', and this is the role he has chosen for himself.

Although he wins the sexual favours of his landlady, what he really wants is her respect and love. For her part, she cannot bring herself to love this socially inept gladiator. What appeals to her sexually also disgusts her in equal measure socially: his size and physical strength. 'So big. So stupid.' And indeed whenever he can't get his way Machin expresses himself physically and like Steinbeck's Lennie he tends to break fragile things. When Margaret Hammond criticises a man for having weak hands, and so by definition not to be a real man, Machin looks down at his own huge hands: 'Hands? What have hands got to do with it?' Men's hands, says Heinrich Böll's eponymous hero in *The Clown* are made for hitting and for paying money.[9] Machin is good at both.

It has to be admitted that Machin's choice of lover is an unfortunate one. Although a respectable working-class widow with a young family, Margaret Hammond, it transpires, may have been indirectly responsible for her husband's death through suicide. She is unable to allow herself to give the kind of secure love to a partner that she had denied to her husband. His polished boots stand in the grate as both memorial and reprimand. She gives herself to Machin when making love but warns him: 'I've nothing more to give you.' And yet she tries, and indeed at one point puts the boots away. Unfortunately this symbolic act does not make Machin any less big or stupid.

To her he is no folk hero but a 'big ape on a rugby field'. He is unable to accept that the more gifts he showers on her, the more he prises her out of the shell of working-class respectability which means so much to her, the more she resents him. The more she turns from him in consequential desperation, the more gifts he bestows. Her response to his kindness is that he does these things not because he loves her but because it 'makes him feel big'.

The decisive episode in their relationship occurs when Frank finally persuades her to come out to dinner with him. He has bought her a fur coat especially for the occasion and does not notice the disapproval of the neighbour who is to baby-sit for them, though Margaret Hammond herself is painfully aware of it. At the best restaurant in town Machin acts with such gross discourtesy to the waiting staff as acutely to embarrass his partner. When she rebukes him he replies surlily: 'We're paying for it! That's all they're interested in.' She knows now what she always suspected: there is no way she can love this bully. She tries with increasing desperation to persuade Machin to leave the lodgings, telling him that he makes her feel dirty. Incredulous he asks why. She replies spitefully: 'If you deal with dirt you get dirty.' He strikes her in pain and anger. Yet the more she rejects him the harder he tries until eventually when he openly declares his love for her she spits in his face. He leaves her at last and shortly after Margaret dies of a brain haemorrhage.

Lindsay Anderson, the film's director, does not seek to construct a social polemic; his characters are rich and are treated not as symbols at all but as individuals. Margaret Hammond is a very complex woman and Frank Machin, though he expresses that crude sense of masculinity that characterised the portrayal of working-class men in the cinema of the 1960s, has at the same time an innate sensitivity of which even he is scarcely aware: he is very vulnerable emotionally.[10] This story has much about it of a tragic nature, but for our purposes the element which I have concentrated on concerns a man who needs to rise above the claustrophobia of his class and yet is quite lost without the support structure of that class. Like Joe Lambton he must escape from his background and in the increasingly prosperous area of sport his talents allow him to do so.

Orwell's socialist working-class values, described in Chapter 3, are not in the forefront of these two films, but they provide instead the backdrop. In *This Sporting Life* we see sequences of staged rugby league games involving Machin against a backdrop of genuine footage showing the crowds from contemporary matches. This is the Yorkshire working-class that Orwell cherished and from which our characters are struggling to extricate themselves. Orwell's community-conscious working-class was beginning to fray seriously at the edges and the agents of change were the increased prosperity referred to earlier and the increasing social opportunities brought first by the war and then by the 1944 Education Act. Two of socialism's goals were slowly being achieved, then, but at the expense of the social cohesiveness and egalitarian values by which socialists like Orwell set so much store. This was the irony of traditional socialism in its northern heartland: its political and economic successes had begun to destroy the social cohesion that had promoted it.

The theme of social change and its consequences is addressed through the medium of individual human experience. Our leading characters are not typical in any sense, and yet they may be seen to embody something of the spirit of a new age. We share their individual triumphs and disasters but unlike them we are able to put their stories into the broader, more representative context of the 1960s.

Working-class values: the 1990s

The twenty years that followed witnessed the decline of all the major labour-intensive industries in the north of Britain. Yorkshire lost the Hull fishing industry in its entirety, a large part of its steel-making capacity, the heart of its textile industry and most of its pits, including even some of the most modern and productive. The vibrant, cocky world of Lambton and Machin was brought to its knees and even Yorkshire's fabled cricket team, the ultimate talisman and source of tribal pride, lost its habit of winning.[11] The importance of the latter should not be underestimated, for only Yorkshiremen could play for Yorkshire whereas other counties bought and sold in the transfer markets. In all respects then, including cricket, it seemed that by the 1980s the market economics of Conservative governments had done for Yorkshire and indeed for most of the north of Britain.

In his remarkable *Notes from a Small Island* the American Bill Bryson, who himself settled in Yorkshire, wrote:[12]

One of the great surprises to me upon moving north was the extent to which it felt like another country... Mostly what differentiated the North from the South ... was the exceptional sense of economic loss, of greatness passed ... If you draw a line between Bristol and the Wash, you divide the country into two halves with roughly 27 million people on each side. Between 1980 and 1985, in the southern half, they lost 103,600 jobs. In the northern half in the same period they lost 1,032,000, almost exactly ten times as many. And still the factories are shutting...

Much has been written about Thatcherism and its consequences but we shall restrict ourselves here to a few remarks by Andrew Gamble, one of its foremost critics.[13] The Thatcher governments, he tells us, were committed to the strengthening of market forces throughout society, to the 'rolling back of the state', in order to maximise economic efficiency and thus competitiveness. Labour as a commodity needed to be flexible. Thus the government abandoned the commitment to full employment, sold off public assets, privatised public corporations, broke the public service up into agencies some of which were privatised, reduced the increase in public expenditure and confronted the trade union movement, referring to its leaders as 'the enemy within'. The effects of all this in the north of Britain were dramatic. Thatcher laid waste to Yorkshire if not as systematically then certainly as effectively as William the Conqueror had done after the Norman Conquest. Had there been a Domesday Book compiled at the end of the twentieth century it would have said of much of the county what the original had said: 'hoc est vasta'. The social effects of Thatcherism were caught in a number of films[14] and we shall concentrate here on two, both set in Yorkshire, *Brassed Off* and *The Full Monty*. Both, unlike the two films just discussed, though they had an equally serious intent, were in fact comedies. Neither was based upon a novel and both are examples of popular cinema the impact of which is more overtly visual than the films we have just discussed. They are about ordinary people; their often strong and uncompromising language is unmistakably the language of ordinary people.

Brassed Off is a simple morality tale requiring us to accept an implausible story line and recognise that our heroes will be (mostly) good and heroic, our villains (mostly) evil and villainous and the weak (mostly) virtuous. The film tells the story of the community of Grimley, a small colliery town in the Yorkshire coalfield modelled on Grimethorpe (Orwell visited the coalface here, describing conditions there as 'fearful beyond description'[15]). It focuses particularly on two interlocking themes: the attempt of the Coal Board, on behalf of the Conservative government, to close the pit and the battle of the pit's brass band to win through for the first time ever to the Grand Finals to be held in London's Albert Hall. The bandsmen, we discover, are on the point of mutiny because money is short and they fear the pit's closure.

Enter a young woman, born in Grimley (and in fact the childhood sweetheart of Andy, one of the younger miners), who has trained as a quantity surveyor 'down South' and is working on the feasibility study which could save Grimley if the issue of closure were to go to an official review. She happens to be the granddaughter of a legendary miner and horn player, and by some helpful coincidence has inherited and plays her grandfather's horn. She is allowed to play with the band because she is 'one of them' and anyway turns out to be a superlative horn player. Later she admits to Andy that she is working 'for the bosses' but on the men's behalf, explaining that she could not tell this to the rest of the men because they would not understand. Andy replies that he does not understand either: the pit will not go to review because the men will vote by four to one to accept the management's enhanced redundancy package and the pit will close. She argues that he and those like him will surely vote against acceptance – so he must have hope. No, not hope, he replies: principles.[16] The decision to close the pit, he declares with absolute confidence, was taken at least two years ago 'while you were at College' (shorthand for 'down South': enemy territory).

Gloria's arrival saves the band from disintegration, much to the relief of the conductor Danny who believes that they have a genuine chance of winning through to the semi-finals in Halifax and then going on to contest the Grand Finals. But on the day that they win the semi-finals at Halifax's historic Piece Hall the result of the ballot is declared: the men have voted for acceptance of closure by four to one. There will be no review and so with closure, semi-final victory or no, the band will not now be able to afford their trip to the Finals in London. It is now that Danny's son, a trombonist in the band, discovers that his father has been rushed to hospital, dying. Phil is unable to bring himself to tell his father of the bandsmen's decision not to go to the Finals.

Meanwhile the disgraced Gloria, on discovering that her feasibility study had been nothing but a piece of window-dressing (just as Andy had predicted), hands in her notice and sells her car to make possible the band's trip to the Finals after all. At the Albert Hall the band plays with such grace and power as to win, and Danny, mysteriously up from his deathbed, makes a rousing speech in which he rejects the magnificent trophy on political grounds. The band exchanges the platform for the moral high ground, but just as the attendant is about to put the trophy away, one of the bandsmen comes back to take it. 'He said you were refusing it', says the attendant. 'Don't be so bloody soft!' And so the band heads back north having won a moral victory and the trophy.

The film can be seen to explore the themes that were elucidated by Orwell fifty years earlier concerning northern working-class values. First and most important is the strength and palpable sense of community amongst the miners, underpinned by the family structures. The film begins with lights strangely bobbing unconnectedly, which gradually identify themselves as the helmet lights of miners coming off shift; they are in fact very much connected. As they leave the pit they drive past their women, in makeshift shelters with the sign 'Victory to the Miners' printed in large letters. We hear a thin rendition of the great battle song from the strike of 1984: 'The mine-ers, unite-ed, will nev-er be de-feated'. We understand the irony: Thatcher was able to set miner upon miner and they were, all of them, decisively defeated.

The band is a symbol of Orwellian community values. As Danny tells them, the band has been going for 110 years: 'They can close the pit, take our jobs, but they'll never shut us up.' In truth Danny is far more than a spokesman for community values: his love of music is almost pathological. As their world crumbles around them, Danny still single-mindedly pursues a place in the Grand Finals, and when his son remonstrates on behalf of the band that there are more important things in life than music, he replies quite simply: 'Not in my life there isn't.' This idiosyncrasy is used to powerful effect when Phil, distraught at his father's fatal illness, his wife's desertion and his own recognition that penury will force him to vote for closure, spectacularly attempts his own life. Unsuccessful he is taken to the same hospital as his father who asks him if he has 'lost his marbles'. 'Maybe', Phil replies, 'I've lost everything else: wife, kids, house, job, self-respect, hope. But that's nowt is it dad? Cos it's music that matters.' Danny is devastated.

Later, when declining the trophy, Danny tells the Albert Hall audience that music doesn't matter, winning the Finals doesn't matter. The government, he says, had destroyed the coal industry, destroyed homes, lives and communities over the previous ten years. The Grimley pit has been closed with the loss of 1,000 jobs. But it isn't just jobs: it is the will to win, to fight, and to live that has been lost. 'If we were seals or whales it wouldn't be allowed to happen, but we're not. We're just ordinary, honest, decent human beings without hope.'

The sense of community value is captured by the miners' attitude to those who will vote for closure. Scabs are simply excommunicated. And yet the community has been so thoroughly eaten away by consumerism that the miners *know* that the vote against closure will be lost. The management has made them an offer few can refuse. Even Phil has no option but to vote for closure and when, after his suicide attempt, his mates collect him for a drink, he tells them how he voted. 'Drink wi' scabs, do you?' 'Come on Phil lad, stop being a drama queen and come and have a wet wi' us.' They understand the pressures; they know that Phil, one of them, has been broken. But he is still one of them. Here is the first major break with Orwell's socialist themes. The community and its values have been damaged perhaps beyond repair: not by the

Thatcherism of the 1980s but by the consumerism inaugurated in the 1960s. It gave the miners something to lose.

What of Orwellian family values? Phil's family life is a war zone. Orwell's long-suffering and accepting working-class wife and mother of *Coming Up for Air*, the eternal maker of Yorkshire puddings, has been replaced by an equally long-suffering but non-accepting individual, willing and able to act on her own behalf. Sandra, Phil's wife, hasn't enough money to survive, is unable, for example, to pay her bill at the Co-op, having added it up wrongly. Apologising to her friend at the counter she says: 'Me and sums – not best of friends. Me and money – total friggin' strangers.'

We discover that Phil played a prominent role in the 1984 strike and was jailed as a consequence. He had been out of work until eventually reinstated and their finances had never recovered. Their lives are shaped by poverty and by the millstone that even limited property ownership brings to them. Sandra can see only one way out of the morass: to vote for closure. 'Ain't life just shit!' she tells Phil. Like the community, the family has been eroded since Orwell's day. Set up by consumerism only to be floored by Thatcherism.

Phil's attempts to earn extra money as Coco the Clown at children's parties have a modest success, but one well-to-do hostess divines that clowning is not his full-time job. No, says Phil, he is a miner. 'You remember, love: dinosaurs, dodos…miners.' Phil uses his clowning money not to help Sandra and the children but to buy a better trombone for the band, to please his father, and on his return home finds the bailiff's men threatening to clear the house. He begs the men to wait until the vote. 'Oh aye, Coco the Scab is it?' Again, Orwell's prescient point: 'middle-class' people are simply not in a position to combine like the traditional working-class: they have mortgages to pay. When she discovers the receipt for the trombone, and the bailiff's men make a second appearance and strip the house, Sandra leaves, taking the children with her.

Women are a far stronger force in the Grimley community than they were in Orwell's North. Their strength is variously depicted: they 'man' the picket, they have a say in what their husbands do, and they are consulted. As Sandra shows, they are prepared to leave their men. On the other hand the miners, when driving past their wives at the picket, described their activities as pissing in the wind. 'Can they do that, women, piss in the wind?' No, it is agreed: but so much of what they do is equally ineffectual. Orwell would just about have recognised the women of Grimley. They contribute substantially to the community, but there are no women in the band before Gloria arrives and the lives of the miners revolve around the club, in which we see no women.

The centre of the community is the pit and its band wrapped around by the tribalism of Yorkshire about which Orwell wrote. When first Gloria comes to the band rehearsal Danny will not allow her to play. 'Sorry love, no outsiders.' But of course she is not an outsider. Later, when the victorious band, on its way home, passes the Houses of Parliament their rendition of 'Land of Hope and Glory' is intended ironically. There is no hope, still less glory in Grimley, and its people do not feel themselves to be represented in the Mother of Parliaments. In his final clowning appearance Phil – Coco the Scab – tells the children that when God created the world his angels told him that they had plenty of bodies left but no brains or hearts or vocal cords. ' "Stitch them up all the same", says God, "smack smiles on their faces and teach them to talk out of their arse". And so God created the Tory party.' The Conservative Party has always been predominantly the party of the south of England. In 1997 and again in 2001 not a single constituency in the Yorkshire industrial heartland (the People's Republic as it was known) was taken by the Tories. This was Yorkshire's small revenge on the party of Margaret Thatcher. But if the film celebrates the kind of values Orwell had written about it does so, to coin Andy's phrase, more as a gesture of principle than hope. The supreme irony is that although its brass band has won the Finals the community has lost its pit, its *raison d'être*, and is doomed.

Moving on now to *The Full Monty*, we become immediately aware of two major differences between small-town Grimley and cosmopolitan Sheffield. The community of Sheffield contains many blacks and Asians, and women are not only out of the kitchen but also into positions of economic power. The film opens with a short promotion film for the city of Sheffield, Yorkshire's second city (though not in its own eyes). It is described as 'the jewel in Yorkshire's crown'. 'Thanks to steel', we are told, 'Sheffield really is a city on the move.' We now advance twenty-five years to discover to where the city has moved. We are in an empty steel foundry where two young men, ex-steel workers, and a boy are trying to 'liberate' a girder worth £20 which will allow one of them, Gary (Gaz), to pay maintenance money so that he can continue to see Nathan, his son, who lives with his mother and her new partner. Suddenly they hear music: the brass band of the steelworks is marching past to rehearsal. 'Still going?' asks Gaz. 'Only thing that is', replies Dave. They find themselves locked in by the security guard and can only escape via the canal. They finish stranded on the top of an abandoned car in the canal, their girder fallen into the water.

164 of British Socialism

Soaked they trek home only to pass a group of young women queuing to go into what had been the working men's club but is now a nightclub hosting a performance by the Chippendales, the male strippers. Gaz offers the women his own sexual services when they tire of looking at 'them poofs' but discovers that Dave's wife is there to watch the show. Gaz attacks Dave for 'allowing' her to go and is not won over by the riposte that it's her money. Is Dave simply going to allow 'some poof to wave his tackle' in front of his wife? Where is his pride? So Gaz climbs in with Nathan to 'rescue' Dave's wife Jean. He finds himself in the former men's toilet and hides when three women, one of whom turns out to be Jean, come in. After a bout of 'laddish' behaviour one of them, to gales of laughter, uses the urinal like a man: 'I wasn't in the Girl Guides for nothing.' When this is later reported to the group of ex-steelworkers at the employment exchange the act is seen as symbolic. 'When they start pissing like us we're finished.' In a few years men will be obsolete, and they will simply have no use: 'like skateboards'. Dave proposes a counter argument: after all, the women were only at the club to see men, thus presumably reinforcing male dominance. But women have the money. The men are there to earn a living by pleasing them.

A revolution has taken place. The transformation of the economy, under way in Grimley with the collapse of labour-intensive industry, is near to completion in Sheffield where service industries, dominated by women, have replaced manufacture as the chief employer. Women earn the money. Both Gaz's and Dave's wives offer to find their men work, though both men consider the work to be beneath them: '£2.50 an hour in the Black Hole of Calcutta', says Gaz. Symbolically the men of Grimley note that their women cannot piss into the wind like men. In go-ahead Sheffield they can.

What of family life in Sheffield? One of the film's motifs is Gaz's attempt to keep contact with his son. His wife will be granted sole custody if he cannot meet maintenance payments of £700. How can he do that on the dole? Gaz likes to think of himself as a free spirit, but a free spirit that needs to find maintenance money so badly that he is driven to consider stripping. He is consumed by the love of his son. Another motif is Dave's relationship with Jean. Dave's loss of employment and hope has made him impotent. Rather than reject him his wife gives him every support, though as she tells her friends: 'Dave's given up. Work, me, everything.' But again, Sheffield had moved on from Orwell's Yorkshire and even from Grimley in the sense that it is not simply the standard family that is portrayed affectionately. After all, Gaz and his wife are separated yet he fights to retain the love of his son. The homosexual relationship that forms between two of the group is shown to be enriching and is fully accepted by the others.

Conversely the one relationship that fails to survive in any form is Gerald's and he is proudly middle-class: 'I've got standing, me.' Gerald goes home to discover his goods being repossessed. His wife, mortified that he had not told her of his redundancy at the steel foundry, throws him out. Their life is full of consumables that only separate them. They have a garden full of ornamental gnomes that each has bought the other, unaware that neither likes gnomes.

Dave and Gaz befriend Lomper, a security guard at the former steelworks, and between them hatch a plan to put on their own strip show in order to make money. Gaz and Lomper are driven by desperation; Dave, at first anyway, simply by friendship with Gaz. They need to involve their old foreman, the middle-class Gerald, who is an experienced ballroom dancer. He rejects Gaz's scheme as hare-brained, and anyway, he has an interview for a new job. They effectively ruin his job prospects, however, and he eventually throws in his lot with them: he badly needs the money. Gerald has his reservations but Gaz is persuasive: Gerald can teach them to dance and together – tribal pride here – they will do a Yorkshire version of the Chippendales. 'If them buggers can, we can!'

So they audition for additional performers and though they have at best a limited success, the project moves forward. Gerald has problems getting them into a routine but slowly they improve. Gaz decides to have posters printed and stuck up around Sheffield advertising 'Hot Metal – We Dare to Bare'. Some young women accost them – why should they bother to pay to see them when they can see the real thing? Because, says Gaz impulsively, we go all the way. His fellow performers immediately rebel: they will become a laughing stock. Wrong, says Gaz, 'nobody laughs at a man with £1,000 in his pocket'.

By now, however, everybody knows who they are; and the local headline reads 'Steel Strippers Exposed'. They discover that over 200 tickets have been sold and so decide to go ahead. Even Gerald, with his 'standing' and his new job, will participate, just the once. 'You've got the rest of your life to wear a suit', Gaz tells him. Dave, meanwhile, has told his wife what has been happening. What a stupid idea it was, he says; who would ever want to see him dance? But Jean is able to give him the necessary confidence by replying with such conviction: 'Me, Dave, I do.' The men turn up to the gig only to discover that what was to have been a women-only audience is in fact mixed, with many of their mates present. With huge misgivings, then, the five do their routine all the way to 'the full Monty'.

Why have a group of Yorkshire steelworkers, steeped in a culture of male dominance, taken to stripping in public? They have been pushed by loss of self-respect, loss of income, independence. For each it becomes a shared struggle against economic hardship – taking on the system together. For those who go to the show it is quite simply fun: but it is more, a community gesture of solidarity, truly a Yorkshire version of the Chippendales. This tribalism is far more inclusive than Grimley's. Sheffield is, after all, more cosmopolitan, more used to incomers. The community is clearly multiracial and has no problems recognising differing sexual orientations: you might be black or Asian, you might be 'queer', but you are working-class and you are Yorkshire, and these are the things that really matter. But you are expected to fit in. Orwell wrote that the northern working-class found that those who earned a lot of money were actually figures of fun[17] and it is in this egalitarian sense that communal tribalism dominates the film.

If the film ends in what some critics have described as a magnificent gesture of triumph we would have to be blind not to recognise the ironic reality of the broader canvas depicting a much more encompassing defeat. That final *reductio ad absurdum* represents the eclipse of the North's greatness as a centre of manufacture; it represents the eclipse of men as the dominant force in society. In their place come the service and entertainment industries and dominance by women. This is the end of Orwell's working-class value system, even if it does go down with a fight. In parenthesis, this story is not a triumph for femininity over masculinity. These women could be said to have usurped masculinity. They piss like men.

We may conclude this analysis of film by noting that Orwell proved an insightful guide to the values of the communities that the films depict. The later films appear to depict the two communities brought to their knees by Thatcherism. From the earlier films, though, we recognise that the softening-up process owed everything to growing affluence. Just as Orwell predicted, affluence threatened the social cohesion and thus political influence of these communities through the 1980s and 1990s. Thatcherism, in so far as it removed from the state any obligation to protect the ailing industries of the North (and elsewhere), provided only the *coup de grâce*. In 1972 the National Union of Mineworkers brought down a Conservative government; in 1984 Thatcher exacted her very well planned revenge. Between 1984 and 1994, 140 pits were closed with the direct loss of one quarter of a million jobs.

There remains one element of northern working-class life that Orwell referred to without developing but which the two 1990s films allow to unfold with skill and affection. What sustained the miners of Grimley and the steelworkers of Sheffield was not just the strength of family and community life, the tribal pride and the feeling of equality, but also a triumphant sense of humour which somehow allowed them to hang on to that notion of common decency which had been so influential in shaping Orwell's politics and indeed the politics of what these days is dismissively called 'Old Labour'. But that was all they hung on to. As Danny said in his Albert Hall speech, they had lost everything else. Orwell's last desperate belief was that if there was any hope for the future (for his kind of socialism) it lay with the proles. But the proles were last seen 'taking their kit off' for £1,000 in a Sheffield pub.

Conclusions

Brassed Off and *The Full Monty* were both popular and successful films, not only in the United Kingdom, and they enjoyed considerable critical acclaim. They provoked a strong response wherever they were shown. Going to a film, like going to see a play, is a communal experience and so can often be a more direct and intense one than reading a book.[18] Moreover cinema reaches a wider audience even than literature and can thus provoke more discussion and a more general response at least in the short term. It is undoubtedly the case that cinema can influence politics. If one were seeking to account for the growth of Scottish national sentiment in the 1990s, for example, the effect of the film *Braveheart* could not be ignored. But films should not be thought of as rivals to books. In seeking to understand *Brassed Off*, for example, we may well be drawn towards, not away from, literature: *Wigan Pier* or *Love on the Dole* are likely to come down off the shelf for a reread. Indeed it is generally well-established that the filming of a novel will increase sales of that novel, often coaxing out a new edition.

What finally of the argument that those, like the average student of politics, who have no knowledge of the complexities of the cinema as process or art form cannot, without first acquiring that knowledge, benefit from studying film? It would be odd to suggest that an understanding of the processes and techniques of film-making and of cinema as a form of narrative could be anything other than an advantage to the students of politics trying to understand film, but a lack of such knowledge should not constitute a barrier. Good films are not made primarily for cinema critics, just as good books are not written primarily for professors of English literature. Both are produced, at least in the main, to communicate with ordinary people.

The films we have considered in this chapter help us to understand part of the decline of traditional socialism as a political force in the United Kingdom. Set in the heartland of that ideology and among the kind of people who gave it such strength as a political force, we can gain an understanding of part of the processes of decay. Orwell's socialism constituted a value system that not merely drew strength from the economic and social disadvantage of its principal adherents but actually required that disadvantage in order to thrive. Orwellian socialism was vulnerable to programmes of economic and social improvement just as statist socialism was vulnerable to monopolistic inefficiencies. The Labour Party's success in pursuing welfare policies that made life better for many (but not all) and at the same time in controlling major labour-intensive manufacturing and service industries (nominally) in the interests of the workers were to prove the undoing of socialism. It created a world that idealists like Jimmy Porter in *Look Back in Anger*[19] detested because of its self-evident failures but a world that nevertheless positively encouraged working-class children to forsake their class.

In the mid-1970s even Labour Party leaders were acknowledging that the days of the postwar Keynesian consensus were over. Chancellor of the Exchequer Denis Healey called for sweeping cuts in public expenditure and even the Keynesian Secretary of State for the Environment Anthony Crosland told local authorities that 'the party's over'.[20] By this time traditional working-class communities were as unable to resist the tide of economic liberalism as were socialist intellectuals to construct a credible collectivist alternative economic strategy. Socialism as both an ideology and a political force was always more than an expression of working-class interests and values. Nevertheless much of its intellectual and moral strength came from and was nourished by this class base. That momentous meeting of workers and socialists in Bradford in 1893 out of which the Labour Party eventually came[21] created a political force that never established itself independently of that base and an ideology that always owed it loyalty. What the psephologists refer to as class dealignment,[22] so clearly inimical to socialism for precisely this reason, was in part the indirect consequence of the success of Labour governments, especially that of the 1945–50 Attlee government.

On the strength of the examples considered in this Postscript, film as a narrative form proves well-suited to depicting the effect of events or developments such as political and social change on communities and individuals. It has a directness that speaks to the audience but can also invoke a subtlety and pathos that render scenes and characters unforgettable. We began by hypothesising that what film could not easily provide was the kind of intellectual or ideational context to its stories that was part and parcel of imaginative literature. To get the most out of a film, then, we have to take in quite a lot in the way of intellectual background. Yet this is why our brief foray into film suggests that it is a particularly appropriate medium for an age that abjures metanarratives. When Margaret Thatcher declared that there was no such thing as society she brought the curtain down on British socialism as a viable political movement at least for the foreseeable future. Our films show the working-class, backbone of the Labour Party and residue of Orwellian hope, weakened by affluence, broken by neo-liberalism, finally exiting stage left, naked, with a song. A more powerful narrative of the decline of working-class socialism would be difficult to imagine.

Notes

1 Narrative and Politics

1. I shall not attempt to define narrative in any detail but instead take Sterne's option in *Tristram Shandy*. Tristram defines a nose as a nose – 'nothing more or less' (p. 225). Thomas M. Leitch points out that we all know what stories are – fortunately – 'for it is excessively difficult to say just what they are' (*What Stories Are: Narrative Theory and Interpretation* (University Park and London: Pennsylvania State University Press, 1986) p. 3). For present purposes narrative and imaginative literature will generally be used synonymously, though in the Postscript of this study we will also be considering film as a narrative form.
2. Hoggart, Richard, *Speaking to Each Other*, Vol. 2, *About Literature* (London: Chatto & Windus, 1970) p. 19.
3. Auden, W.H., 'The American Scene', in *The Dyers Hand* (London: Faber & Faber, 1948) p. 313.
4. Hoggart, *Speaking to Each Other*, p. 19.
5. Leavis, F.R., *The Common Pursuit* (London: Chatto & Windus, 1958) p. 198.
6. Sartre, J.-P., *What is Literature?* (London: Methuen University Paperback, 1967) p. 124.
7. Charques, R.D., *Contemporary Literature and Social Revolution* (London: Martin Secker, 1933) p. 5.
8. Whitebrook, Maureen, 'Politics and Literature', *Politics*, 15(1) (1955) 55–62.
9. Barker, Rodney, *Political Ideas in Modern Britain* (London: Methuen, 1978).
10. Arblaster, Anthony, *The Rise and Decline of Western Liberalism* (Oxford: Blackwell, 1984).
11. Johnson, Peter, *Politics, Innocence and the Limits of Goodness* (London: Routledge, 1989).
12. Quin, Kenneth, *How Literature Works* (London: Palgrave Macmillan, 1992).
13. Quin, *How Literature Works*, p. 9.
14. Doctor Johnson is quoted as remarking: 'Great abilities … are not required for an Historian; for in historical composition, all the greatest powers of the human mind are quiescent. He has facts only to his hand; so there is no exercise of invention. Imagination is not required in any high degree … Some penetration, accuracy and colouring will fit a man for the task, if he can give the application which is necessary' (*Boswell's Johnson* (London: Cygnet Classics, 1968) p. 46).
15. Eagleton, Terry, 'The Rise of English', in Dennis Walder (ed.), *Literature in the Modern World* (Oxford: Oxford University Press, 1990) p. 25.
16. Eagleton, Terry, 'Marxist Criticism', in John Barrell (ed.), *Poetry, Language and Politics* (Manchester: Manchester University Press, 1988) p. 208.
17. Hirsch, E.D., Jnr, 'The Babel of Interpretation', in Walder (ed.), *Literature in the Modern World*, p. 64.
18. Quin, *How Literature Works*, p. 18.
19. Quin, *How Literature Works*, p. 20.

20. Orwell, George, 'Why I Write', *Decline of the English Murder and Other Essays* (Harmondsworth: Penguin, 1965 edn).
21. Quin, *How Literature Works*, p. 93.
22. Crick, Bernard, *George Orwell: A Life* (London: Secker & Warburg, 1980) p. 85.
23. Forster, E.M., 'Anonymity: An Enquiry', in *Two Cheers for Democracy* (London: Edward Arnold, 1951) p. 89.
24. Mellor, D.H., 'On Literary Truth', *Ratio*, 10 (1968) 150–68. My italics.
25. Auerbach, Eric, *Mimesis* (Princeton, NJ: Princeton University Press, 1968) p. 496.
26. Clark, Margaret, 'The Politics of Literature', *British Review of New Zealand Studies*, 7 (1994) 18–29.
27. Benjamin, Walter, 'Theses on the Philosophy of History', in Hannah Arendt (ed.), *Illuminations* (New York: Schoken Books, 1969) p. 159.
28. Rorty, Richard, *Contingency, Irony and Solidarity* (Cambridge: Cambridge University Press, 1989) p. 7.
29. Fischer, Michael, in Alan Malachowski, *Reading Rorty* (Oxford: Basil Blackwell, 1990) p. 241.
30. From his poem 'I am', *Selected Poems of John Clare 1793–1864* (Leeds: E.J. Arnold and Son, 1964) p. 70.
31. See for example Ingle, Stephen, *George Orwell: A Political Life* (Manchester: Manchester University Press, 1993) ch. 4.
32. Auerbach, *Mimesis*, p. 353.
33. Lukacs, Georg, 'The Ideology of Modernism', in John Barrell (ed.), *Poetry, Language and Politics* (Manchester: Manchester University Press, 1988).
34. Lukacs, 'Modernism', p. 81.
35. Quin, 'How Literature Works', p. 212.
36. Extract from a radio interview (1990) quoted in Lukacs, 'Modernism', p. 210.
37. Lukacs, 'Modernism', p. 103.
38. Charques, *Contemporary Literature and Social Revolution*, p. 51.
39. Woolf, Rosemary, *Art and Doctrine: Essays on Medieval Literature* (London: Hambleton Press, 1986) p. 196.
40. Golding, William, *Rites of Passage* (London: Faber & Faber, 1980).
41. Orwell, George, 'Inside the Whale', *Collected Essays, Journalism and Letters* (*CEJL*) (London: Secker & Warburg, 1968) Vol. 1, pp. 493–526.
42. Orwell, George, 'Charles Dickens', *CEJL*, Vol. 1, pp. 413–59.
43. Julien Benda, *La Trahison des clercs* (Paris: Grasset, 1927) *passim*.
44. We might wish to distinguish, in this debate, between 'literature' and propaganda. In the latter we may assume that the writer is concerned to promulgate the virtues of one of Orwell's 'smelly little orthodoxies' and is not concerned primarily with communicating an aesthetic experience. The study of propaganda is as important as it is interesting but I am not concerned with it here. More problematical for my argument is the writer or producer of 'faction' or documentary where essentially a story or an account is portrayed as literally true. As we will see from the example of Jack London's work, this can be a literary exercise but only on certain conditions. I have said that literal or historical truth is secondary to the enterprise of narrative but in some cases the intention might be to transmit an experience that is intentionally or unintentionally based on a historical untruth. This becomes particularly contentious when the subject of the story is recent, for example the two television films

that appeared in 2002 to commemorate the events of 1972 in Derry/ Londonderry known as Bloody Sunday. Neither of the two documentaries, Paul Greengrass's *Bloody Sunday* or Jimmy McGovern's *Sunday*, could be said to have aimed for impartiality but the latter was considered by *The Times* critic Jo Joseph to 'repeatedly sacrifice dramatic complexity for argumentative certainty'. Joseph considered that McGovern was 'so busy assigning blame, and assuring us that all is fact and nothing fiction', that the drama suffers.

For those who believe there is no truth, only 'truths', this is not a problem. Yet we might agree that if a writer or film-maker *chooses* to say something about recent historical events they should at least not knowingly lie, or even pretend to knowledge that they do not have. We may be confident that if their portrayal of events *is* clearly historically flawed or prejudiced it is not, as Joseph hints, likely to achieve more than a passing influence.

45. Quoted in Belsey, C., *Critical Practice* (London: Methuen, 1980) p. 13.
46. Eagleton, 'The Rise of English', p. 23.
47. For example, Quin, *How Literature Works*, pp. 55–63.
48. In an interview published in *The Times Higher Educational Supplement*, 26 July 1996.
49. See Jauss, Robert, 'Literary History as a Challenge to Literary Theory', in Walder Dennis (ed.), *Literature*, p. 73.
50. Crosland, C.A.R., *The Future of Socialism* (London: Cape, 1956).

2 'The Terrible Stone Face'

1. London, Jack, *The People of the Abyss* (London: The Journeyman Press, 1977).
2. See Hynes, Samuel, *The Edwardian Turn of Mind* (London: Oxford University Press, 1968) pp. 18–22.
3. London, *The People of the Abyss*, pp. 24–5.
4. Shaw, Bernard, *Mrs Warren's Profession* in *Plays Unpleasant* (Harmondsworth: Penguin, 1972 edn) p. 247.
5. Shaw, *Widowers' Houses*, in *Plays Unpleasant* (Harmondsworth: Penguin, 1972 edn) p. 59.
6. Shaw, *Widowers' Houses*, p. 71.
7. Shaw, Bernard, Preface to *Widowers' Houses*, pp. 25–6.
8. This attack was in *St James' Gazette* and is quoted in the Preface to *Mrs Warren's Profession, Plays Unpleasant*, p. 201.
9. Wells, H.G., *The Wife of Sir Isaac Harman* (London: Odhams, 1914) esp. p. 193.
10. Shaw, Bernard, *Major Barbara* (Harmondsworth: Penguin, 1972 edn) p. 88.
11. Shaw, *Major Barbara*, p. 97.
12. Shaw, *Major Barbara*, p. 142.
13. Morrison, Arthur, *A Child of the Jago* (Harmondsworth: Penguin, 1946).
14. Keating, P.J., *The Working Classes in Victorian Fiction* (London: Routledge & Kegan Paul, 1971).
15. Quoted in Keating, *Victorian Fiction*, p. 83.
16. Tressell, Robert, *The Ragged Trousered Philanthropists* (St Albans: Panther, 1972).
17. See Ball, F.C., *One of the Damned* (London: Weidenfeld & Nicolson, 1973).
18. Tressell, *The Philanthropists*, p. 227.
19. Quoted in London, *The People of the Abyss*, p. 123.

20. Sassoon, Siegfried, 'Memoirs of an Infantry Officer', in *The Complete Memoirs of George Sherston* (London: Faber, 1972).
21. Orwell, George, *The Road to Wigan Pier* (Harmondsworth: Penguin, 1965 edn) pp. 16–17.
22. Greenwood, Walter, *Love on the Dole* (Harmondsworth: Penguin, 1975 edn) p. 50.
23. Booth, Charles, *Life and Labour of the People in London* (London: Palgrave Macmillan, 1892–7) 10 vols.
24. Rowntree, B. Seebohm, *Poverty: A Study of Town Life* (London: Palgrave Macmillan, 1902).
25. Hynes, *The Edwardian Turn of Mind*, p. 54.
26. Silone, Ignazio, *Fontamara* (London: Journeyman Press, 1975).
27. Brady, Frank (ed.), *Boswell's Life of Johnson* (London: Signet Classics, 1968) p. 297.
28. Gissing, Algernon and Ellen, *Letters of George Gissing to Members of His Family* (London, 1927) p. 169.
29. Hardy, Thomas, *Jude the Obscure* (London: Macmillan, 1972 edn) p. 337.
30. Hardy, *Jude the Obscure*, p. 125.
31. Swingewood, Alan, *The Novel and Revolution* (London: Palgrave Macmillan, 1975) p. 129.
32. Gissing, George, *The Nether World* (Brighton: Harvester, 1974) p. 109.
33. Gissing, *The Nether World*, p. 113.
34. Goode, John, Introduction to Gissing, *The Nether World*, p. vii.
35. Spencer, Herbert, *The Man versus the State* (London: Watts, 1950) *passim*.
36. Especially *The Hope of Pessimism*. See Gardner, P.L., *Schopenhauer* (Harmondsworth: Penguin, 1971).
37. *Saturday Review*, 21 August 1886, p. 261.
38. H.G. Wells, *Kipps, The Story of a Simple Soul* (London: Palgrave Macmillan, 1926) p. 393. First published 1905.
39. Goode, John, 'Gissing, Morris and English Socialism', *Victorian Studies* (December 1968) 201–26.
40. Wells, H.G., *Tono Bungay* (London: Macmillan, 1909).
41. Wells, *Tono Bungay*, p. 108. My italics.
42. Wells, *Tono Bungay*, p. 108. My italics.
43. Wells, H.G., *The New Machiavelli* (London: John Lane, 1911).
44. The very antithesis of the 'Socialism' of the infant Labour Party (Book 3, ch. 8).
45. Well, H.G., *A Modern Utopia* (London: Chapman & Hall, 1905) offers a picture of a world run according to these principles by a self-selective aristocracy, the samurai. We shall be considering the samurai in more detail in Chapter 6.
46. Wells, H.G., *War of the Worlds* (London: Heinemann, 1898).
47. Wells, H.G., *The Time Machine* (London: Heinemann, 1895).
48. Wells, H.G., *First Men on the Moon* (London: Newnes, 1901).
49. Wells, H.G., *Food of the Gods* (Clinton, Mass.: Airmont Classics Series, 1965), first published 1904.
50. Shaw writes expressly on the inefficiencies of capitalism in *Everybody's Political What's What* (London: Constable, 1944) ch. XVIII.
51. These arguments are set out in Shaw's *Intelligent Woman's Guide to Socialism, Capitalism, Sovietism and Fascism* (London: Constable, 1949 edn) pp. 374–7.
52. Priestley, J.B., The *Edwardians* (London: Heinemann, 1970) p. 57.

3 Power to the People?

1. I have explored these differences in respect of two prominent Victorian socialists, William Morris and Bernard Shaw, and have tried to explore the ramifications of these differing interpretations for their politics. See Ingle, Stephen, 'Socialist Man: William Morris and Bernard Shaw', in B.C. Parekh (ed.), *Concepts of Socialism* (London: Croom Helm, 1975) pp. 72–95.
2. This is, of course, an oversimplification but it allows a fundamental distinction to be made, delineating on the one hand those who see socialism as representing a complex system to be run for the good of all by a trained elite and those for whom the greatest good is to create a system which incorporates and allows to flourish the values of ordinary men and women. I have pursued this distinction in more depth in my book *The British Party System*, 3rd edn (London: Pinter, 1999) ch. 5.
3. Pearson, Hesketh, *Bernard Shaw: His Life and Personality* (London: Methuen, 1961) p. 68.
4. Shaw, George Bernard, *Essays in Fabian Socialism* (London: Constable, 1932) p. 131.
5. Quoted in Adam, Ruth, *What Shaw Said* (London: MacDonald, 1966) p. 57.
6. Harris, Frank, *Bernard Shaw, an Unauthorized Biography* (London: Gollancz, 1931) p. 5.
7. Speech given on 26 March 1914, quoted in Chappelow, Alan, *Shaw 'The Chucker Out'* (London: Allen & Unwin, 1969) p. 288.
8. Shaw, George Bernard, *Bodley Head Collected Plays of Bernard Shaw* (London: Bodley Head, 1951) Vol. X, p. 210.
9. Shaw, *Essays in Fabian Socialism*, p. 158.
10. From *Time and Tide*, 2 February 1945, quoted in Chappelow, *The Chucker Out*, p. 321.
11. Chappelow, *The Chucker Out*, p. 322.
12. Preface to *The Apple Cart*, in Shaw, Bernard, *Plays Political* (Harmondsworth: Penguin, 1986) p. 22.
13. Shaw, Bernard, *Intelligent Woman's Guide to Socialism, Capitalism, Sovietism and Fascism* (London: Constable, 1949 edn) pp. 452–3.
14. Shaw, Bernard, *Major Barbara* (Harmondsworth: Penguin, 1972 edn) p. 142.
15. Hulse, James W., *Revolutionists in London – a Study of Five Unorthodox Socialists* (Oxford: Clarendon Press, 1970) p. 113.
16. *Cosmopolis*, 3 (September 1896) 659.
17. Shaw, *Major Barbara*, p. 142.
18. Quoted in Chappelow, *The Chucker Out*, p. 197.
19. A draft for a radio talk, quoted in Chappelow, *The Chucker Out*, p. 199.
20. Letter to R. Page Arnott, 5 November 1947.
21. Wells, H.G., *New Worlds for Old* (London: Constable, 1908) p. 22.
22. Wells, H.G., *New Worlds for Old*, p. 26.
23. Mackenzie, Norman and Jean, *The Time Traveller* (London: Weidenfeld & Nicolson, 1973) p. 267.
24. Wells, H.G., 'Discovery of the Future', *Nature*, 6 February 1902.
25. West, Anthony, the son of Wells and Rebecca West, wrote a biography of his father entitled *H.G. Wells: Aspects of a Life* (New York: Random House, 1984).

26. Wells, H.G., *The Island of Doctor Moreau* (Harmondsworth: Penguin, 1971) p. 198. First published 1898.
27. Wells, H.G., *Shape of Things to Come* (London: Hutchinson, 1933) p. 262.
28. Dennis, Norman and Halsey, A.H., *English Ethical Socialism* (Oxford: Oxford University Press, 1988).
29. Dennis and Halsey, *English Ethical Socialism*, p. 6.
30. See Davis, Lawrence, 'Morris, Wilde, and Marx on the Social Conditions of Individual Development', *Political Studies*, XLIV (1996) pp. 719–32.
31. Morris, William, 'Art Under Plutocracy', in Morton, A.L. (ed.), *Political Writings of William Morris* (London: Lawrence & Wishart, 1973). All essays subsequently referred to are taken from this edition.
32. Morris, William, 'Art and Socialism'.
33. Morris, William, *News from Nowhere*, in Morton A.L. (ed.), *Three Works by William Morris* (London: Lawrence & Wishart, 1973) p. 269.
34. Hall, Stuart, 'The Question of Cultural Identity', in his edited collection *Modernity and its Futures* (Cambridge: Polity Press, 1992) pp. 273–316.
35. See 'The English People', *Collected Essays, Journalism and Letters (CEJL)* (London: Secker & Warburg, 1968) Vol. 3, pp. 1–37.
36. 'The Art of Donald McGill', *CEJL*, Vol. 3, pp. 155–64.
37. Orwell, George, *The Road to Wigan Pier* (Harmondsworth: Penguin, 1963 edn) p. 104. The political importance of family was emphasised, too, by Solzhenitsyn, who says of his peasant Spiridion in *First Circle* (New York: Bantam Books, 1968, p. 461):

> His country was – family
> His religion was – family
> Socialism was – family.

38. Review of *Caliban Shrieks* by Jack Hilton, *CEJL*, Vol. 1, pp. 148–50.
39. Letter to Cyril Connolly dated 8 June 1937, *CEJL*, Vol. 1, pp. 280–2.
40. Orwell, *Wigan Pier*, pp. 156–62.
41. Bellow, Saul, *Mr Sammler's Planet* (London: Weidenfeld & Nicolson, 1970). Mr Sammler is an expert in the field of imaginative writers and politics and has studied a number of the authors with whom we deal here.
42. See 'London Letter' to Partisan Review, *CEJL*, Vol. 4, pp. 185–90.
43. Eco, Umberto, *The Name of the Rose* (London: Picador, 1984) pp. 205–6.
44. See 'Notes on the Way', *CEJL*, Vol. 2, pp. 15–18.
45. See 'As I Please', *Tribune*, 3 March 1944.
46. See Ingle, Stephen, *George Orwell*, pp. 108–13.
47. Quoted in Jackson, Robert Louis, *Dialogues with Dostoevsky* (Stanford, Calif.: Stanford University Press, 1993) pp. 296–7.
48. See, for example, Pearson, Geoffrey, *Hooligan: A History of Respectable Fears* (Basingstoke: Palgrave Macmillan, 1983).
49. Huxley, Aldous, *Point Counter Point* (Harmondsworth: Penguin, 1971) p. 59.
50. Greene, Graham, *Brighton Rock* (London: Heinemann Bodley Head, 1970).
51. Plant, Raymond, 'Antonyms of Modernist Political Thought: Reasoning, Context and Community', in James Good and Irving Velody (eds), *The Politics of Post Modernity* (Cambridge: Cambridge University Press, 1998) p. 77.

52. Orwell, George, *Coming Up for Air* (Harmondsworth: Penguin, 1986 edn).
53. Orwell, *Coming Up for Air*, pp. 9–11.
54. Orwell, *Coming Up for Air*, pp. 140–1.
55. Orwell, *Coming Up for Air*, p. 11.
56. Orwell, *Coming Up for Air*, p. 23.
57. Orwell, *Coming Up for Air*, p. 40.
58. Orwell, *Coming Up for Air*, p. 66.
59. Orwell, *Coming Up for Air*, p. 112.
60. Houllebecq, Michel, *Atomised* (London: Vintage, 2001) p. 201.
61. Orwell, *Coming Up for Air*, p. 192.
62. Orwell, *Coming Up for Air*, pp. 213–14.
63. Orwell, 'Charles Dickens', *The Penguin Essays of George Orwell* (Harmondsworth: Penguin, 1994) pp. 35–78.
64. Gissing, George, *Demos: A Story of English Socialism* (Brighton: Harvester Press, 1972).
65. Henry Straker was the chauffeur of John Tanner, the central character of Shaw's *Man and Superman*.
66. Lawrence F. Kaplan argues along very similar lines, though naturally his model for the development of modern China was not expressly a Shavian one. See 'China and Freedom', in *Prospect*, 67 (October 2001) 28–33.

4   Narrative and the Sword

1. Harding, Neil, 'Socialism and Violence', in B.C. Parekh (ed.), *The Concept of Socialism* (London: Groom Helm, 1975) p. 204.
2. Sorel set these ideas out most fully in *Reflections on Violence*, Jeremy Jennings, ed. (Cambridge: Cambridge University Press, 2000). The book was first published in 1908. For a full discussion of his theories see Roth, Jack J., *The Cult of Violence: Sorel and the Sorelians* (London: University of California Press, 1980).
3. Harding, 'Socialism and Violence', p. 209.
4. See Fanon's *The Wretched of the Earth* (London: MacGibbon & Kee, 1965).
5. Quoted in Cleaver, Eldridge, *Post-Prison Writings and Speeches* (London: Panther Books, 1971) p. 55.
6. Orwell, George, *Homage to Catalonia* (Harmondsworth: Penguin, 1966) p. 119.
7. Quoted in Chappelow, Alan, *Shaw 'The Chucker Out'* (London: Allen & Unwin, 1969) p. 181.
8. Orwell, George, 'Catastrophic Gradualism', *CEJL*, 4, pp. 15–19. For a full examination of Orwell's attitude to revolution, see Ingle, Stephen, ch. 4, 'The World Set Free', in *George Orwell: A Political Life* (Manchester: Manchester University Press, 1992) pp. 57–82.
9. See Hampshire, Stuart, *Public and Private Morality* (London: Cambridge University Press, 1978) p. 50.
10. Although a great deal has been written on this subject, Steve Buckler's *Dirty Hands: The Problem of Political Morality* (Aldershot: Avebury Press, 1993) provides a very useful review.
11. Sartre, Jean-Paul, *Crime Passionel* (English translation; London: Methuen World Classics, 1961), first published in 1949, p. 95.

12. See Walzer, M., 'Political Action: The Problem of Dirty Hands', in Marshall Cohen *et al.* (eds), *War and Moral Responsibility* (London: Princeton University Press, 1972) p. 65.
13. Walzer, 'Political Action: The Problem of Dirty Hands', p. 65.
14. See Smart, J.J.C. and Williams, Bernard, *Utilitarianism For and Against* (London: Cambridge University Press, 1973).
15. Kant's position is set out in Weldon, T.D., *Kant's Critique of Pure Reason* (Oxford: Clarendon Press, 1958).
16. Berki, R.N., 'Machiavellism: A Philosophical Defence', *Ethics*, 81 (1970–71) pp. 107–17.
17. Orwell, George, *Homage to Catalonia* (Harmondsworth: Penguin, 1962), first published 1938.
18. Nagel, Thomas, 'War and Massacre', in Cohen *et al.* (eds), *War and Moral Responsibility*, p. 22.
19. Reported in *Daily Telegraph*, 19 October 1997.
20. For example, McKee, Patricia, *Public and Private: Gender, Class and the British Novel* (Minneapolis: University of Minnesota Press, 1997).
21. See Goodwin, Robert E., 'Utility and the Good', in Peter Singer (ed.), *A Companion to Ethics* (Oxford: Blackwell, 1991), pp. 241–8.
22. Hampshire, *Public and Private Morality*, p. 49.
23. Machiavelli, N., *The Discourses*, Vol. I (Harmondsworth: Penguin, 1970) ch. 9, p. 139.
24. Warren, Robert Penn, *All the King's Men* (New York: Bantam Books, 1951) p. 393. First published 1946. My italics.
25. Huxley, Aldous, *Grey Eminence* (London: Triad Paperbacks, 1982), first published 1944.
26. See Holland, R.F., *Against Empiricism: On Education, Epistemology and Value* (Oxford: Blackwell, 1980) esp. ch. 9.
27. Koestler, Arthur, *The Gladiators* (London: Hutchinson, 1965), first published 1939.
28. Koestler, Arthur, *Darkness at Noon* (Harmondsworth: Penguin, 1964), first published 1940.
29. Koestler, Arthur, *Arrival and Departure* (Harmondsworth, Penguin, 1969), first published 1943.
30. Koestler, *The Gladiators*, p. 125.
31. Koestler, *The Gladiators*, p. 51.
32. Koestler, *The Gladiators*, p. 293.
33. Koestler, *The Gladiators*, p. 319.
34. Koestler, *The Gladiators*, p. 223.
35. Ezard, John, *The Guardian*, 4 March 1983.
36. Koestler, *Darkness at Noon*, pp. 40–1.
37. Gramsci, Antonio, *Selections from the Prison Notebook* (London: Lawrence & Wishart, 1971) pp. 125–40.
38. Koestler, *Darkness at Noon*, p. 122.
39. Koestler, *Darkness at Noon*, p. 124.
40. Koestler, *Darkness at Noon*, p. 189.
41. Koestler, *Darkness at Noon*, p. 206.
42. Crossman, Richard (ed.), *The God That Failed* (London: Hamish Hamilton, 1950).

43. Crossman, *The God That Failed*, pp. 69–70.
44. Crossman, *The God That Failed*, p. 77.
45. Crossman, *The God That Failed*, p. 81.
46. Koestler, Arthur, *The Yogi and the Commissar* (London: Jonathan Cape, 1945).
47. The original was written in 1942; this second essay was written two years later and is included in the same volume.
48. Orwell referred to Spartacus as the prototypical revolutionary leader, *Collected Essays, Journalism and Letters* (London: Secker & Warburg, 1968) Vol. 3, p. 237.
49. Djilas, Milovan, *The New Class: An Analysis of the Communist System* (London: Allen & Unwin, 1966) p. 162.
50. Morris, William, *News from Nowhere*, in A.L. Morton (ed.), *Three works by William Morris* (London: Lawrence & Wishart, 1973) pp. 286–317.
51. Morris, *News from Nowhere*, pp. 310–11.
52. Morris, *News from Nowhere*, p. 314.
53. Morris, *News from Nowhere*, p. 317.
54. Morris, *News from Nowhere*, p. 310.
55. London, Jack, *The Iron Heel* (London: Everett, 1912).
56. Orwell, George, *Homage to Catalonia* (Harmondsworth: Penguin, 1966).
57. Orwell, 'Looking Back on the Spanish War', *Homage to Catalonia*, p. 239.
58. The egalitarianism of *Nowhere*, by contrast, is underpinned by the fact that the community produces only to meet observable, measurable community needs. Morris made it abundantly clear that in seeking to maintain equality in its widest application he would be willing to sacrifice the chance of a better standard of living. Snowball has no such qualms.
59. An obvious parallel to the debate between Stalin and Trotsky over worldwide revolution versus socialism in one country, the debate in which Koestler's Bogrov took the losing side.
60. Hyndman, H.M., *Record of an Adventurous Life* (London: Macmillan, 1911) p. 432.
61. See Rorty, Richard, 'The Last Intellectual in Europe', in *Contingency, Irony and Solidarity* (Cambridge: Cambridge University Press, 1989) pp. 169–88.
62. Quoted by Wolf, Leonard, in C.M. Joad, *Shaw and Society* (London: Odhams, 1953) p. 44.
63. Malraux, André, *Man's Estate* (Harmondsworth: Penguin, 1975) p. 167.
64. Huxley, Aldous, *Eyeless in Gaza* (Harmondsworth: Penguin, 1972) p. 207.

5 Narrative and the Law

1. Shaw, George Bernard, *Essays in Fabian Socialism* (London: Constable, 1932) pp. 235–6.
2. Prodi, Romano, *Europe As I See It* (Cambridge: Polity Press, 2000). Translated by Allan Cameron.
3. See 'The Revolutionist's Handbook' in *Prefaces by Bernard Shaw* (London: Odhams Press, 1938) pp. 167–95.
4. Wilson, E., *The Triple Thinkers* (London: Oxford University Press, 1939) p. 241.
5. Wilson, *The Triple Thinkers*, p. 240.
6. This argument is developed fully in Chappelow, Alan, *Shaw 'The Chucker Out'* (London: Allen & Unwin, 1969) pp. 104–29.

7. For an account of this debate see Holroyd, Michael, *Bernard Shaw: The Pursuit of Power*, Vol. 2 (London: Chatto & Windus, 1989) pp. 257–9.
8. Shaw, *Essays in Fabian Socialism*, pp. 235–6.
9. See Harrison, Brian, *The Transformation of British Politics 1860–1995* (Oxford: Oxford University Press, 1996) pp. 70–2.
10. First printed in *The Clarion* in 1905.
11. 'New Radicalism' (published 1887) in L. Crompton (ed.), *The Road to Equality* (Boston, Mass.: Beacon Press, 1971) p. 31.
12. *Fabian Election Manifesto*, 1892.
13. Preface to *The Apple Cart* in *Prefaces by Bernard Shaw*, p. 326.
14. Gibbs, A.M., *Shaw* (Edinburgh: Oliver & Boyd, 1969) p. 29.
15. Shaw, 'The Simple Truth about Socialism' in L. Crompton (ed.), *The Road to Equality*, p. 163.
16. Shaw, *Intelligent Woman's Guide to Socialism, Capitalism, Sovietism and Fascism* (London: Constable, 1949 edn) p. 376.
17. Aristotle, *The Politics* (Harmondsworth: Penguin, 1969 edn) p. 132.
18. This argument is explored in some depth in Chappelow, *Shaw 'The Chucker Out'*, pp. 131–61.
19. *Observer*, 24 September 1944.
20. Quoted in Hugo, Leon, *Bernard Shaw, Playwright and Preacher* (London: Methuen, 1971) p. 131.
21. *Prefaces by Bernard Shaw*, p. 325.
22. *Prefaces by Bernard Shaw*, p. 329.
23. In *On Authority and Revelation* (Princeton, NJ: Princeton University Press, 1955) p. 195, Kierkegaard had warned: 'The art of statesmanship will [in a democracy] become a game. Everything will turn upon getting the multitude pollenated ... absolutely indifferent as to whether they understand anything or no.'
24. Shaw, George Bernard, *Man and Superman* (Harmondsworth: Penguin, 1948 edn) p. 251.
25. Smith, J.P., *Unrepentant Pilgrim* (London: Gollancz, 1966) p. 151.
26. Smith, *Unrepentant Pilgrim*, p. 151.
27. 'The Simple Truth about Socialism', in L. Crompton (ed.), *The Road to Equality*, p. 190.
28. 'The Revolutionist's Handbook', in *Man and Superman*, p. 264.
29. For example, Gibbs, *Shaw, passim*.
30. *Thus Spake Zarathustra*, in W. Kaufman (ed., trans.) *The Portable Nietzsche* (New York: Vintage Books, 1968) p. 126.
31. Philmus, R.M. and Hughes, D.H., *Early Writings of H.G. Wells* (London: University of California Press, 1975) p. 218.
32. *Notes from the Underground*. See Jackson, R.L., *Dialogues with Dostoevsky* (Stanford, Calif.: Stanford University Press, 1993) ch. 6.
33. Wells, H.G., *Boon* (London: Fisher Unwin, 1915) p. 152.
34. Quoted in Nicholson, N., *H.G. Wells* (London: Arthur Brooker, 1950) p. 43.
35. Quoted in Philmus and Hughes, *Early Writings*, p. 185.
36. 'Human Evolution', in Philmus and Hughes, *Early Writings*, p. 218.
37. Wells, H.G., *Experiments in Autobiography* (London: Gollancz, 1934) p. 771.
38. Wells, H.G., *The Shape of Things to Come* (London: Corgi Books, 1967 edn) p. 287.

39. See Parrinder, P., *H.G. Wells* (Edinburgh: Oliver & Boyd, 1970) *passim*.
40. Orwell, 'Wells, Hitler and the World State', *Collected Essays, Journalism and Letters*, Vol. 2, p. 142.
41. Wells, H.G., *Food of the Gods* (Clinton, Mass.: Airmont Classics Series, 1965) p. 46.
42. Wells, *Food of the Gods*, p. 99.
43. Wells, *Food of the Gods*, p. 143.
44. Wells, *Food of the Gods*, p. 174.
45. Wells, *Food of the Gods*, pp. 187–90.
46. Orwell, 'Wells, Hitler and the World State', *Collected Essays, Journalism and Letters*, Vol. 2, p. 141.
47. Huxley, Aldous, *Eyeless in Gaza* (Harmondsworth: Penguin, 1972), first published in 1936.
48. Huxley, *Eyeless in Gaza*, p. 13.
49. Huxley, *Eyeless in Gaza*, p. 150.
50. Huxley, *Eyeless in Gaza*, p. 292.
51. Huxley, *Eyeless in Gaza*, p. 293.
52. Huxley, *Eyeless in Gaza*, p. 294. My italics.
53. The character Rampion, in Huxley's novel *Point Counter Point* (1928), represents Lawrence and expounds some of his more political ideas.
54. Lawrence, D.H, 'Sex versus Loveliness', in *Selected Essays* (Harmondsworth: Penguin, 1976) p. 18.
55. 'Democracy', in Lawrence, *Selected Essays*, p. 95.
56. Woodcock, George, *Dawn and the Darkest Hour* (London: Faber & Faber, 1972) p. 14.
57. Lawrence, D.H., 'The State of Funk', in *Selected Essays*, p. 97.
58. Huxley, *Eyeless in Gaza*, p. 12.

6   The New Jerusalem

1. Wilde, Oscar, 'The Soul of Man under Socialism', *Selected Essays and Poems* (Harmondsworth: Penguin, 1954) p. 34.
2. Schklar, Judith, 'Political Theory of Utopias: From Melancholy to Nostalgia', *Daedalus*, 94 (Spring 1965) p. 376–81.
3. See Morton, A.L., *The English Utopia* (London: Lawrence & Wishart, 1952).
4. See for example Engels's sustained attack on utopianism in *Socialism: Utopian and Scientific*, ed. George Novac (New York: Pathfinder Press, 1972), first published 1892.
5. Bellamy, Edward, *Looking Backwards* (New York: Signet Classics, 1964), first published in 1888. Bellamy's was one of the most widely read of utopian novels and largely inspired Morris's *News from Nowhere* as an ethical socialist riposte to Bellamy's scientific vision.
6. Walsh, Chas., *From Utopia to Nightmare* (London: Geoffrey Bles, 1952) p. 22.
7. Morris, Willam, 'Art under Plutocracy', in A.L. Morton (ed.), *Political Writings of William Morris* (London: Lawrence & Wishart, 1973).
8. Morris develops this argument in 'Art under Plutocracy' where he declares: 'the best artist [is] a workman still, the humblest workman [is] an artist'.
9. Some tasks, he concedes, are inherently distasteful and so may not be performed artistically. Wherever it can be managed these tasks should be

mechanised. Where not they must be shared around as much as possible, so as not to burden any particular individual or group.

10. Morris, 'The Lesser Arts', in *Political Writings*.
11. Morris, 'Art and Socialism', in *Political Writings*.
12. Morris, 'Useful Work versus Useless Toil', in *Political Writings*.
13. Morris, 'Art and Socialism'.
14. Morris, 'Art and Socialism'.
15. Morris, William, *News from Nowhere*, in A.L. Morton (ed.), *Three Works by William Morris* (London: Lawrence & Wishart, 1973) p. 203.
16. Morris, *News from Nowhere*, p. 203.
17. Morris, *News from Nowhere*, pp. 209–10.
18. Morris, *News from Nowhere*, p. 258.
19. Morris, *News from Nowhere*, ch. XIV.
20. Morris, *News from Nowhere*, pp. 336–7.
21. Morris, *News from Nowhere*, p. 357.
22. Morris, *News from Nowhere*, p. 362.
23. Morris, 'The Society of the Future', in *Political Writings*.
24. Hewlett, Maurice, *National Review* (August 1891).
25. It is intriguing to remember that Bentham's prison, the panopticon, was similarly transparent. See Goodwin, Barbara and Taylor, Keith, *The Politics of Utopia* (London: Hutchinson, 1982) p. 63.
26. Hewlett, Maurice, *National Review*.
27. Thompson, E.P., *William Morris: Romantic to Revolutionary* (London: Merlin Press, 1977) p. 187.
28. Wells, H.G., *The Time Machine*, in H.G. Wells, *Selected Short Stories* (Harmondsworth: Penguin, 1970), first published 1895.
29. Wells, *The Time Machine*, p. 59.
30. Ascherson, Neil, 'Beware perfect comfort and security, the Morlocks will have their hour', *Independent*, 26 May 1995.
31. Morris, William, *A Dream of John Ball*, in A.L. Morton (ed.), *Three Works by William Morris*.
32. See Ingle, Stephen, 'Socialist Man: William Morris and Bernard Shaw', in B.C. Parekh (ed.), *The Concept of Socialism* (London: Croom Helm, 1975) pp. 72–94.
33. Morris, William, *News from Nowhere*, p. 275.
34. Morris, *News from Nowhere*, p. 288.
35. Huxley, Aldous, *Brave New World* (Harmondsworth: Penguin, 1973 edn) p. 24. First published in 1932.
36. Huxley, *Brave New World*, p. 44.
37. Huxley, *Brave New World*, p. 173.
38. Huxley, *Brave New World*, p. 67.
39. Huxley, *Brave New World*, p. 88.
40. Huxley, *Brave New World*, p. 74.
41. Huxley, *Brave New World*, p. 182.
42. Huxley, *Brave New World*, p. 185.
43. Huxley, *Brave New World*, p. 187.
44. Hawkes, Nigel, 'How does tomorrow look today?', *The Times*, 26 July 1994.
45. Houllebecq, Michel, *Atomised* (London: Vintage, 2001) p. 187.
46. Huxley, Aldous, *Island* (Harmondsworth: Penguin, 1974 edn) *passim*.

47. Day, Gary, 'The Passage from Hubris to Humility', a review of David Bradshaw (ed.), *The Hidden Huxley: Contempt and Compassion for the Masses* (London: Faber, 1994).
48. Burgess, Anthony, *A Clockwork Orange* (Harmondsworth: Penguin, 1962).
49. Wells, H.G., *A Modern Utopia* (London: Collins & Son, 1905) p. 5.
50. Wells, *A Modern Utopia*, p. 4.
51. Shaw's Perivale St Andrew was, after all, only the first stage in a long development which would eventually lead to something far more ambitious when 'lives that have no use, meaning or purpose will fade away'.
52. Orwell, 'Wells, Hitler and the World State', *Collected Essays, Journalism and Letters* (London: Secker & Warburg, 1968) Vol 2, p. 142.
53. Wells, H.G., *A Modern Utopia*, p. 2.
54. Joseph Conrad was much more favourably impressed. He wrote to Wells in 1905 that in reading this account 'no civilised man, in his infinite variety, need, when reading that book, feel "left" for a single moment'.
55. Wells made just such a tour in the company of fellow Fabian – and political scientist – Graham Wallas in 1903.
56. Wells, *A Modern Utopia*, pp. 5–6.
57. Wells, *A Modern Utopia*, p. 72.
58. Wells, *A Modern Utopia*, p. 70.
59. Wells, *A Modern Utopia*, p. 157.
60. Wells, *A Modern Utopia*, p. 169.
61. Wells, *A Modern Utopia*, p. 170.
62. Wells, *A Modern Utopia*, p. 73.
63. Bacon, Francis, *The New Atlantis, Ideal Commonwealths*, rev. edn (London: Collier, 1901).
64. Wells, *A Modern Utopia*, p. 45.
65. Wells, *A Modern Utopia*, p. 95.
66. Wells, *A Modern Utopia*, p. 100.
67. Baines, J., *Joseph Conrad* (London: Weidenfeld & Nicolson, 1960) p. 232.
68. Wells, *A Modern Utopia*, pp. 184–8.
69. Wells, *A Modern Utopia*, p. 215.
70. Wells, *A Modern Utopia*, p. 216.
71. Whilst it is true that Orwell borrowed heavily from works such as Zamyatin's *We* (1924), Koestler's *Darkness at Noon* (1942) and Burnham's *The Managerial Revolution* (1942), *Nineteen Eighty-Four* was rightly regarded by George Woodcock as 'the culmination of twenty years of writing'. Even so we should recognise that Orwell did not intend this book to be his last testament.
72. Orwell, George, *Nineteen Eighty-Four* (Harmondsworth: Penguin, 1960 edn) pp. 62–3.
73. Orwell, *Nineteen Eighty-Four*, p. 61.
74. In 'The Road to 1984', *Political Science Quarterly*, 81(4) (December 1966), George Kateb dismisses Orwell's definition of power as simply a description of sadism. Isaac Deutscher, too, argued that Orwell had succumbed to what he called the 'mysticism of cruelty'.
75. See Ingle, Stephen, *George Orwell: A Political Life* (Manchester: Manchester University Press, 1993) pp. 4–6.
76. See Jackson, Robert Louis, *Dialogues with Dostoevsy* (Stanford, Calif.: Stanford University Press, 1993) p. 191.

77. As Pascal noted, 'le coeur a ses raisons que la raison ne connaît pas'.
78. In *The Social Crisis of Our Time* (London: Hodge, 1950) Röpke emphasised the importance of family life in preserving democratic values. His analysis of the 'volitional paralysis' that might make totalitarianism possible is similar to Orwell's picture of Oceanian culture at many points.
79. Orwell, *Nineteen Eighty-Four*, p. 110. Orwell depicts family life in Oceania through the Parsons: see pp. 22–4.
80. Orwell, *Nineteen Eighty-Four*, p. 45.
81. See, for example, Young, John Wesley, *Totalitarian Language* (London: University of Virginia Press, 1991).
82. Orwell, *Nineteen Eighty-Four*, p. 126.
83. Raymond Williams remained of the view that Orwell had limited the critical scope of his novel by implying that the nature of Winston's revolt was chiefly sexual. See his *Orwell* (London: Fontana Modern Masters, Fontana/Collins, 1971).
84. Orwell, *Nineteen Eighty-Four*, p. 51.
85. In St Thomas More's *Utopia* (1516), for example, there was no private property.
86. Either power is intrinsically malevolent or it unerringly draws to it those who use it malevolently. This is scarcely a distinction that matters for Orwell.
87. Orwell, *Nineteen Eighty-Four*, p. 239.
88. Houllebecq, *Atomised, passim*.
89. With the modern advances in robotics even Huxley's rigid hierarchy will become unnecessary.
90. Houllebecq, *Atomised*, p. 191.

7   The Power of Narrative

1. Adams, John R., *Harriet Beecher Stowe* (New York: Twayne Books, 1963) p. 144.
2. Hanne, Michael, *The Power of the Story, Fiction and Political Change* (Providence, RI: Berghan Books, 1994).
3. In a paper to the 1998 conference of the American Political Science Association in Boston, James Wagman decribed the book as 'the literary explosive with which to destroy the public amnesia which covered the crimes of Stalin'.
4. Heer, Nancy W., *Politics and History in the Soviet Union* (London: MIT Press, 1971) p. vii.
5. Hanne, *The Power of the Story*, p. 150.
6. See Allensworth, Wayne, 'Solzhenitsyn and the Russian Question', in *The Russian Question: Nationalism, Modernisation and Post-Communist Russia* (Lanham, Md: Ruaman & Littlefield, 1998) pp. 57–97.
7. Hanne, *The Power of the Story*, p. 184.
8. Hanne, *The Power of the Story*, p. 147.
9. Quoted in Hanne, *The Power of the Story*, p. 198.
10. Sinclair, Upton, *The Jungle* (New York: Doubleday, Page & Co.) 1905.
11. Paton, Alan, *Cry the Beloved Country* (New York: Charles Scribner's Sons) 1948.
12. See Barnes, Barry, 'Thomas Kuhn', in Quentin Skinner (ed.), *The Return of Grand Theory* (Cambridge: Cambridge University Press, 1985) pp. 85–100.
13. Thomas Docherty (ed.), *Postmodernism: A Reader* (Hemel Hempstead: Harvester Wheatsheaf, 1993) p. 36.

14. Alexander, K.W. and Hobbs, A., 'What Influences Labour MPs', *New Society*, 13 December 1962.
15. Preface to *Mrs Warren's Profession* in *Prefaces by Bernard Shaw* (London: Odhams Press, 1938) pp. 219–36.
16. Preface to *The Shewing Up of Blanco Posnett* in *Prefaces by Bernard Shaw*, pp. 400–40.
17. Preface to *Mrs Warren's Profession*.
18. Orwell's comment comes to mind: 'The minds of us all, and therefore the physical world, would be perceptibly different if Wells had never existed', *Collected Essays, Journalism and Letters* (London: Secker & Warburg, 1968) Vol. 1, p. 164.
19. Quoted in Chappelow, Alan, *Shaw 'The Chucker Out'* (London: Allen & Unwin, 1969) pp. 104–29.
20. Almost all of the sixty-and-over age group claimed to have read 'quite a lot' of Shaw and Wells.
21. Seventy per cent claimed to have done most of their reading before entering politics or early in their political careers. Further evidence of this can be found in the fact that only 38 per cent of the sixty-and-over age group had read at least a 'fair amount' of Orwell, who of course became successful only after they had entered on their careers.
22. See Ingle, Stephen, *The British Party System*, 3rd edn (London: Pinter, 1999) pp. 154–60.
23. Mayhew, Christopher, *Party Games* (London: Hutchinson, 1969) p. 154.
24. *New Statesman*, 30 September 1994, pp. 22–4.
25. See Philp, Mark, 'Michael Foucault', in Quentin Skinner (ed.), *The Return of Grand Theory* (Cambridge: Cambridge University Press, 1985).
26. Rorty, Richard, *Contingency, Irony and Solidarity* (Cambridge: Cambridge University Press, 1989) p. 7.
27. Fischer, Michael in Alan Malachowski (ed.), *Reading Rorty* (Oxford: Basil Blackwell, 1990) p. 241.
28. Orwell, George, 'A Hanging', *The Penguin Essays of George Orwell* (Harmondsworth: Penguin, 1994) pp. 14–18.
29. Crick, Bernard, *George Orwell: A Life* (Harmondsworth: Penguin, 1992) p. 151.
30. Rorty, Richard, *The Consequences of Pragmatism: Essays 1972–1980* (Brighton: Harvester, 1982) pp. 165–7.
31. Included in Skelton, Robin, *Poetry of the Thirties* (Harmondsworth: Penguin, 1964) pp. 54–9.
32. O'Farrell, John, *Things Can Only Get Better* (London: Black Swan, 1999) p. 260.
33. Hanne, *The Power of the Story*, p. 17.
34. Marr, Andrew, 'Orwellian thought', *Independent*, 25 March 1996.
35. O'Brien, Conor Cruise, *Writers and Politics* (London: Chatto & Windus, 1965) pp. 32–3.
36. Purves, Libby, 'We still need Orwell', *The Times*, 15 April 1997.
37. Marquand, David, 'The life after the death of socialism', *Guardian*, 5 June 1991.

Postscript: The Implosion of Values

1. See Beer, S.H., *British Politics in the Collectivist Age* (1964), but published in the United Kingdom as *Modern British Politics* (London: Faber, 1965).

2. For a full account of these developments see Ingle, Stephen, *The British Party System*, 3rd edn (London: Pinter, 1999) pp. 121–5.

3. Gledhill, Christine, 'Developments in Feminist Culture', *Quarterly Review of Film Studies*, 3(4) (1978) p. 464.

4. See Hill, John, *British Cinema in the 1980s* (Oxford: Oxford University Press, 1999), especially ch. 1, 'The British Cinema and Thatcherism'.

5. Williams, Raymond, 'A lecture on realism', *Screen*, 18(7) (Spring 1977) pp. 61–74.

6. In Braine's book Lambton muses on these new surroundings that this must be 'England'. He had never seen it before.

7. For example, Richard Mutimer in *Demos* or Clara Hewett in *The Nether World*.

8. In recent years rugby union has itself become professional and has enticed former league players into the union game. Indeed ex-league players have subsequently represented Scotland, Wales and even England. Time was when league players were entirely ostracised by the RFU and other national unions and union players were allowed no contact with them.

9. Böll, Heinrich, *The Clown* (London: Marion Boyars, 1980 edn) p. 196.

10. See Anderson, Lindsay, 'Sport, Life and Art', *Film and Filming* (February 1963) p. 16.

11. Yorkshire had always been by far the most successful county side. They won the county championship in 1968, the third of three consecutive championship successes, but they did not win another championship for thirty-three years.

12. Bryson, Bill, *Notes from a Small Island* (London: Black Swan Books, 1996) p. 212.

13. Gamble, Andrew, 'The Thatcher Decade in Perspective', in Patrick Dunleavy *et al.*, (eds) *Developments in British Politics* (London: Palgrave Macmillan, 1990).

14. Quoted in Hill, John, *Sex, Class and Realism* (London: British Film Institute, 1986) p. 135.

15. Orwell, diary entry for 21 March 1936, *Collected Essays, Journalism and Letters (CEJL)* (London: Secker & Warburg, 1968) Vol. 1 pp. 209–12.

16. In *The Origins of Totalitarianism*, Hannah Arendt argues that one of the preconditions of totalitarianism is that 'the worst have lost their fear and the best have lost their hope' (Cleveland, Ohio: Meridon Books, 1958) p. 446.

17. Orwell, 'The Art of Donald McGill', *CEJL*, Vol. 3, pp. 155–64.

18. I watched *Brassed Off* with a predominantly middle-class audience in Scotland. It was a packed house. At the end the audience broke into spontaneous and prolonged applause.

19. Osborne, John, *Look Back in Anger*, perhaps the most famous of the kitchen-sink dramas, was first staged in 1956.

20. See Shaw, Eric, *The Labour Party Since 1945* (Oxford: Blackwell, 1996) ch. 6.

21. See Callaghan, John, *Socialism in Britain* (Blackwell: Oxford, 1990) ch. 4.

22. See Crewe, I., Barrington, B. and Alt, J., 'Partisan Dealignment in Great Britain 1964–74', *British Journal of Political Science*, 7(2) (April 1977).

Bibliography

Adam, Ruth, *What Shaw Said* (London: MacDonald, 1966).

Adams, John R., *Harriet Beecher Stowe* (New York: Twayne Books, 1963).

Alexander, K.W. and Hobbs, A., 'What Influences Labour MPs', *New Society*, 13 December 1962.

Allensworth, Wayne, 'Solzhenitsyn and the Russian Question', in *The Russian Question: Nationalism, Modernisation and Post-Communist Russia* (Lanham, Md: Ruaman & Littlefield, 1998) pp. 57–97.

Anderson, Lindsay, 'Sport, Life and Art', *Film and Filming* (February 1963) 16.

Arblaster, Anthony, *The Rise and Decline of Western Liberalism* (Oxford: Blackwell, 1984).

Aristotle, *The Politics* (Harmondsworth: Penguin, 1969 edn).

Ascherson, Neil, 'Beware perfect comfort and security, the Morlocks will have their hour', *Independent*, 26 May 1995.

Auden, W.H., 'The American Scene', in *The Dyers Hand* (London: Faber & Faber, 1948).

Auerbach, Eric, *Mimesis* (Princeton, NJ: Princeton University Press, 1968).

Bacon, Francis, *The New Atlantis, Ideal Commonwealths*, rev. edn (London: Collier, 1901).

Baines, J., *Joseph Conrad* (London: Weidenfeld & Nicolson, 1960).

Ball, F.C., *One of the Damned* (London: Weidenfeld & Nicolson, 1973).

Barker, Anthony, *Political Ideas in Modern Britain* (London: Methuen, 1978).

Beer, S.H., *British Politics in the Collectivist Age* (1964), published in Britain as *Modern British Politics* (London: Faber, 1965).

Bellamy, Edward, *Looking Backwards* (New York: Signet Classics, 1964).

Bellow, Saul, *Mr Sammler's Planet* (London: Weidenfeld & Nicolson, 1970).

Belsey, C., *Critical Practice* (London: Methuen, 1980).

Benda, Julien, *La Trahison des clercs* (Paris: Grasset, 1927).

Benjamin, Walter, 'Theses on the Philosophy of History', in Hannah Arendt (ed.), *Illuminations* (New York: Schoken Books, 1969).

Berki, R.N., 'Machiavellism: A Philosophical Defence', *Ethics*, 81 (1970–71) 107–17.

Böll, Heinrich, *The Clown* (London: Marion Boyars, 1980 edn).

Booth, Charles, *Life and Labour of the People in London* (London: Palgrave Macmillan, 1892–7) 10 vols.

Brady, Frank (ed.), *Boswell's Life of Johnson* (London: Signet Classics, 1968).

Bryson, Bill, *Notes from a Small Island* (London: Black Swan Books, 1996).

Buckler, Steve, *Dirty Hands: The Problem of Political Morality* (Aldershot: Avebury Press, 1993).

Burgess, Anthony, *A Clockwork Orange* (Harmondsworth: Penguin, 1962).

Burnham, James, *The Managerial Revolution* (Harmondsworth: Penguin, 1975).

Callaghan, John, *Socialism in Britain* (Blackwell: Oxford, 1990).

Chappelow, Alan, *Shaw 'The Chucker Out'* (London: Allen & Unwin, 1969).

Charques, R.D., *Contemporary Literature and Social Revolution* (London: Martin Secker, 1933).

Clark, Margaret, 'The Politics of Literature', *British Review of New Zealand Studies*, 7 (December 1994) 18–29.

Cleaver, Eldridge, *Post-Prison Writings and Speeches* (London: Panther Books, 1971).

Crewe, I., Barrington, B. and Alt, J., 'Partisan Dealignment in Great Britain 1964–74', *British Journal of Political Science*, 7(2) (April 1977).

Crick, Bernard, *George Orwell: A Life* (London: Secker & Warburg, 1980, reprinted by Penguin in 1992).

Crompton, L. (ed.), *The Road to Equality* (Boston, Mass.: Beacon Press, 1971).

Crosland, C.A.R., *The Future of Socialism* (London: Cape, 1956).

Crossman, Richard (ed.), *The God That Failed* (London: Hamish Hamilton, 1950).

Davis, Lawrence, 'Morris, Wilde, and Marx on the Social Conditions of Individual Development', *Political Studies*, XLIV (1996) 719–32.

Day, Gary, 'The Passage from Hubris to Humility', a review of David Bradshaw (ed.), *The Hidden Huxley: Contempt and Compassion for the Masses* (London: Faber, 1994).

Dennis, Norman and Halsey, A.H., *English Ethical Socialism* (Oxford: Oxford University Press, 1988).

Docherty, Thomas (ed.), *Postmodernism: A Reader* (Hemel Hempstead: Harvester Wheatsheaf, 1993).

Eagleton, Terry, 'Marxist Criticism', in John Barrell, *Poetry, Language and Politics* (Manchester: Manchester University Press, 1988).

Eagleton, Terry, 'The Rise of English', in Dennis Walder (ed.), *Literature in the Modern World* (Oxford: Oxford University Press, 1990).

Eco, Umberto, *The Name of the Rose* (London: Picador, 1984).

Engels, Friedrich, *Socialism: Utopian and Scientific*, ed. George Novac (New York: Pathfinder Press, 1972).

Fanon, Frantz, *The Wretched of the Earth* (London: MacGibbon & Kee, 1965).

Fischer, Michael, in Alan Malachowski (ed.), *Reading Rorty* (Oxford: Basil Blackwell, 1990).

Forster, E.M., 'Anonymity: An Enquiry', in *Two Cheers for Democracy* (London: Edward Arnold, 1951).

Gamble, Andrew, 'The Thatcher Decade in Perspective', in Patrick Dunleavy *et al.*, *Developments in British Politics*, vol. 3 (London: Palgrave Macmillan, 1990).

Gardner, P.L., *Schopenhauer* (Harmondsworth: Penguin, 1971).

Gibbs, A.M., *Shaw* (Edinburgh: Oliver & Boyd, 1969).

Gissing, George, *Demos: The Stay of English Socialism* (Brighton: Harvester, 1972).

Gissing, George, *The Nether World* (Brighton: Harvester, 1974).

Gissing, Algernon and Ellen, *Letters of George Gissing to Members of his Family* (London, 1927).

Gledhill, Christine, 'Developments in Feminist Culture', *Quarterly Review of Film Studies*, 3(4) (1978) 464.

Golding, William, *Rites of Passage* (London: Faber & Faber, 1980).

Goode, John, 'Gissing, Morris and English Socialism', *Victorian Studies*, vol. XII, no. 2 (December 1968) pp. 201–26.

Goode, John, Introduction to Gissing, *The Nether World* (Brighton: Harvester, 1974).

Goodwin, Barbara and Taylor, Keith, *The Politics of Utopia* (London: Hutchinson, 1982).

Goodwin, Robert E., 'Utility and the Good', in Peter Singer (ed.), *A Companion to Ethics* (Oxford: Blackwell, 1991) pp. 241–8.

Gramsci, Antonio, *Selections from the Prison Notebook* (London: Lawrence & Wishart, 1971).

Greene, Graham, *Brighton Rock* (London: Heinemann Bodley Head, 1970).

Greenwood, Walter, *Love on the Dole* (Harmondsworth: Penguin, 1975 edn).

Hall, Stuart, 'The Question of Cultural Identity', in his edited collection *Modernity and its Futures* (Cambridge: Polity Press, 1992) pp. 273–316.

Hampshire, Stuart, *Public and Private Morality* (London: Cambridge University Press, 1978).

Hanne, Michael, *The Power of the Story, Fiction and Political Change* (Providence, RI: Berghan Books, 1994).

Harding, Neil, 'Socialism and Violence', in B.C. Parekh (ed.), *The Concept of Socialism* (London: Croom Helm, 1975).

Hardy, Thomas, *Jude the Obscure* (London: Palgrave Macmillan, 1972 edn).

Harris, Frank, *Bernard Shaw, an Unauthorized Biography* (London: Gollancz, 1931).

Harrison, Brian, *The Transformation of British Politics 1860–1995* (Oxford: Oxford University Press, 1996).

Hawkes, Nigel, 'How does tomorrow look today?', *The Times*, 26 July 1994.

Heer, Nancy W., *Politics and History in the Soviet Union* (London: MIT Press, 1971).

Hill, John, *British Cinema in the 1980s* (Oxford: Oxford University Press, 1999).

Hirsch, E.D., Jnr, 'The Babel of Interpretation', in Dennis Walder, *Literature in the Modern World* (Oxford: Oxford University Press, 1990).

Hoggart, Richard, *Speaking to Each Other*, vol. 2, *About Literature* (London: Chatto & Windus, 1970).

Holroyd, Michael, *Bernard Shaw: The Pursuit of Power*, vol. 2 (London: Chatto & Windus, 1989).

Houllebecq, Michel, *Atomised* (London: Vintage, 2001).

Hugo, Leon, *Bernard Shaw, Playwright and Preacher* (London: Methuen, 1971).

Hulse, James W., *Revolutionists in London: A Study of Five Unorthodox Socialists* (Oxford: Clarendon Press, 1970).

Huxley, Aldous, *Point Counter Point* (Harmondsworth: Penguin, 1971).

Huxley, Aldous, *Eyeless in Gaza* (Harmondsworth: Penguin, 1972).

Huxley, Aldous, *Brave New World* (Harmondsworth: Penguin, 1973 edn).

Huxley, Aldous, *Island* (Harmondsworth: Penguin, 1974 edn).

Huxley, Aldous, *Grey Eminence* (London: Triad Paperbacks, 1982).

Hyndman, H.M., *Record of an Adventurous Life* (London: Palgrave Macmillan, 1911) p. 432.

Hynes, Samuel, *The Edwardian Turn of Mind* (London: Oxford University Press, 1968).

Ingle, Stephen, 'Socialist Man: William Morris and Bernard Shaw', in B.C. Parekh (ed.), *The Concept of Socialism* (London: Croom Helm, 1975) pp. 72–94.

Ingle, Stephen, *George Orwell: A Political Life* (Manchester: Manchester University Press, 1993).

Ingle, Stephen, *The British Party System*, 3rd edn (London: Pinter, 1999).

Jackson, R.L., *Dialogues with Dostoevsky* (Stanford, Calif.: Stanford University Press, 1993).

Jauss, Robert, 'Literary History as a Challenge to Literary Theory', in Walder, *Literature in the Modern World* (Oxford: Oxford University Press, 1990).

Johnson, Peter, *Politics, Innocence and the Limits of Goodness* (London: Routledge, 1989).

Kaufman, W. (ed., trans.), *The Portable Nietzsche* (New York: Vintage Books, 1968).

Keating, P.J., *The Working Classes in Victorian Fiction* (London: Routledge & Kegan Paul, 1971).

Kierkegaard, Soren, *On Authority and Revelation* (Princeton, NJ: Princeton University Press, 1955).

Koestler, Arthur, *The Yogi and the Commissar* (London: Jonathan Cape, 1945).

Koestler, Arthur, *Darkness at Noon* (Harmondsworth: Penguin, 1964).

Koestler, Arthur, *The Gladiators* (London: Hutchinson, 1965).

Koestler, Arthur, *Arrival and Departure* (Harmondsworth: Penguin, 1969).

Lawrence, D.H., *Selected Essays* (Harmondsworth: Penguin, 1976).

Leavis, F.R., *The Common Pursuit* (London: Chatto & Windus, 1958).

Leitch, Thomas M., *What Stories Are: Narrative Theory and Interpretation* (London: Pennsylvania State University Press, 1986).

London, Jack, *The Iron Heel* (London: Everett, 1912).

London, Jack, *The People of the Abyss* (London: The Journeyman Press, 1977).

Lukacs, Georg, 'The Ideology of Modernism', in John Barrell, *Poetry, Language and Politics* (Manchester: Manchester University Press, 1988).

Machiavelli, N., *The Discourses*, vol. I (Harmondsworth: Penguin, 1970) ch. 9, p. 139.

McKee, Patricia, *Public and Private: Gender, Class and the British Novel* (Minneapolis: University of Minnesota Press, 1997).

Mackenzie, Norman and Jean, *The Time Traveller* (London: Weidenfeld & Nicolson, 1973).

Malraux, André, *Man's Estate* (Harmondsworth: Penguin, 1975).

Marquand, David, 'The life after the death of socialism', *Guardian*, 5 June 1991.

Marr, Andrew, 'Orwellian thought', *Independent*, 25 March 1996.

Mayhew, Christopher, *Party Games* (London: Hutchinson, 1969).

Mellor, D.H., 'On Literary Truth', *Ratio* (1968) 10.

Milovan, Djilas, *The New Class: An Analysis of the Communist System* (London: Allen & Unwin, 1966).

Morris, William, 'Art under Plutocracy' and other essays in A.L. Morton (ed.), *Political Writings of William Morris* (London: Lawrence & Wishart, 1973).

Morris, William, *A Dream of John Ball*, in A.L. Morton (ed.), *Three Works by William Morris* (London: Lawrence & Wishart, 1973).

Morris, William, *News from Nowhere*, in A.L. Morton (ed.), *Three Works by William Morris* (London: Lawrence & Wishart, 1973).

Morrison, Arthur, *A Child of the Jago* (Harmondsworth: Penguin, 1946).

Morton, A.L., *The English Utopia* (London: Lawrence & Wishart, 1952).

Nicholson, N., *H.G. Wells* (London: Arthur Brooker, 1950).

O'Brien, Conor Cruise, *Writers and Politics* (London: Chatto & Windus, 1965).

O'Farrell, John, *Things Can Only Get Better* (London: Black Swan, 1999).

Orwell, George, 'As I Please', *Tribune*, 3 March 1944.

Orwell, George, *Nineteen Eighty-Four* (Harmondsworth: Penguin, 1960 edn) pp. 62–3.

Orwell, George, 'Why I Write', *Decline of the English Murder and Other Essays* (Harmondsworth: Penguin, 1965 edn).

Orwell, George, *The Road to Wigan Pier* (Harmondsworth: Penguin, 1965 edn).

Orwell, George, *Homage to Catalonia* (Harmondsworth: Penguin, 1966).

Orwell, George, 'Charles Dickens', *Collected Essays, Journalism and Letters* (*CEJL*) (London: Secker & Warburg, 1968) vol. 1, pp. 413–59.

Orwell, George, 'Inside the Whale', *CEJL* (London: Secker & Warburg, 1968) vol. 1, pp. 493–526.

Orwell, George, Letter to Cyrill Connolly dated 8 June 1937, *CEJL* vol. 1, pp. 280–2.

Orwell, George, review of *Caliban Shrieks* by Jack Hilton, *CEJL* vol. 1, pp. 148–50.

Orwell, George, 'Wells, Hitler and the World State', *CEJL* vol. 2, pp. 139–45.

Orwell, George, 'Notes on the Way', *CEJL* vol. 2, pp. 15–18.

Orwell, George, 'The Art of Donald McGill', *CEJL* vol. 3, pp. 155–64.

Orwell, George, 'The English People', *CEJL* vol. 3, pp. 1–37.

Orwell, George, *Coming Up for Air* (Harmondsworth: Penguin, 1986 edn).

Orwell, George, 'A Hanging', *The Penguin Essays of George Orwell* (Harmondsworth: Penguin, 1994) pp. 14–18.

Parrinder, P., *H.G. Wells* (Edinburgh: Oliver & Boyd, 1970).

Pearson, Geoffrey, *Hooligan: A History of Respectable Fears* (Basingstoke: Palgrave Macmillan, 1983).

Pearson, Hesketh, *Bernard Shaw: His Life and Personality* (London: Methuen, 1961).

Philmus, R.M. and Hughes, D.H., *Early Writings of H.G. Wells* (London: University of California Press, 1975).

Philp, Mark, 'Michel Foucault', in Quentin Skinner (ed.), *The Return of Grand Theory* (Cambridge: Cambridge University Press, 1985).

Plant, Raymond, 'Antonyms of Modernist Political Thought: Reasoning, Context and Community', in James Good and Irving Velody (eds), *The Politics of Post Modernity* (Cambridge: Cambridge University Press, 1998).

Platt, Steve and Gallagher, Julia, 'From Bevan to the Bible', *New Statesman*, 30 September 1994, 22–4.

Priestley, J.B., *The Edwardians* (London: Heinemann, 1970).

Prodi, Romano, *Europe As I See It*, trans. Allan Cameron (Cambridge: Polity Press, 2000).

Purves, Libby, 'We still need Orwell', *The Times*, 15 April 1997.

Quin, Kenneth, *How Literature Works* (London: Palgrave Macmillan, 1992).

Röpke, Wilhelm, *The Social Crisis of Our Time* (London: Hodge, 1950).

Rorty, Richard, *The Consequences of Pragmatism: Essays 1972–1980* (Brighton: Harvester, 1982).

Rorty, Richard, *Contingency, Irony and Solidarity* (Cambridge: Cambridge University Press, 1989).

Roth, Jack J., *The Cult of Violence: Sorel and the Sorelians* (London: University of California Press, 1980).

Rowntree, B. Seebohm, *Poverty: A Study of Town Life* (London: Palgrave Macmillan, 1902).

Sartre, Jean-Paul, *Crime Passionel* (London: Methuen World Classics, 1961).

Sartre, J.-P., *What is Literature?* (London: Methuen University Paperback, 1967).

Sassoon, Siegfried, 'Memoirs of an Infantry Officer', in *The Complete Memoirs of George Sherston* (London: Faber, 1972).

Schklar, Judith, 'Political Theory of Utopias: From Melancholy to Nostalgia', *Daedalus*, 94 (Spring 1965) 376–81.

Shaw, Bernard, *Essays in Fabian Socialism* (London: Constable, 1932).

Shaw, Bernard, *Everybody's Political What's What* (London: Constable, 1944).

Shaw, Bernard, *Man and Superman* (Harmondsworth: Penguin, 1948 edn).

Shaw, Bernard, *Intelligent Woman's Guide to Socialism, Capitalism, Sovietism and Fascism* (London: Constable, 1949 edn).

Shaw, Bernard, *Bodley Head Collected Plays of Bernard Shaw* (London: Bodley Head, 1951).

Shaw, Bernard, *Major Barbara* (Harmondsworth: Penguin, 1972 edn).

Shaw, Bernard, *Mrs Warren's Profession*, in *Plays Unpleasant* (Harmondsworth: Penguin, 1972 edn).

Shaw, Bernard, *Widowers' Houses*, in *Plays Unpleasant* (Harmondsworth: Penguin, 1972 edn).

Shaw, Bernard, *The Apple Cart*, in *Plays Political* (Harmondsworth: Penguin, 1986).

Shaw, Eric, *The Labour Party Since 1945* (Oxford: Blackwell, 1996).
Silone, Ignazio, *Fontamara* (London: Journeyman Press, 1975).
Skelton, Robin, *Poetry of the Thirties* (Harmondsworth: Penguin, 1964).
Smart, J.J.C. and Williams, Bernard, *Utilitarianism For and Against* (London: Cambridge University Press, 1973).
Smith, J.P., *Unrepentant Pilgrim* (London: Gollancz, 1966).
Spencer, Herbert, *The Man versus the State* (London: Watts, 1950).
Swingewood, Alan, *The Novel and Revolution* (London: Palgrave Macmillan, 1975).
Thompson, E.P., *William Morris: Romantic to Revolutionary* (London: Merlin Press, 1977).
Tressell, Robert, *The Ragged Trousered Philanthropists* (St Albans: Panther, 1972).
Walsh, C., *From Utopia to Nightmare* (London: Geoffrey Bles, 1952).
Walzer, M., 'Political Action: The Problem of Dirty Hands', in Cohen Marshall *et al.* (eds), *War and Moral Responsibility* (London: Princeton University Press, 1972) p. 65.
Warren, Robert Penn, *All the King's Men* (New York: Bantam Books, 1951).
Weldon, T.D., *Kant's Critique of Pure Reason* (Oxford: Clarendon Press, 1958).
Wells, H.G., *The Time Machine* (London: Heinemann, 1895).
Wells, H.G., *War of the Worlds* (London: Heinemann, 1898).
Wells, H.G., *First Men on the Moon* (London: Newnes, 1901).
Wells, H.G., 'Discovery of the Future', *Nature*, 6 February 1902.
Wells, H.G., *A Modern Utopia* (London: Chapman & Hall, 1905).
Wells, H.G., *New Worlds for Old* (London: Constable, 1908).
Wells, H.G., *Tono Bungay* (London: Palgrave Macmillan, 1909).
Wells, H.G., *The New Machiavelli* (London: John Lane, 1911).
Wells, H.G., *The Wife of Sir Isaac Harman* (London: Odhams, 1914).
Wells, H.G., *Boon* (London: Fisher Unwin, 1915).
Wells, H.G., *Kipps, The Story of a Simple Soul* (London: Palgrave Macmillan, 1926).
Wells, H.G., *Experiments in Autobiography* (London: Gollancz, 1934).
Wells, H.G., *Food of the Gods* (Clinton, Mass.: Airmont Classics Series, 1965).
Wells, H.G., *The Shape of Things to Come* (London: Corgi Books, 1967 edn).
Wells, H.G., *The Time Machine*, in *H.G. Wells: Selected Short Stories* (Harmondsworth: Penguin, 1970).
Wells, H.G., *The Island of Doctor Moreau* (Harmondsworth: Penguin, 1971).
West, Anthony, *H.G. Wells: Aspects of a Life* (New York: Random House, 1984).
Whitebrook, Maureen, 'Politics and Literature', *Politics* 15(1) (1995) 55–62.
Wilde, Oscar, 'The Soul of Man under Socialism', *Selected Essays and Poems* (Harmondsworth: Penguin, 1954).
Williams, Raymond, *Orwell* (London: Fontana Modern Masters, Fontana/Collins, 1971).
Williams, Raymond, 'A lecture on realism', *Screen* 18(7) (Spring 1977) 61–74.
Wilson, E., *The Triple Thinkers* (London: Oxford University Press, 1939).
Wolf, Leonard, in C.M. Joad, *Shaw and Society* (London: Odhams, 1953) p. 44.
Woodcock, George, *Dawn and the Darkest Hour* (London: Faber & Faber, 1972).
Woolf, Rosemary, *Art and Doctrine: Essays on Medieval Literature* (London: Hambleton Press, 1986).
Young, John Wesley, *Totalitarian Language* (London: University of Virginia Press, 1991).
Zamyatin, Yevgeny, *We* (Harmondsworth: Penguin, 1972).

Index

35668733